A Disreputable Priest:

Being Gay in Anti-Gay Cultures

Ian Corbett

GILEAD
B O O K S
PUBLISHING

Gilead Books Publishing
Corner Farm
West Knapton
Malton
North Yorkshire YO17 8JB UK

www.GileadBooksPublishing.com

First published in Great Britain, May 2015

2 4 6 8 10 9 7 5 3 1

Copyright © Ian Corbett 2015

British Library Cataloguing in Publication Data:

A CIP catalogue record for this book is available from the British Library.

ISBN-13: 978-0-9932090-0-0

All scripture quotations, unless otherwise indicated are from the Good News Bible ©1994 published by the Bible Societies/HarperCollins Publishers Ltd UK, Good News Bible ©American Bible Society 1966, 1971, 1976, 1992. Used with permission.

Every effort has been made to obtain copyright permission of all material quoted. In the event of obtaining further permissions, these will be acknowledged in future editions.

The publisher makes every effort to ensure that the papers used in our books are made from trees that have been legally sourced from well-managed and credibly certified forests by using a printer awarded FSC & PEFC chain of custody certification.

Cover design: Nathan Ward

Cover illustration: Anna Tash

To Desmond Tutu, Archbishop Emeritus of Southern Africa; Khotso Makhulu, Archbishop Emeritus of Central Africa; and to those friends and family on three continents who have supported, sustained and cared for me so persistently despite all my faults and failures.

Contents

Acknowledgements

I would like to thank all the friends who have supported me in this project, especially Fiona Bell, who typed the manuscript and made many helpful suggestions; Alan Lomas, who read the draft; Andrew Crompton, who unwittingly provided the title; Brenda Meakins and Albert Radcliffe for their poems; and to Shiou Tsai for computer help and advice.

Special gratitude is due to several people in the USA, where most of the work was first written – to the Very Revd Dr Ian Markham, Principal of Virginia Theological Seminary (where I spent a happy sabbatical term,) for his advice and encouragement, and to the staff and students (especially the appropriately named Mike Angell) for their hospitality; to Mary Sojourner, a feisty eco-warrior and author for her faith in me and readiness to let me quote her; to Barry and Steve Simpson for their friendship and hospitality, and allowing me to quote from their weekly bulletins; to Win and Meredith Blevins, novelists extraordinaire, for encouraging me to believe I could do this, and for their bucolic camaraderie; to Martha Rice and Vince Wilcox for their deep friendship and nurture through difficult times.

Thanks to the Revd Richard Kirker, founder and former secretary of the Lesbian and Gay Christian Movement, for what seems like a lifetime of love and inspiration.

Above all, my deepest gratitude to Chris Hayes of Gilead Books for having the courage to take me on; and to Gaby, widow of the late Philip Wetherell, whose book is published by Gilead.[1] Philip and Gaby were both colleagues of mine in USPG.

Finally, since this work was completed and since I turned seventy, new love has at last unexpectedly entered my life, so thanks to Thomas and other friends who now sustain me – a miracle that ends this confession on perhaps a more confident note than the main text suggests.

> *A psychologically complete and honest confession of life would require so much indiscretion...that it is simply out of the question.*
> Sigmund Freud[2]

> *Can a memoir be more than "a garbage of confessions, recollections and reminiscences?"*
> Sir Walter Scott

My Lord God, I have no idea where I am going, I do not see the road ahead of me, I cannot know for certain where it will end.

Nor do I really know myself, and the fact that I think I am following your will does not mean that I am actually doing so.

But I believe that the desire to please you does in fact please you. And I hope that I have that desire in all that I am doing. I hope that I will never do anything apart from that desire.

And I know that if I do this you will lead me by the right road, though I may know nothing about it. Therefore, I will trust you always, though I may seem to be lost and in the shadow of death. I will not fear for you are ever with me, and you will never leave me to my thoughts alone.

Thomas Merton, Thoughts in Solitude[3]

Section 1

A Love Letter

I killed my mother.

I believed I killed my mother.

She died of a coronary thrombosis – her second – probably occasioned by being overweight. She once made a comment that her obesity had been caused by my birth, and I learned only in my sixties that this could not be true. Yet this conviction has shadowed and disturbed my life with its terrible responsibility and burden of guilt.

Death has been a regular companion, however – pupils, friends, and the "dispensable" people with whom I have worked – and the letter with which I begin this memoir is a requiem for what they have given me and a cry of anguish for all I have lost.

It is addressed to a dead friend and lover. He died of an undiagnosed disease that over took him rapidly and terrifyingly. I needed to make some sense and meaning out of his life and mine. It helped me to write to him, and it compelled me to relate the course of events that led to our relationship and, in so doing, to confront personal issues that I hope will resonate with you who now share this journey with me as I seek clarity and wholeness.

Ian Corbett
Malvern

1. Thoughts in Solitude

There is no road – we make the road by walking
Anon

Shamwari Wangu, My Friend

This is for you. You are as dead as I am alive and yet there is a sense in which I shall always be yours.

I sit disconsolately on the edge of the brooding cliffs of the San Juan River. At this end of a furnace hot, dusty day I gaze at the far bluffs which pulsate with a vermillion glare as though lit from within then soften to pink, then rose and pass through majestic purple into nocturnal blackness. The valley disappears in post–alpenglow gloom. I find the dark empty abyss disturbingly alluring.

Further to the East the red sandstone merges into a colourless limestone with volcanic debris, apparently thrown around in the tumultuous wrath of a deranged monster. That horizon is quite devoid of beauty, stark and uninviting. Yet, that too, like the fiery rock here, mirrors my inner rage and loneliness – alone, isolated, abandoned.

Hell, Ndlovu, I'm trying to hold on but your hand slips from mine more and more.

My mind becomes misted. Even your face – and so beautiful a face – sometimes fades. Memory plays tricks, too, as time passes. Do I remember you as you were? Have I reinvented you in my thoughts? How much do I save or reject? I don't even know any of your family and friends. You are drifting away, leaving me...

I thought I needed a desert, both without and within, a place of space and without distraction so that I would not lose you completely. I fear this may have been one gamble too far. Without you, I have become a wanderer, unable to settle again. This, I admit, has not been without advantage. The word "wander" derives from the verb "to wind" and is associated with the German word "wandeln", to change. I have certainly grown in my wanderings. The wanderer does not find change a threat but rather an invitation to new possibility. The wanderer is free. I have roamed great tracts of the Earth. Mentally and spiritually, too, I have travelled no frontier too far, no depth too deep. My soul is full of wanderlust! How grimly ironic, then, that my pilgrimage has failed to bring me closer to you. I cannot face that I may have to let you go.

I feel confused. I need your words of encouragement, the radiance of your presence. You told me I have a gift of loving and that I must follow my gift into a wonderful adventure of discovery. But without you I have lost my way, and I am afraid of my gift. I cannot embrace it. I lack courage. I know only disappointment.

Dearest Ndlovu, I am trying to inhabit my aloneness. I am taught that even bleakness can be transformed into belonging. But I cannot **feel** that your love revealed to me that "friendship is one of the most beautiful places, in which longing reaches initial fulfilment and is then further deepened, refined and transfigured". We were close not only at a physical but at a spiritual level, revering each other's mystery. I have lost not just you but the very art of loving.

A far horizon all around. The early stars begin to reflect light from the limitless distance of the cosmos. Pascal said "The eternal silence of these infinite spaces frightens me". I feel lost and insignificant in this wild beauty. Haunted by the past, perhaps I feel guilty about you; though I know I could not have been there when you died.

Why did you have to die? Perhaps my anger really finds its source in you, for leaving me bereft and damaged. But I also rage at myself because I was not always faithful. Were you? My guilt locks me in a mental prison. I have become my own jailor. Someone once wrote "When you make the past your jailor you destroy your future". I have lost the key and have no sense of self-compassion.

You have trapped me, Ndlovu. I know I need to integrate my faults and guilt and begin a journey of healing, find new creativity. Yet now I would rather die with you than live without you.

But Ndlovu my anger is not yet spent for I have a greater adversary. An English friend – we loved each other deeply – once, at a very depressed time in his life, stood on top of a hill in the bleak Pennines Range in Northern England and cursed God – yelled at him and accused him of being indifferent to his misfortune. Years later, we held each other on that same hill and hoped we had made his peace with the Creator. Now I wish that I had the courage to stand, shout and shake my fist at him from this crag. We were all abandoned by him Ndlovu. He's been defeated by the juggernaut of free will that his

Utopian plans let loose. So let me, a priest, stand here and curse God our betrayer!

I'll tell of my wanderings, Ndlovu. Expelled from Zimbabwe, your country, by the Anglican Church, by a power-fixated Bishop who seemed to see his role akin to that of a Nineteenth Century tribal chief. He didn't even tell me himself – he left that to the incredulous immigration authorities. Why? Because I tried to reflect what I then perceived as the love of God for all human beings by working with disadvantaged youth and developing a strong, perhaps to him threatening youth movement? Or because I am gay – no evidence needed, supposition or rumour enough for him. Disposed of because of who I am, my identity trampled.

Desmond Tutu says that to oppress or misuse any human being is not heresy but blasphemy for it is to "spit in the face of God" in whose image we are made. This happened a year after finishing an arduous assignment in the barren mountains of Lesotho, working clandestinely with the African National Congress during the death throes of apartheid. The rest I will have to tell you more about. Tell you more! Are you there? It feels as though I am talking to you – and it helps. You succour me from beyond the grave.

You know our last meeting was difficult – so little time and our futures equally unsure. Then it happened – and you were not there.

I survived two jobs in the Kalahari region, its outer mirroring my own inner desert. I was then invalided back to England with myalgic encephalomyelitis and was off work for two years. Of course that bastion of Christian love, The Church, abandoned me: I was employed by no particular diocese so nobody had any responsibility for me. I existed on social security, a salutary experience, as I do not know how a less literate person than me could have penetrated its labyrinthine regulations. I remember embracing an African American quite spontaneously in an underground station, just for the joy of it. He was marvellous, understood and hugged me while reminding me that I was now in England and had better control myself unless I wanted to land in hospital, jail or both!

I cannot survive without African love (and I know I shall have to explain that) which now arrives only by mail. But sensing that I needed aboriginal society I eventually took up work with the Ojibway/Saulteaux "Indians" in Canada, after a short and tumultuous period at Tuam Cathedral in the West of Ireland. (I lived in a village called Cong and one wag dubbed me "Queen of Tuam and King of Cong").

But speaking out on Gay issues was not acceptable to the Anglican establishment. The God forsaken reservations I worked on were like having inner city problems in a forest wilderness location. I was so needing your love, anybody's love, but again the Church failed. The money ran out and I had to move on.

So here I am, now after seven years in Navajoland, with so much to share with you in the forlorn hope that you can still listen and guide me and, and if you cannot bring us closer, then – and I can scarcely force myself to say this – teach me how to let you go and live without you. But now the mists close in.

2. Falling in Love

The Zambezi River flows from the North West to become the eventual border between Zambia and Zimbabwe after plummeting dramatically in what Livingstone called The Victoria Falls. If you approach by this route it is a slow moving majestic water course nearly two kilometres in width. Despite tourist intrusions it still resembles the Koranic Paradise with myriad birds and animals, and elegant sinuous Africans gracing its shores. Approaching from any other direction you are aware first of its sound, even miles away, a low subterranean rumble. Long before arrival you become aware of its visual presence in a persistent explosion of spray reaching high above the forest canopy, and then you are there at Mosi wa Tunya, "The smoke that thunders", an indescribable and intimidating spectacle of water, sound and light. That calm river plunges into catastrophe, turning ninety degrees as it roars into its canyon. When the river is high the whole scene is viewed through a gossamer mist overhung by a perpetual rainbow, the spray itself sustaining a luxurious tropical forest. When the river is low the full interplay of rock, water and blooms is seen in all its vastness and spectacle. It never ceases to thrill and amaze. Livingston felt that even angels in flight must have paused to look upon so wondrous a sight.

This is where we met, Ndlovu. I was on vacation, driving from my base in Lesotho to visit friends in Harare and you were, well, working. The wonderland of Mosi wa Tunya seemed to me to hold its breath for a moment as you appeared, a rival to its own beauty. Africans certainly know how to dress! This slim, athletic figure of easy gait, walked alongside me, dressed in polished shoes, immaculately pressed trousers and a gleaming white shirt that was the perfect frame for a chocolate brown unblemished face and chest. I usually pass up such opportunities owing to shyness and nervousness, and I hurried on. You caught me up. You were soaked from the spray. We white tourists were prepared with our raincoats. You hardly noticed the conditions. But this gave me an opening which I seized.

"Would you like to share my raincoat?" I asked, "It is quite large enough for two".

I remember the exact words. My heart was beating fast but you were in complete control. "Thank you" you replied and, laughing, "Though I doubt it will make much difference now". Our first words. An easy togetherness. My heart raced less but was almost bursting with a sensation of joy and thanksgiving. How could I, a vagrant, ageing European be with a young man of my dreams? I pulled out of my coat and threw it round both our shoulders, and so we walked the rim of the falls our arms around each other, admiring the views and talking without ceasing. At one point my arm fell around your waist and you did not resist. We knew then. As we retraced our steps we endured several disapproving looks but we laughed and held each other tighter because it was our day and the world could share our happiness or be damned.

We returned to my hotel for a drink. I couldn't bear to let you go. I wanted to prolong this afternoon indefinitely. At the bar on the hotel roof we looked across at the falls and furtively clasped hands, yours warm strong and certain. We talked about everything, about "cabbages and kings". Inevitably the issue of our work arose. You were not thrown by hearing I was a priest: indeed, we were both amused by the situation we were in. But how surprised I was to hear that you had turned in a good position and were now smuggling emeralds! Apparently, the Falls, which occur near a meeting of the borders of Zimbabwe, Zambia, Botswana, Namibia and Angola, afford easy opportunities for dodging customs posts and passing illegally from one country to another. Porous border posts indeed! You produced a couple of gems in evidence. I was horrified, not at your occupation but for your safety. Your smile, your laugh, again. You assured me you could take care of yourself and needed the money to further your education. As we talked on into the evening you even came up with the ingenious plan of my becoming your agent and conduit into Lesotho, opening up a new market. After all, who would expect a priest. It was then my turn to laugh at the audacity of the scheme, and at how smoothly we had arrived at this intimacy. It grew late. Neither of us wanted to part. "Where are you staying?" I recall asking, trying to appear merely curious while my heart thumped against my chest. At a caravan site, it appeared, with people who, you made clear, would not miss you for a night, though you needed to be back there by dawn. I didn't enquire as to the reason. I didn't care. We were to be together that night.

We went inside and showered. I was wild with delight. Your declared beauty so far was nothing compared to your naked loveliness. We were both hesitant and unsure at first but, as we lay side by side, we slipped closer, turned and embraced. I remember all the details, Ndlovu, because I need you to know how you showed me possibilities of loving and being loved that I had never imagined. I was crying. You, perhaps, did not really understand, but you held me in that tight, muscular but infinitely gentle embrace that is my abiding memory of Africa, an embrace that speaks both of protection and unlimited giving. We made love. Your passion was so gentle yet insistent. I knew with you a totally uninhibited joy, freedom, peace and desire that I have experienced neither before nor since.

Nowhere was God more real than here. You had led me into a deeper awareness of the depths of love than any preacher. This was living, to feel this bonding with you and yet also, through you, an interconnectedness with the entire cosmos, that all things are related. Richard Wagner knew this. In the second act of his music drama, "Tristan und Isolde", you are in no doubt that their love is being fed by something cosmic, infinite, above and beyond themselves. Sorry – this means nothing to you. But you had shown me, existentially, what great artists had indicated to me but dimly. I was at peace, at one, through you. At – one – ment.

But now I remember your smile, your stroking hands, your infinite "tendresse", as we drifted into sleep in each other's arms. When I awoke, you had already gone. I felt angry at first but I soon realised that you had been kind to us and spared us the agonies of parting. We had already exchanged addresses, and so was to begin that long flow of letters between us until – you were no longer there. It was not an ideal communication because you found it harder than I to express emotions in words, but we shared many joys and sorrows, and the photographs I had taken of you in the hotel room that night also kept you alive daily in my thoughts and prayers. The proof of the goodness and genuineness of our encounter was that, despite the aching agony of separation, I was strengthened and empowered by that meeting, and given a renewed hope and vision that has never completely left me. We affirmed one another in a total way. If we had never corresponded again we would both have been inspired and changed for the better. I cannot resist adding that this exposes the inadequacy of the notion that the "one night stand" is necessarily a morally inferior human encounter. Why do we judge relationships by their longevity rather than by their depth? In one night you broke open my life and exposed it to new possibilities for ever.

3. Innocence Lost

I realize now that our relationship could never have happened had I not been prepared for it. I mean that, having lived in Africa among Africans, for a few years had helped me to appreciate the potential richness of relationships. I would never have been so forward to a fellow European. And for that I have to thank my coming to Lesotho. It happened in the most unexpected way, and has taught me that it is better to make the space to be open to possibility than to limit the future by over planning it.

I had been a priest for eighteen years in Manchester, England. I was too radical to fit in easily with the Anglican establishment but the Diocese was perhaps unique in having Bishops, first Patrick Rodger and then Stanley Booth-Clibborn, together with senior staff who were discerning in giving people their heads and encouraging younger clergy even when we were disruptive. I had previously been a secondary school teacher on a huge housing estate in Birmingham, where I had my second conversion experience (the conventional first we'll come to later), namely, a conversion to people. Having been brought up in a sheltered, lower middle class environment, attended a selective secondary school and Cambridge University, it was an eye opener to be exposed to the seething mass of the great unwashed, whom I had been conditioned to beware of. These kids were marvellous, full of life, love, and joy, and there has scarcely ever been a time in my life when day after day, without fail, I have risen eager to embrace all the possibilities of a new dawn. And, after offering their love so unconditionally, these young people proceeded to educate me.

There is a sort of teasing seductiveness in the relationship between teens and teacher. It is fun, and harmless for the most part. It is a way young people learn to mature in a safe environment. These friendships across the age barrier are important to both parties, affirming them both in their lovability, and exchanging much needed affection. Part of the anger I feel within arises from the frustration with the current obsession with paedophilia, and health and safety which makes such contact impossible now. Of course, adults who sexually abuse minors must be punished with the full force of the law but that is primarily a question of the misuse of power. No longer can old men sit on park benches with their arm around a questioning child. In our self righteous quest for moral purity (mercifully absent in Africa) we have destroyed a whole area of human growth and potential. That world of the young in heart and the young in years learning from and supporting one another has been banished by the censorious and desecrated ancients whose embittered lives they wish to visit on all of us as standard and without deviation. This mutual affection for and reliance on me and the young was underscored in my first parish, which is why I raise the issue now. It was very much the "lost generation" who befriended me and, I might add, often protected me in this huge, soulless agglomeration of council housing estates outside Bolton, Lancashire. I became a sort of unofficial chaplain to a local Hells Angels group and made a conscious decision to grow my hair long and dress in denims – in the end, I was always a mod rather than a rocker so no leathers for me! It worked and I was part of their scene. It also helped when I moved to Bolton itself largely to do college chaplaincy work. This was a very precious time of initiation, into all sorts of music new to me, into soft drugs, into the world of hippiedom and flower power. It was a marvellous time, and a good time, and, for many of us ageing hippies it was a time of vision that has marked us forever. I was also initiated into "coming out".

This happened one night in my flat when a group of students – inevitably of psychology and philosophy – decided late on that it was too far to walk home so they would stay. Unprepared for this I was alarmed and perhaps a little scared. Alastair, a Scot of lissom beauty, slept with me and taught me in a gentle, mature, understanding way both to be myself and accept myself. I had really thought that nobody knew! This has so often been my experience – the extraordinary sense of responsibility and spontaneous self giving shown to me by the young. It became a staple food for my life, an anchor and a refuge. I could not have achieved what I have without this home of youthful affection to come in and out of. When I entered college the very next morning people commented on my new zest, confidence and transformation!

It was when I moved to inner city Manchester that my involvement with ethnic minorities really began because I lived in an area populated by West Indians, Asians and students of all racial backgrounds, and my church and its neighbour operated a community programme staffed partly by African and Asian workers, including Muslims and Hindus.

The West Indian Centre was housed in the parish's former school and was run by a formidable mountain of a man, Beresford Edwards, who could successfully intimidate the City Council if funding was ever threatened. He was a lawyer and operated a highly successful legal advice centre. I was invited on to the committee of the centre. It met weekly on the same night as the reggae disco.

My first time I turned up at 9pm, the appointed time, to find nobody I recognised present. The disco was heaving and I enjoyed squeezing through a gladsome throng perfumed by the strong odour of marijuana and a hundred personal deodorants – lots of "Hi, man's and physical contact – great, I thought, I feel at home. About 10pm. I noticed a fellow committee member, and around half an hour later the meeting started. In the middle of the table stood several bottles of whisky which soon had to be replenished. The din from the disco was obsessive and overpowering, aggravated by frequent openings of the door as the only telephone in the building was in this office and there seemed to be a constant need to phone for taxis. Few minutes were taken, and the pattern seemed to be that, as everyone was so drunk, nobody had clear memories of the last meeting so we virtually started all over again each time. I certainly staggered home very much the worse for wear that night. But what a marvellous way of holding committee meetings! The work got done in spite of them. Having spent thousands of desperate hours in grey meetings of handkerchief - chewing boredom I can confidently assert that they are usually a total waste of time and that their goals are best achieved by networking activist cells.

One day Beresford sat me down and said, "I'm going to give you a history lesson - about your country", and proceeded to devastate me by exposing me to the truth about my people, my culture, my history. So conditioned was I by my grammar school and exclusive university education that I could scarcely give credence to what I heard. But it changed me and my perspectives and I could never see my own context in the same uncritical way again. This was re-enforced by study and five years experience in the inner city. I had thought I was so avant-garde, but I hadn't known the half of it. I actually rose in the ecclesiastical hierarchy. I suppose all wise establishments try to absorb and so neutralise dissent. I became the youngest ever Canon of Manchester Cathedral, and was eventually responsible for the continuing education (or in-service training) of the clergy. Needless to say this appointment by my friend Bishop Stanley, was not universally popular, especially among those like Father Lowe who described the liturgy of my church as "death of God with incense", a label of which I was rather proud. Then – and we have arrived, Ndlovu – into my life walked Michael Worsnip.

He was a remarkable person, that rare phenomenon, a radical white South African who, in the days of apartheid, was a member of the African National Congress. He had begun ordination training but had been forced to flee the country for political reasons. He sought out Stanley as the most radical bishop on the bench and as one who had also worked in Kenya and understood something of Africa. Stanley agreed to ordain him if he embarked on a Masters course in Theology and came to me for his pastoral training. He was immediate trouble. He walked out of his first Sunday service in the parish to which he had been assigned because it was Parade Sunday and he could not stand the sight of these regimented children in what he described as paramilitary uniforms. Months later, after a Stewardship Campaign, he observed, upon receiving the collection during the final hymn that the offering looked no larger than usual so he walked down the aisle, handing people money from the collection plate commenting that if this was all they could afford to give they clearly needed the cash themselves. But we bonded instantly and I was soon the student learning, for the first time in depth, the awful realities of the South African situation. He very soon became frustrated at the inability of the English to understand the urgency of matters there and, not lacking courage, he visited South Africa to spy out the possibilities of work. He was detained but released and so judged the situation shakily viable with the support of some senior bishops there. The post he landed was that of General Secretary of the Christian Council of Lesotho. Lesotho is a small independent country totally surrounded by South Africa. Its government was then a military one, imposed by its powerful neighbour, but at least it was a step away from apartheid and the full force of the draconian secret police system. As the ANC knew very well it was an ideal place from which to sow dissension in South Africa and would be a good base for Michael. So off he went upon graduating, making me promise to visit. He would write, equally insistently, which puzzled me. Eventually he wrote to say he had arranged with the bishop for me to do some clergy training: if I would pay my passage the local church would look after me. Wanting to see Michael, and never having been to Africa, I was sorely tempted.

Stanley agreed to a sort of sabbatical leave and a church educational trust met my airfare. Though initially British Airways seemed unable to locate Lesotho, which didn't fill me with confidence, a ticket was booked and I flew to Johannesburg, catching my first sight en route of the Atlas Mountains in Morocco, little imagining that within a year I would be standing on the summit of Toubkal, the highest peak in North Africa. But I was on my way to Southern Africa, and to you, and, unsuspected by me, a clever trap of Michael's devising.

4. Paradise Found

Lesotho! Le-soo-too. The very name breathes the softness, sweetness and sensuality of the people. It is perched on the Western edge of the mighty Drakensberg mountains, whose Zulu name, uKhahlamba, the Barrier of Spears, resonates with the harsh alpine wilderness that these gentle people inhabit, forced up into its lofty confines from the rich plains of the Free State by the progress of the Great Trek and later colonial encroachments. It is a land of enchantment, almost entirely above the tree line, ranging from eight thousand to thirteen thousand feet, of the purest air and water, the highest country in the world to be inhabited over almost its entire surface, with some of the highest mountain passes. It is small, about the size of Belgium, but feels vast owing to its towering ranges and consequent slowness of transportation.

It was love at first sight. Despite the difficulties of getting there involving a long walk at Johannesburg airport to this tiny aeroplane (which convinced me I was about to be taken by the security police) and several terrifying dips into "air pockets" en route at the mercy of every wind, I stepped on to free African soil both shaken and stirred. The panorama was breathtaking. The name of the capital city, Maseru, means "the place of red sandstone". The mountains were glowing in the softness of sunset: there were warm vermillion tints, burnt ochre highlights and earthy browns. These mountains were to become a landscape that breathed and spoke to me, a home of infinite wonder. The next morning the sky was to explode in brilliant reds, yellows and oranges, the sun rising as a huge shimmering orb of gold. I think it was the first time I had witnessed a simultaneous sunrise and moonset. The mountain tops were painted in soft blues, light purples and touches of reflected red. I was to learn how to read and interpret these sky signs and mountain faces, and to know their healing properties. The early mornings would glow with an unearthly light as one great peak after another gleamed at their top most points a dazzling orange pink mass, with their lower parts still in opalescent shadows of violet and blue. This radiance never ceased to feel too much for mortal mind to grasp. One was a trespasser in a holy place. My love affair with these mountains is well expressed by Moss Campion - although he is talking of other mountains I was to come to know in America.

With each hour the mountains show a new aspect of themselves, a new colour, a new mood. Clouds gather then shred apart under a blinding blue sky; water trickles everywhere, fresh from the snow fields; yellow and purple flowers poke through the glistening soil; occasionally a slide of rock rumbles down from above, echoing between the buttresses... The beauty is endless, so vast and ever changing it can never be held, owned, or captured by the mind...It is frustrating in its utter unpossessableness, its infinite otherness, its austere separateness. Under its spell the heart first opens – and then must break under the pang of its yearning...Panting as I climb to the top of a ridge-line I can feel my heart beat pounding in my head, as if entrained with my thoughts. It roars in my chest, as I am met at the crest by sunlight, bursting through clouds in great coronal streamers. My heart is breaking and it is the yearning born of too great beauty that is the cleaver. Irradiated with sun glow I am struck by the truth of the assertion made most forcefully by the Sufis, that the broken heart was the gift supreme because it generated the magnetic force that drew the divine to you. So if you were smart you wouldn't even want to have that wound healed by the usual consolations. The broken heart was like a beacon for the Absolute. It was meant to bleed.[4]

Some extracts from my journals also reveal my obsession with the mountains.

Not many visitors to Roma proceed beyond the university or one of its many Catholic institutions for it was here that Father Gerard established his first mission in the middle of the nineteenth century. But if you climb out of the valley at its far end, up a precipitous track that clings to the hillside across from an imposing sandstone canyon, you drop a little from the plateau so gained into the lovely secluded valley of the Little Makhaleng River. Over to your right soar the modest heights of Popa and Popanyane whose elegantly sculptured slopes sometimes harbour rare mountain reedbuck. To the left rears the impressive bulk of Thabana-li-Mele, The Mountain of the Nipples, so called because of its shapely twin peaks. This offers one of the most rewarding mountain walks in a country full of them. As this is a rare free-standing peak in Lesotho, mountain and valley vistas open up at every turn as soon as you begin to climb and there are many horse and pedestrian tracks to follow. From the plateau ridge half way up the ascent there is a stunning panorama of almost the entire Makhaleng valley reaching far down into the southernmost depths of Lesotho at Mohale's Hoek. Thabana-li-Mele is in fact the first mountain you can clearly identify in Lesotho as you approach the country from Zastron in the Free State. Although one summit is strictly for rock climbers only (and a particularly difficult challenge), children from one of the tiny plateau villages will show you how to scramble up the other, from which vantage point it seems that you can survey half the misty recesses of Lesotho and admire the nearest three thousand metre peak to the North, Machache, which is accessible by horse from this side but which falls shearly a thousand metres to the lowlands below from its far face. The complete silence is broken only by bird cry or the distant jingle of cow bells.

After crossing the high plateau once you have climbed out of the lush green Roma valley you descend passing little villages of thatched rondavels hugging the hillsides with the endlessly waving children darting in and out, into the majestic broad valley of the mighty Makhaleng River. Accross its silver flow you are confronted by the seemingly impassable barrier of the Thaba Putsoa (Blue Mountains), until you look carefully and make out the track snaking upwards for miles ahead. There used to be an almost impossible hairpin bend on a one in two gradient, and, if you made that, you would eventually cross the range at just under three thousand metres, an awe inspiring mountain wilderness of icy, windswept boulders, sub alpine vegetation and forever receding distant peaks. A more gradual descent brings you to the grasses and wheat fields of the lovely Semonkong Valley, though you are still above the tree line. The village has the air of a Wild West frontier post, with the rail for tethering horses outside Fraser's Store. Scruffy little urchins wearing shreds of blankets and gum boots will offer to take you to the Malutsenyane Falls, the highest in Southern Africa where the roaring waters, heard long before they are seen, plunge nearly two hundred metres into the high walled narrow gorge below. Perched on high cliffs opposite the cascade, with the vultures wheeling overhead, sheep graze on impossible ledges at the falls edge (the locals will tell you they change into snakes to reach them), and surrounded by further mountain tops you realise that you are gazing on an utterly primeval scene, a landscape in one of the most ancient ranges in the world in the heart of Lesotho, that has changed almost not at all since time immemorial. It has also been a journey into the past.

Scaling the peaks of the Natal Drakensberg is one of those occupations that changes your life, alters your perspectives and becomes the centre around which other events diminish in significance. Each climb is so different from any other, yet equally dramatic that it etches itself in the memory with vivid clarity. One experience must stand for many. I approached Cleft Peak, once considered the highest point of the range, from Cathedral Peak Hotel. An energetic hike brings you to the summit of the Little Berg, with its rolling hills and deep rivers, and a typical clear spring tasting like nectar. From here the stark immensity of the mountain wall ahead is intimidating. Excitement mounts as the Camel is circumvented on a high, hanging, path before a narrow rock scramble brings you to the top of the appropriately named Qooo la ma Soja (Bridge of the Soldiers) or Organ Pipes Pass, with its remarkable rock sculptures. A steep and tiring walk brings you on to the escarpment rim, and the last pull up on the stately dome of Cleft Peak is a real exertion after such exposure. But the reward is beyond the power of telling. To the East, far below in the misty depths, the hills of Natal stretch away towards the Indian Ocean. To the West the further mountain peaks of Lesotho glare ominously. From North to South there extends the uninterrupted line of the Northern Drakensberg escarpment: On the one horizon Mdedelo (Cathkin Peak) juts out menacingly, held to Champagne Castle by Monk's Cowl, while on the other far horizon Phofung (Mont-aux-Sources) and The Sentinel challenge the clouds, with the serrated peaks of the remote Mnweni region in the middle distance and, in the foreground the majestic ridge of The Bell and Cathedral Peak. But what holds the attention immediately ahead are lower ridges of crazy spires and gothic shapes, such as The Chessmen, which constitute a fairy tale world in which you can discern your own ruined castles and cathedrals. You can also understand the beautiful Zulu name for these mountains, uKhahlamba, a Barrier of Spears. As I lay exhausted on the very edge of the plunging cliffs the unbelievable happened. The many wind currents around the crags began to produce their own melodies, occasionally coalescing into strange harmonies, truly the music of the spheres. And, as I looked out over the void, only a few metres away a lammergeyer hung on the thermals over the abyss, fixing me with a fierce eye. Lastly, there descended the eternal peace of the mountains. I descended with a sense of benediction, of quiet joy, which not even the thrills of a family of baboons and a rare sighting in these parts of a black mamba could dispel.

If my favourite wise saying is "when in doubt, go higher", it is also true that mountains teach humility, an acceptance of life and a proper sense of one's place in the world.

But Africa became my home, and remains so in exile, not only because of the land but primarily because of the people. From the genuinely warm and friendly welcome of airport officials to the silent young man who was outside my door each morning to ascertain whether all was well, to the hundreds of others who would enter my life, I have never experienced anything to touch the depth and beauty of African friendship – and this was known mainly through the love of simple, rural people. If love involves "paying attention to another in an act of gracious self-forgetting" then I experienced it in all its glory and generosity here. I found myself profoundly accepted as I am, with deep understanding, and knew friendship as the greatest gift of God. This love was not sentimental but realistic, creative, truly affectionate and impatient with barriers or conventions. Coming from a pressurised life in England I found myself restored and liberated. There was great healing to be found in the extreme physicality of the Basotho, always touching, holding hands in conversation or walking, embracing. Their deep friendly eyes saw into you. They taught me that the body is much sinned against, that it is sacred and sacramental, suffused with truth, the mirror of the soul.

How can Africans be so different to us Westerners, how can they be so much more whole? Is it because they are the living link to our roots in primitive man and have preserved more of the essence of true humanity? Have they been less corrupted than us? They are certainly both more innocent and more discerning. At the beginning it is uncomfortable to live with the probing scrutiny, honesty and directness of your hosts. They are very open and expect you to be so, and are full of alarming questions like, "how much do you earn?" or "why are you not married?" They do not value personal space as much as we do: if your door is open you will be visited. Once, young visitors simply would not take the hint to leave and continued our conversation sitting on the side of the tub while I bathed. I discovered that those who have so little in western terms appear to have so much. If your life is radically reduced to essentials then those things that really matter – the family, friendship, the land, food, fun, singing, dancing, prayer and worship – are truly at the centre of life, which is lived with a love and directness that are initially overwhelming. My one question after my first month, in a letter to England, was, "can you have a sort of aesthetic breakdown from being exposed to too much beauty?" A favourite saying is, "motho ke motho ba batho ba bang – a person is a person only through other persons", a key concept of relatedness that informs the idea of "ubuntu", connectedness, our making sense only in terms of our relationships.

But back to my arrival! I also learnt another lesson that day: be infinitely patient and adaptable in Africa. There was nobody to meet me as my message about my landing time had not got through. Eventually Michael was contacted and appeared to collect me – much relief and hugging! Then, on our journey to his home, I learnt that I was not to direct some clergy training (for which I was prepared) but to run the seminary (for which I was not). Lelapa la Jesu (The

Family of Jesus) was situated in the University Town of Roma, and its warden had departed suddenly with a nervous breakdown. I wondered what I was in for! After a delightful weekend with Michael, his wife Jane and a freedom fighter call Tito, whom I was to come to know well much later, I was deposited at the seminary. Touchingly, the students were all gathered in the lecture room in blind faith that someone would turn up to teach them. Leaving my luggage at the door I embarked immediately and unprepared to take my first ethics class.

I need have had no fears. I think we fell in love with each other in those first few days. There were just eight students, some from Johannesburg, the rest from Lesotho. They were a delight. I discovered being acting warden meant being the only resident member of staff. I had to teach every subject on offer that term, some of which I had not studied seriously since my own days in seminary. My early mornings were spent in keeping one lecture ahead of the students. But a regular visitor, for days at a time, was Father Martin Mkwibiso, a lovely old priest who was one of the best educated in Lesotho and a great asset and support.

It was a steep learning curve. I learnt from the South African students the appalling horrors of life in the townships under the apartheid regime: all of them had known close family and friends murdered. I learnt from the Basotho their customs and culture, and soon realised how well having been a shepherd boy, used to solitude, prepares you for ordination. I learnt never to use words like "stupid" with which Africans were regularly regaled by whites, and to be unfailingly polite, patient and attentive, as they were. It was a humbling experience but riddled with laughter as Africans can never remain too serious for too long. My accent and mannerisms were mercilessly exposed. And I came to realise that laughter was a great tool for survival under extreme conditions. It was on the weekend trip to Sehlabathebe, noted below from my journals, that I became convinced that I was being guided to return to Lesotho to work permanently. My "second conversion", to people, was being re-enforced. I knew they had needs I could help meet, and I knew I needed them. Imagine my joy on returning to discover that the students had been thinking the same. What brought an ageing English priest and vibrant young Africans so closely together is difficult to define. However, let me tell you about the trip.

Sehlabathebe, "the place of the shield", referring to the shape of this little plateau perched on the Southern

Drakensberg on the Eastern border of Lesotho, must be one of the most remote and evocative national parks in the world. Access is usually from Quthing in the South West, where, after passing locations redolent of colonial history such as Fort Hartley and Mount Moorosi, in the broad Senqu (Orange) river valley, at the confluence with the Quthing river, the magnificent south perimeter road heaves you up great sandstone mountain cliffs, reminiscent of the Grand Canyon, over a spur of Mount Austen and back along the Senqu, but now high above it. The far bank is access to some of the remotest parts of Lesotho for there is no bridge across the Senqu except near Quthing. Eventually the great mass of Mount Listsang dominates the sky line, a massif just asking to be climbed, as it does the Tsoelike Valley as you bear round it (not having forgotten a short diversion to the border post of Qacha's Nek for petrol, for there will be no more on our route). This cliff track above the limpid, winding river is better than the main road we have left and, after Ramatseliso's Gate, affords lovely views of Natal way down to the right as well as grim, weather scarred peaks to the left. The village of Sehlabathebe seems like the end of the world, its few buildings scattered haphazardly over the moonscape without meaning or purpose. Typically for Lesotho the last few miles are the worst, the track into the park seemingly not maintained and in places all but impassable.

But the rewards for perseverance are great. You can stay in a splendid lodge originally built for the former prime minister, a rogue called Chief Jonathan, though you need to be fully self-reliant. You can take a walk to the peaceful Tsoelike Falls, a two day hike down the spectacular Bushman's Pass into Natal and back, or a climb up Thaba 'Ntso (Mountain of the Eagle), a triple peaked mountain, otherwise known as the Devil's Knuckles, which affords unforgettable vistas over Natal on one side and Lesotho on the other. The first time I visited was with a team from the Biology Department of the National University, led by Professor Robin Meakin, a well known English eccentric and the archetypal mad scientist. We had gone to investigate an insect unique to the rock pools of the area which is both red-blooded and transparent. We found it and took specimens but all Robin's photographs were a failure as it turned out he had forgotten to put any film in his camera. We did, however, enjoy sightings of various buck and birds, including the strikingly red-bosomed jackal buzzard and that king of the Drakensberg, the lammergeyer and wondered at the marvellous sand stone arches there.

We were determined to return by the other route through the central mountains. On the day of our departure it had clearly snowed again overnight on the higher peaks but we persuaded Robin it was his imagination and set off on an icily cold but sunny day into adventures unknown. We drove through some threateningly raging torrents, clearly fed by melting snow, and entered the formidable Motaneng Pass. It was difficult to discern our route ahead though, as we approached the sheer mountainside, an animal track was visible zigzagging upwards. Imagine our horror to discover, as we drew closer, that this was in fact the road. The bends were so tight that it proved impossible to negotiate them in one manoeuvre, necessitating reversing towards sheer precipices of hundreds of metres in depth and, of course, we encountered snow near the summit. But once there the views were superb, snow clad peaks marching away from us in all directions. The descent was no less fearsome because now the snow had begun to melt, and we needed to stop every few metres to wipe mud from the tyres to prevent us slipping over the edge to a certain death. Robin's driving abilities were certainly more impressive than his photographic ones and, after a daring dash across a tumultuous white water tributary we arrived safely on the banks of the Upper Orange River.

Or so we thought. Having stopped briefly in the mountain village of Sehonghong (where Lesotho Airways fly up the mountain side to its airstrip, having descended into the valley first, following the reverse procedure to depart) we arrived again at the bank of the Senqu, delightedly spotted a flock of bald Ibis on a sand bank, and then noticed to our consternation that the track ahead of us had eroded away into the river. We were faced with the alternatives either of retracing our steps all the way to Sehlabathebe (including the Motaneng Pass) and recovering our original route, or of rebuilding the road. We rebuilt the road. Two hours later we were on our way only to shortly lose yet another hour after discovering we had taken the only possible wrong turn. The scientists noticed that the sun was in the wrong place! Fortunately the low Komakoma Bridge over the Senqu was just navigable and we reached Thaba Tseka, the capital village (almost a new town) of the Central District by dusk. There was no hotel. There was no petrol. Fortunately there was petrol two hours and two mountain passes further on at Mantsonyane, high above its river, but the hotel seemed more like a brothel so we soldiered on. At about ten o'clock we collapsed into the friendly lodge at Molimo Nthuse which nestles in a cleft on the pass above the appropriately named village – "God help me".

My letter to Ndlovu got no further than this – it was left unfinished. I close this section with a shorter one that I did send, to all my friends abroad to greet them for Christmas and New Year 1990 – 91.

Lelapa La Jesu Seminary,
National University of Lesotho,
P. O. Roma 180.
Lesotho
New Year 1991

Dear Friends,

Leaving 1990 feels like coming out of a long Lesotho thunderstorm: much sound and fury, moments of extraordinary beauty and feelings of anxiety, tension and being battered. No, my long honeymoon period with this country and its people is not over, but darker realities have also been in evidence these last twelve months:

I suppose they had to come eventually – no more than Plato's philosopher-kings can we live on mountain tops forever (even in Lesotho).

It has been a more turbulent year in the seminary. We have had more students than ever before (and we are now beginning to serve other Provinces than our own, Botswana in 1990 and Zaire in 1991), but no more staff: I remain the only resident and full time staff member of any description. Indeed, I have been described as "exploited" which is not an epithet commonly applied to whites in these parts! This has meant that conditions have suffered here, not least the quality of my own teaching, and this has contributed to mild student unrest (though they remain, in general, it must be said, marvellously loving and co-operative). As you know, when I become overtired I become irritable, which destabilises the situation further. It is an awful affliction which I do not seem to be able to control adequately.

We've had several minor and one serious dispute, the latter involving a week long boycott of services, classes and even some meals (a sure sign of seriousness!). This arose over my handling of a theft of money: the students and I had different views over culpability, and I stood firm against unproven assumptions about local villagers. Sadly, I am convinced that it is an inside job, but there is little real evidence.[5] The situation showed, however, how fragile the community can be and how emotionally charged it can become. We shall probably never now find proof. My relationship with the ordinands was peacefully resolved by us: they do tend to be passionate in both love and war! But the episode is indicative of the strains that can affect us all – and, of course, I am always in a minority of one! On the positive side, weathering such tensions is also a sign of real community building, and I do feel that the underlying trend is one of continued growth and maturity.

Parish work has been heavy, too. Our new church, St John the Evangelist, Ha Monyooe (so decided by local folk, I must confess, because John is the same name as Ian – a memorial I neither expected nor desired but one which speaks volumes about the warmth of the people), which so many of you have helped to build, was finally consecrated last September on a glorious day with the mountains visible to the horizons all around our rocky ridge. There was a splendid mass, hundreds of visitors (including representatives from all the local churches) and much feasting, singing and dancing. It was a very moving occasion for me – the first church, however modest, that I have ever built – but, fortunately, the Basotho do not allow you to be withdrawn and tearful, at least not until I could curl up with some local friends at the end of a very long day. The very existence of the building has already increased congregations considerably. We have also opened up four other mission centres so, even with the help of the ordinands, the increase in work is considerable – and, of course, we still need to walk to villages up the Helvellyns and Skiddaws of Lesotho, or go by horse, or drive over nonexistent roads! We have also begun an ambitious project with the local Roman Catholic Seminary to assist villages near the university in various community development issues. This has got off to a rather uncertain start but I am confident it will stabilise and grow. It's a marvellous opportunity for our students and for the improvement of my Sesotho.

In 1990 it would have nice to say, in view of the foregoing, that the university had been a haven of peace and godly learning but I fear this was not the case. The release of Nelson Mandela last February was the symbol of new life breaking out in our region, a promise of resurrection. The university should be a place where ideals of democracy and freedom are nurtured and so it was not accidental that the first stirring of independent political life in Lesotho this decade, came, in part, from our campus, both staff and students. The seminary was given the great honour by the organisers to lead the procession through the streets of Maseru celebrating what one theologian likened to the second coming of Christ (Mandela's release – not, I think, as extravagant an eschatology as appears at first sight). We found ourselves leading a different sort of demonstration a few months later. The Student's Union were in dispute with the university administration over an astronomic increase in fees. As corruption is rife here we supported the students, not least when they were patronised and finally threatened with physical force. We harboured them in our premises when the police and army came in and stayed with them outside the gates overnight when they chose to voluntarily leave the campus.

There was, as usual, much singing, and I found myself preaching, without preparation, at my first major demonstration, rather emotionally I must admit, but to responses no sermons usually elicit! When my negotiations with the police failed the next morning I persuaded the Roman Catholic Seminary to admit them all to prevent their forcible removal.

The students went to court and it says something for the independence of the Lesotho judiciary that they won an injunction to be re-admitted to campus. This was extraordinary, all the villages turned out in support, and the seminary led the huge procession back on the campus – dancing! The issues are still being debated but I think we gave a warning that has been heeded. Two minor but problematic consequences for me have been firstly, that my profile has become much higher and 'ntate Ian is now even more in demand and, secondly, that I have become very unpopular with some government and university personnel. But, of course, that is the inevitable consequence of standing for the truth in our region. Amidst all this activity it was sickening to hear that a predecessor of mine and an active member of the ANC, Michael Lapsley, had lost both his hands and an eye in a parcel bomb explosion at his home in Zimbabwe:

please remember him in your prayers as he convalesces and give thanks for the remarkable faith that sustains him.

Yet all this is not the limit of my activities.

For some, like being responsible for post-ordination training in the Diocese there is little time, others are best left unsaid, and counselling, as you will realize with me, is a major occupation. The result seems to be that two thirds of the way through each year I tire seriously and pick up the first bug that comes along. In 1989 it was glandular fever and in 1990 a lethal combination of pneumonia and tic- bite fever that has left me very low. This must call my future here into question, much as I love being here. The medicine I need is, of course, an assistant member of staff. Throughout the Province sympathetic noises are being made but no Bishop seems able to find me anyone: at the time of writing I have less help promised this year than last. U. S. P. G., who support me here and have generously extended my contract for a further year, have quite rightly said that they will not support a renewed contract unless help is found. So the longer term future is in the balance...

It is really impossible to comment briefly on the political situation.

Despite the appalling disasters across our borders there really are signs of hope. But if you take the lid off a boiling cauldron it is bound to boil over. We are not so much entering the Promised Land after our Exodus events, but are rather in the Wilderness, maybe searching for Sinai. Generally so-called black-on-black violence does not happen unless it is instigated by the security forces or lunatic right wing groups. In Lesotho itself the military government is making contorted moves towards an easing of our own dictatorship and state of emergency but we cannot accept freedom as a gift from the army nor its puppet constituent assembly, which has been described as a gathering of political mercenaries. The most promising political event here has been a well sustained teacher's strike (my role was only in supporting individuals), which was inconclusive but marks an end to the enslavement of the Basotho to fear and despair. As in South Africa growing union activity will be crucial.

From the public to the private domain – my personal life is utterly chaotic and marvellously happy, and there just isn't time for it all! It is such a joy to be loved across so many apparent barriers, to be so accepted and tolerated.

I wish I could share with you things that have been shared with me and to describe how I am succoured from the very depths of heart and soul but some things cannot be spoken. Students from the university and friends in the villages will be with me forever. Even the most combative ordinand said to me recently, "we might fight but you have to stay" (that probably means more to me than many less critical comments)! I now also have some marvellous friends in Zimbabwe and one came back with me for a few memorable weeks last year. And I must refer at least once to this scenically magnificent part of the world. Last winter I discovered the Vumba in Zimbabwe, a pocket of mountains in the eastern highlands that it is easy to bypass. And there, on one of the highest hills, is a distinctly English teashop set in a sort of hanging gardens that must be Eden rediscovered – and with beautiful young people that made it like the Koranic view of Paradise, too! Beautiful mountains and beautiful people in conjunction must be what heaven is like. My annual climbing expedition in the Drakensbergs was a little limited by post-pneumonic exhaustion but I did follow the route of the Langalibalele rebellion up and down the escarpment and spent some refreshing days in splendid isolation, often in utter silence and with not a human being to be seen. I've come to appreciate more the so called Little Berg, the mountains in front of the main Drakensberg range: you are high enough for marvellous views but also get the most stunning impressions of the escarpment itself which, of course, you cannot see either when you are on it or when you are much further away. The spring flowers were overwhelming this year though I saw few birds and animals.

So it has been an action packed and exhausting year. There is just too much to digest. Some of it is faintly disturbing. Sometimes I feel poised between two cultures while belonging to neither, now rather remote from the U.K. but not really a white Mosotho (though I am sometimes called such, which I value). It is all a little redolent of E. M. Forster's classic "A Passage to India" with its crux of the impossibility of really belonging to what you love. I shall never be able to convey to you what being here means to me but I have never felt such passion for a whole people and certainly never for a land, for rock and earth...

Yet underneath the clamour the quiet ecstasy is still there. The national motto is "Khotso, Pula, Nala" – peace, rain, prosperity.

There is the deep peace of the great rivers, the silent mountains, the serene shepherd boys (how like Celtic spirituality), which I have probably found at just the right time in my life. Certainly the rain of God's abundant blessings has never seemed so real, the "prosperity" of inner contentment and the ability to be satisfied with less. This never takes me away from you; indeed it is easier to be with you here than separated by fewer miles in talkative little England. While being full of gratitude for my life here I grow in thankfulness for you. How blessed I am with so many friends who support me ceaselessly with their prayers, letters and gifts. I don't know how to say "thank you" because I am lost for words. If a priest, in Michael Ramsey's words goes to the altar with his people on his heart then that is where you are, and not least when I daily celebrate the Eucharist and know our everlasting togetherness in the spirit. "Oneanothering" is a nice expression I encountered recently for the importance of sticking together...

Ian with Ordinands in an illegal procession in Lesotho following the release of Nelson Mandela from prison

Mock Funeral procession in Bolton

Mont-Aux-Sources in the Drakensberg Range, Lesotho

Tuam Cathedral, Eire

School Teacher | Curate - Bolton | Parish Priest Manchester

Section 2

In this section I shall fill in some of the gaps from my earlier years, before emigrating, return to Africa, and then go on to describe significant experiences in my later life, all in a series of short vignettes.

1. Lancashire – Hell's Angels

I described earlier what I call my "second conversion", my conversion to people. After a somewhat narrow domestic and educational upbringing I suddenly discovered in teaching the wonder of raw humanity and joined, as it were, the human race.

As a young curate I worked on a huge council housing estate, Highfield, on the edge of Bolton near Manchester. Every morning I met God afresh in at least three different ways. First, in the splendour of spectacular sunrises over a sea of roofs and chimneys: nothing guarantees sensational sunrises and sunsets better than industrial haze. Secondly, in the quiet of intimate worship in the Parish Church as the Vicar and I said Morning Prayer together. And thirdly, in a different sort of sea, that of eager, alert young faces in one of our church schools. In the United Kingdom religious education is still part of the school curriculum and religious assemblies are mandatory: the former used to be exclusively Christian and the latter a daily gathering of the school. Now R.E. is multifaith but patchily done, and assemblies are rarer and have a more secular purpose, but this meeting of church and state in education arising in part from the establishment status of the Church of England, in part from the post war Butler Education Act gave maverick clergy like me a chance to make contact with youth and raise life issues with them.

We had a church secondary school. I conducted some R.E. classes and would use the music and literature of the current "Flower Power", hippy era as ways in to discussing matters of vital concern to the students, issues of meaning, love, life and death. I found myself in trouble for discussing questions of human sexuality, allowing them to use the language natural to them in this area. I discovered that an unlikely rock group, Black Sabbath, had, early in their career, produced a rock mass entitled "Ceremony". The Kyrie began with a low, indeterminate sound that gradually emerged as that of human wailing, the whole world baring its hurts and wounds. The dance group would respond to this and then break into an energetic performance of the joyful Gloria. The Lord's Prayer, in a mysteriously haunting setting, made a perfect backdrop to receiving communion. With these pupils and later in my next post, Higher Education Students, we organized some open air festivals in the parks. In those heady days, youngsters often wrote poetry or were in music groups and I felt it was important to provide a platform to showcase their talents and give them the experience of honing and refining their skills in performance as they explored matters both personal and profound. In a similar way I would devise evening services in church around the music and literature they had composed, weaving a theme out of their offerings in the sermon. Such services would often then open into a concert, disco or party.

Luther wrote that the worshipping community needs three arenas: the great cathedrals, where people can gather for solemn liturgy on great occasions; the parish church, whose main service would be the Eucharist, simply done, not aping a cathedral's style; and occasions of worship for "the Turk and the market place", when those on the edge of institutional church life would gather and would be made welcome. It was this last consideration that motivated me here. It is very difficult for people, especially the young, to attend a normal church service, in its formality, stilted and technical language, and high average age, unless that church offers a deep experience of the numinous in worship, great preaching or great music of whatever sort – and not many do. Worship requires far more attention from our church leaders. I wanted young people to experience the wonder of creation and the deep abiding love of its Creator for it. Most people live limited, circumscribed lives and need lifting to wider horizons.

I had no special qualifications for this approach. I was a middle class, Oxbridge trained white male with very limited experience of the world. What bought me out of myself was the warmth and excitement of these young people who invited me to join their world. And I came to realize that I could trust them: they would look after me and not abandon me. I, who was supposed to be "in loco parentis" to them, discovered that I was the one being educated, held and loved. All that is basically required is a deep love for, and openness to, the young. Most adults are afraid of them because their world is largely unknown, inhabited by strange music and disturbing ideas, and because, deep down and unacknowledged, we know that they are the future and will eventually supplant us. As I experienced the idealism and vibrancy of those among whom I worked I became ever more convinced that the future is in good hands. I realized their tremendous capacity for self sacrifice, whether in young kids looking after their siblings in families with inadequate parents, or in care for friends or in efforts to serve the poor and disadvantaged in the local community or overseas – even when they were partially disadvantaged themselves. I came to see that, to be most useful to them, I needed to more fully enter their world and let go of my past and its prejudices, to learn to swim in a new environment.

As a token of my determination, at least for myself, I decided to dress differently, in the fashionable denim jackets and jeans of the day, and to grow my hair long. I eventually looked a lot like Rasputin, and, of course, it was a delicate experiment which could have misfired badly had it not had a sincere intention, but it did, in practice, make me more accessible and broke down barriers. Moreover, I had the privilege of a saintly vicar and a discerning bishop who trusted me to get on with my work without interference.

Its most extreme manifestation was in my ministry to a local informal chapter of Hell's Angels They were the contemporary "Rockers," whose uniform was the decorated black leather jacket and who rode large motor bikes, preferably Triumph Bonneville's. Every summer there would be pitched battles at some seaside resort between "the rockers" and "the mods", gentler souls who dressed in denim, smoked pot, preached peace and listened to more weird, "way out" music than the mainstream rock scene. Of course, my attire indentified me more with the mods, but I discovered that it was the rockers, the Hell's Angels, who were taking over the local community youth centre. Now, I always made a point, as a clergyman, of visiting all the institutions on my patch, from bars to schools, from shops to offices, because the church tends to minister in areas where people sleep rather than where they work or make recreation and, when you encounter people on their ground rather than yours, they tend to be more forthcoming and relaxed. Some of my most intimate and searching counselling has been done in pubs. You run the risk of being misinterpreted, of course, and tales will be told, but that is the price to be paid for doing the job and, in any case, my name and reputation is not the most important thing the Lord has given me to take care of.

My first encounter with the Hell's Angels was not propitious. They would see my dress as an affront, my age (twenty-seven) as a barrier, and my calling as either a joke or a threat. But I was strange enough to be of a little interest and, with perseverance over several weeks, conversations developed. I eventually went with them to the local bar. It was a neighbourhood pub – the only one – so the whole world was always there. As we entered the "tap room" that evening (the opposite to "the lounge" which was comfortable and cosy, but this was where the men went and played darts and cards, the place of "spit and sawdust"), the lads were roundly booed as they filed in and then, as I appeared in the rear, that night in full regalia, cassock and cloak, silence descended: this was just inexplicable!

As time went on they decided I should be brought closer in to their circle. It was customary for initiates to undergo certain tests. In Liverpool, to the west of us, one of these consisted, in the older areas of the city where tall apartment blocks leaned towards each other over narrow alleys, in leaping from one roof to another across the passage way below. Fortunately for me we were on a modern housing development. I underwent minor trials, such as being taken out as a passenger on a bike and having my leg brushed along the sides of vehicles we overtook; and being driven on and off a motorway by various ramps at a huge spaghetti junction nearby at great speed. I survived these and became an accepted member of the group. The fact that I could hold my own in drinking with them also helped. This all gave me an entrée into an unknown world where caring agencies never went. I was the one who would visit them in hospital after sometimes horrendous road accidents. I was the one engaged to approach parents when a girlfriend became pregnant. I was the only one some of them had to confide in. Above all I listened and did not make judgments. Often this took me into very grey moral areas, especially regarding sex, substance abuse and criminal activity. I was present once when they deflated the tyres of a police car. I was once confronted by two of them who arrived at Highfield Youth Club having escaped from prison. They needed accommodation for the night – they were on the run. I had a very accommodating landlady who would probably have obliged, had I not told the full story, but my immediate reaction was to resist putting her in a compromising position so I refused them. They went off into the night and were picked up by the police a few days later. By doing "the right thing" (apart from not reporting them) I made my worst mistake. I should have sheltered them. I am quite sure of that. I had let them down in their hour of greatest need. It was easy to justify the course of action I had taken but I had failed to demonstrate the love I preached.

If you are to fully serve a group you must be loyal to it. This will inevitably involve moral compromise. But the cost of doing the respectable, conventional thing can be to lose the trust of those you are seeking to support and you destroy your own ministry. I have often felt obliged to shield young people from the undiscriminating arm of the law. When I was chaplain to several Colleges of Further Education I would often secrete little packets of marijuana in my office as the police would often frequent the discos looking for easy pickings. The worst thing that someone a little under the influence can face is an aggressive policeman. I also felt caught in the moral confusion and hypocrisy of social mores. In those days we smoked marijuana mixed with tobacco so that its effect was diluted. It was no health hazard and produced no hangover. Smoking marijuana in this way was less harmful than smoking cigarettes or drinking beer to excess, two very common and acceptable social vices. Sometimes the company you keep compels you to a radical view of ethical judgements and even a priest must be true to him/herself and his constituency.

The nonsense to which conventional thinking can lead us was illustrated by my being chaplain to a notorious night club, The Twisted Wheel, in inner city Manchester. A young friend of mine told me of this club he frequented every weekend. It was a haven for drug taking and trafficking. Its advantage was that it collected "the scene" together, rather than its being diffused across the clubs of the city, and so made it easier for both the police and social services to keep in touch with the activity. However, a newly elected city council wanted to close the place down, despite the objections of the police. The owner, facing a dilemma, sought a chaplain and social workers, and he urged the youth to bring their parents! It was the only literally all night club in town, closing at dawn with breakfast. The music was great with live acts and the best DJs. A pleasant odour permeated the place! So I was recruited as the chaplain. Each Saturday I would take the bus to Manchester with my friend, arriving at about 10 pm, meeting his friends in cafes (some marvellous people), learning where they stashed their dope (often between bricks in walls) where they could retrieve it the next morning to help them "come down" gradually, and then "loitering with intent" at the club in my clerical collar, enjoying the music and conversation and sometimes getting involved in very difficult situations. About 3am the owner's driver would take me home with my fee – a large Cuban cigar! After two hours sleep I would arise for a full day in church. But the whole effort failed. I appeared as a witness in court, stressing the advantages of centralising the drug scene in this way so people could the more easily be helped and supported. An elderly, petulant magistrate thought otherwise, the club was closed and the drug scene scattered all over Manchester, just as we had feared.

I remember, too, speaking in court for a young man convicted of "cottageing" that is, seeking sexual satisfaction in a public convenience. Most cases were brought by police acting as "agents provocateurs", a regrettable practice that could cause significant psychological damage to men who might be insecure, desperate and extremely lonely. Many of us were resolved to do what we could to stop this practice. The young man in question, Martin, was openly gay and a well known activist, but in this case was quite innocent and had been "set up". Several of us appeared as character witnesses and my appearance quite perplexed the magistrate. But he threw the case out, and the practice of police provocation largely disappeared – a little battle won in the campaign for equality.

The spiritual resources needed for such work come largely through the relationships that are established and finding that, once you are willing to let go of many former certainties, you do not sink but swim, upheld both by your new constituency but also by that love of God which wells up in all situations where people take the risk to be vulnerable to one another. The love of God expressed through deep personal engagement with Hells Angels, drug addicts, and the gay community has often been more overwhelming than any encounter deriving from the church. The greatest requirement is resilience, hence the need for plenty of sleep and an active prayer life. The church tends to be very conservative in its moral theology, developing systems that fail to take account of individual needs and experience. In the real world of questioning young people you are constantly challenged to stretch your ethical categories to meet ever new situations. For instance I was compelled to reconsider my attitude to the so called "one night stand", usually a torrid sexual experience with someone you "pick up" and may never meet again. It occurred to me, after one such experience of my own which had, in fact, been a very loving and life affirming encounter that we tend to judge the "success" of a relationship by longevity rather than depth. Surely most of us have experienced enriching encounters with individuals we have never met again but whose insights and zest for life have challenged us in some way? Conversely we have known long standing connections with those whose lack of vitality and vision – even, dare one say, some marriages – have left us deeply unsatisfied and may be even drained. Sometimes one assignation of depth can convey a lifetime of experience. I am, of course, not arguing against long standing relationships, which are irreplaceable, but for value in the brief encounter. And some people will know serial relationships rather than the one love of their life. The church needs to acknowledge human reality and develop rites of blessing for these and other great moments of life, such as coming of age, engagement, achieving a first job, business partnerships, friendships, gay relationships. Young people live with risk because learning to live is a risky business, and they encourage all of us to take risks, to "push the envelope", to test the boundaries, to question received tradition and enlarge our vision. They can make us young again.[6]

2. Manchester – The Urban Maze

My first sole pastoral care was the parish of St. John Chrysostom in inner city Manchester. Victoria Park was built in the nineteenth century as an exclusive estate of private mansions, some gloriously restored, some in faded but discernible splendour. Many had declined into apartment dwellings, inhabited by the impoverished, students and representatives of every conceivable race. It was a vibrant, exciting and sometimes dangerous neighbourhood, with large Afro Caribbean and Indo-Pakistani communities on its borders. It was a thrilling place to be. On a Sunday morning I would peer from the altar through the haze of incense to the people gathered for mass, and see a few representatives of the remaining wealth of the area in the near pews, many students, local workers, faces of all colours, university staff, members of the LGBT community, local tramps and even one or two dogs – and I would think, firstly of the slogan of the tabloid newspaper, "The News of the World", "All human life is here", and secondly, what a privilege to be here – this is the kingdom of heaven.

I inherited the typical large rectory and, apart from considerations of just use of property, I could afford to live there only if I took in tenants. I chose students and this proved to be a steep learning curve for us all. Most of us had not lived in community apart from our own homes and it is not an easy situation to adjust to.

I, too, was belatedly finding my place in the world and, though the joys of common life were many, the frustrations could be oppressive – insufficient personal space and time, bearing one another's burdens, mediating in disputes, keeping everyone up to the mark on communal duties such as cooking and, especially, cleaning. But we did all learn to cook very successfully and were soon able to cater gourmet meals to visiting preachers and famous musicians who graced our music programmes. In fact, we grew imperceptibly into a small community of hospitality with an open door, all of us rising to the challenge of being the rectory family. And our own bonds strengthened to the degree that we are all still in touch. The secret of survival here was openness and honesty with one another. When my partner, Gordon, moved in, it had to be by common consent. It is impossible to have secrets in a small, closed commune, impossible to hide anger and resentment, impossible not to affect others for good or ill. My insane urge to encompass everything that a post in pastoral care demands often left me exhausted and spent so that I was scarcely the best host. But the family grew strong enough to cope with that and more than compensated for my weaknesses. I lived in their love and learnt from their young wisdom.

Student life was a major component of parish life and this was always stimulating and challenging. As a preacher and teacher I was kept up to the mark by this intellectual community and reminded of my obligation to make time for study and reflection. As so often, those for whom you are responsible push you towards the elements necessary for your survival and flourishing. I was always nervous of working with this constituency feeling I was intellectually inadequate for such interaction but I was always carried along by the warmth of the companionship and the excitement of debate and, before I realised it, I was indeed managing to produce what was required of me. Pastoral situations were equally demanding: young adults feel deeply "the slings and arrows of outrageous fortune" and go through devastating emotional valleys of death. Intense unremitting concentration is required of the listener. But the secret of this ministry of presence, often silent, is staying with the person and the situation and taking both seriously. Older people develop a sad habit of distancing themselves from the tribulations of the young and looking backwards at them with the spectacles of hindsight and superiority: we tend to treat young adults, and especially children, as apprentice human beings, not fully formed and therefore to be treated with a certain degree of condescension and patronisation. If a problem is serious to a person, whatever our perspective of it may be, it is serious and must be treated as such. How often rifts between parents and children develop because the former fail to treat the latter with sufficient respect and understanding. Respect is the key. If people feel deeply it is the greatest disservice to them to tell them they should not: do we want them to decline into emotional infants or cripples? Such counselling is hugely demanding but immensely rewarding. I have learnt so much about handling relationships through what I have taken from the teens and students I have waited on.

When people feel they have moved into a safe environment remarkable things can happen. I remember a visiting preacher making what was perceived as an ungenerous reference to the LGBT community. It provoked an immediate reaction among members of that fraternity and among the students in the congregation. So we decided to make one of our regular Sunday evening discussion groups in the rectory a discussion of "the church and homosexuality". I invited a charming but trenchant member of the Gay Liberation Front to open it up followed by some careful words about Biblical exegesis from me. Discussion was slow to take fire, the elderly ladies looking bemused. But one of the students was brave enough to seize the moment, "come out" to us all, and introduce his partner. As talk got underway one of the women said she "hated" homosexuality and the student replied that this meant she hated him. We were off! Wise and compassionate dialogue ensued, emboldening one older man to make the revelation of the evening. A respected, retired air force pilot, he confessed that, before flying his first mission in the Second World War and not knowing whether or not he would return, he decided to experiment with "the other sexuality". "It wasn't too bad" he admitted. This really broke the ice and from then the conversation flowed till late. The congregation was strengthened by the openness of some and the empathetic response of others, and next Sunday there were some damp eyes in church and more hugs than usual.

Another significant aspect of this world in microcosm was the presence of ethnic minorities. We and two neighbouring parishes operated what was called The Longsight/Moss Side Community Project, these being the two areas each side of Victoria Park. Cognisant of the existence not only of other nations but also of other religions, we employed, among others, both Muslim and Hindu community workers, Nilofar Siddiqi and Mohini Puri. My relationships with these two communities were warm and cordial. Parish parties would visit the Hindu temple to the south of us for worship and meals and always be well received. I began my study of Hinduism in response, which was to culminate in a visit to India years later. I was fed by what I learnt as one always is in appreciating the beliefs of others and one is stretched to encompass new truths and further revelations. I had to conclude that revelation in Christ was not exclusive or that I had barely understood the cosmic nature of that disclosure. Raimondo Pannikar's marvellous book, *The Unknown Christ of Hinduism*,[7] helped me to a sort of compromise in understanding there. I had to concede the infinite worth and depth of Hindu religious understanding for Hindus. I had to confess that my facile assumptions about Christianity had been made in total ignorance of this rich and fertile tradition. I loved the all-inclusiveness and acceptance of Hinduism and its lack of dogmatic structure and centralised authority. It really was the collected wisdom of a people and deeply democratic. Why could not the Church, which defined God as Love, be at least as inclusive and non judgmental? I was aware of the social problems inherent in Hinduism in India but in the Diaspora it certainly felt like a religion of joy and affirmation, not least in the Diwali ceremony, The Festival of Lights – and, as I was to experience later, especially in evening prayers on the Ganges at Varanasi.

I was equally challenged by Islam. I had no idea that both Jesus and the Blessed Virgin Mary receive extensive treatment in the Qur'an. In visiting Muslim homes I was moved by how young boys could recite passages of scripture by heart. Where did that happen in the church? The South Manchester Mosque was in my parish; the Imam was a school teacher and so spoke good English, a rarity among Imams then. We had many discussions, and he would address the church prayer group on matters of spirituality, always urging us to seek to be better Christians. Again my vision was enlarged. Whatever trepidation I had felt about entering other religious traditions evaporated in the warmth of their reception and in the deepening of my understanding. The act of exploration again drew forth the spiritual qualities necessary to sustain it. A younger Imam was a great shock. I invited him to take part in a Lent course on other religions. He began by referring to the Crusades, which I thought a little tactless. But it was the cornerstone of his argument: this traumatic and bloody experience still resonates, and Muslims see Christians through that lens of oppression, their hands stained with blood. Any apprehension we might have about militant Islam today should be viewed with this in mind. This was salutary and disturbing information for Christians to handle.

I was, in a later job, to experience the Orthodox Jewish Community of Prestwich, Manchester, where I was to live. I knew more about the Jewish religion, of course, but was again humbled by the warm welcome I received everywhere, not least from my neighbours in a street of Jewish households, and was moved to tears by my first experience of a Sabbath supper, realising at once the birth of the Christian Eucharist. I was regularly able to appreciate this through the hospitality of the deputy principal of King David's High School, a true apostle of reconciliation. Surely God is the God of hospitality, as a Japanese theologian surmised.

I mentioned earlier my initiation into the West Indian Centre and my education at the hands of Beresford Edwards. Dealing with the West Indian community was always a joy because people are so warm, vibrant, full of hope and full of humour. Friday nights at the Centre's reggae disco continued to be a riot. When the City of Manchester threatened the Centre with suspension of funds, which they regularly did, owing to failure of audited accounts to appear, Beresford would accuse them of racial prejudice and they always backed down. I made regular court appearances with youth at risk, nearly always admiring in them a daring, determination and self respect that I never had at their age. I attended many meetings in support of Beresford. I had my first experiences of exorcism which was regularly, if not frequently, requested in that community. This required some mature discernment and wisdom. When the trouble seemed to reside in a particular darkened room that people had grown afraid to enter sometimes simply drawing back the curtains and saying some prayers would suffice. On other occasions dark forces were possibly in play. It is normal to perform an exorcism with other clergy or church members but outsiders harboured unfounded fears about entering black areas at night so often it would just be me and the family. The prayers always seemed to work but it was an exhausting business. There were also many from Africa among this community and I am proud to have a Nigerian god son, Obi, who is both a computer geek and a splendid visual artist. The capacity to transcend suffering and the depth of African compassion was a revelation and helped prepare me for work in Africa later.

The GLBT community was well represented in the parish. The Campaign for Homosexual Equality had done sterling work for years in the area of law reform but had become a rather elderly and middle aged group of grandees, revered yet a little apart. There was clearly a need for younger, more vibrant, more activist and politicised organisations and one of them, the Gay Liberation Front, met on occasion in the rectory. I was a founder member of the Gay Christian Movement, as it was first called, and the first priest in Manchester to offer blessings of gay relationships. By then Stanley Booth-Clibborn was Bishop of Manchester and, though he was by far the most left – leaning Bishop on the bench, he found gay relationships difficult to understand. We met once a year over sherry when I would try to convince him that sexual liberation was part of the spectrum of political liberation movements. But, out of respect for me, he trusted me to act appropriately to requests for blessings though he did not want to know any details as he could not give permission! Work with these groups was often a joy and I came to know regulars in the bars who would look out for me to discuss problems that might arise. It is sad that the Church still struggles with this issue which is dealt with further later on. All the groups that the Church has oppressed in the past – women, usurers, female seers (witches), Jews, ethnic minorities, slaves, homosexuals – it has become reconciled to except the last. It is the great test of the churches in our time in laying claim to inclusiveness and being the incarnation of the love of God in the world, the Body of Christ.

The street people, the tramps, were also a regular part of the work. Our many burglaries at the rectory were never their work but that of youthful opportunists. Our callers were often genuine gentlemen of the road who were used to surviving there, either by choice or because some distant disaster had broken them and left them there. They came for food but also to talk. One young man, Peter, we were able to help rehabilitate and he found work locally as a waiter. Once, I went out to a derelict site and sampled "meths" (methylated spirits) with the older men: I don't know how they managed it and it was very clear that it would sooner rather than later destroy them. Two regularly came for breakfast in the rectory with the students after the early mass on Friday morning. A few found the "beauty of holiness" of our High Church liturgy an oasis in the desert of the city. Christmas was always special for me, but in an unusual way. Most of the students had gone home as had many others in the bed-sits if they had anywhere to go, so attendances were actually smaller than at most times of the year. But on Christmas Eve, with the faithful few gathered, including a few of the men of the road, and as the busy city pursued its frenzied search for liquor induced escapism around us, it was easy to feel at one with the Holy Family in the stable that first Christmas night, attended by a few shepherds while the world went its way around them. Thus did the divine glory enter its creation then – and now. Some of my efforts were directed to persuade the civic authorities to better provide for these casualties of our distracted society but there always remained the daily responsibility of caring for individuals without which the organisational work would not have made sense. Too many clergy these days wish to escape into finding institutional solutions to issues as a way of avoiding dealing with individuals with intractable problems. Such clergy can never be found and do not visit. This is a dereliction of duty and a refusal to walk with Jesus among Luke's "anawim", the little ones, the outcasts and dispossessed, which is always the litmus test of Christian ministry and witness.

Whilst seeking to meet this huge range of demanding parish responsibilities I was also, like many promising young clergy, loaded with diocesan responsibilities, serving on various committees, and in particular pioneering ecumenical chaplaincies to Colleges of Further Education, first in Greater Manchester, and then advising nationwide. For all that, as I have suggested, the people we think we are ministering to are often ministering to us and keeping us afloat with their love, support and prayers, such extra burdensome duties tend to crowd out adequate time for prayer and reflection, days off and opportunities just to "chill out". I found I increasingly had no time for myself and those who cared for me, and then exhaustion and depression began to set in, as I have described elsewhere. If you are keen and committed as well as young and inexperienced, it is difficult to avoid the pitfall of taking on too much responsibility and trying to meet everyone's expectations. Not to do so seems like failure and it takes a person of some maturity to realise that it is often in our failures that God acts because we are no longer putting up barriers and keeping him out by trying to achieve everything in our own strength. The church should, of course, be putting resources into monitoring and succouring its young promising clergy but it rarely does, and laity have even less hope of support unless it is from family or friends so people become jaded, disillusioned and alienated from an institution that first uses and drains them and then dumps them. We, in turn, need to look out for those colleagues suffering such exploitation, offer support and challenge the authorities to take responsibility. Bishops should first be servants and carers before they are managers and employers. By and large employees in the medical and secular caring professions are better protected than their colleagues in the Church.

3. Africa – Lelapa La Jesu[8]

I earlier spoke of the manner of my arrival in Lesotho and gave some account of this isolated mountain country. During my preliminary two months there in 1986 I learnt two very important lessons about life in Africa.

Firstly, I had been engaged to lead an in-service training programme for the clergy, something that had never been done before. When I first met the clergy at a conference I was reminded of Wellington's words when he regarded his ragbag army hastily convened at Waterloo to face the escaped Napoleon: "I don't know whether they will terrify the enemy but, by God, they terrify me". They certainly were the wild men of the mountains. One of the nuns rather uncharitably remarked to me that they were all "either drunkards, embezzlers and adulterers, or all three". However, a week before I arrived in Lesotho the Bishop wrote to say he no longer wished me to tackle this (after I had prepared for weeks) but rather to look after the seminary, its warden (principal) having just precipitately resigned. In other words, be prepared for the unexpected, and to have the best laid plans set aside. In remote rural areas crises arise, resources are few and communications difficult so improvisation is the order of the day. One can only try to be prepared for anything and everything! This is also a test of calmness under fire, resilience and resourcefulness. Those with predetermined methods and agendas need not apply!

Secondly, the home of my predecessor which became my temporary home and later permanently, told a salutary tale. Rodney Schofield had built a wattle fence around the house behind which to develop an English garden. On his departure, parts of the fence had been removed. When I returned the following year the fence had disappeared entirely. He had done the classic ex-patriot thing: to allay his anxiety and to preserve a little of his supposed identity he had sought to create a little corner of England in Africa and to protect himself and his family from the unknown world beyond the fence. To the African this fence spoke not of need for privacy, which they did not appreciate, but of excluding them. Otherwise, why would you build a fence? If your children wandered local people (who are marvellous with children) would return them. Why hide your garden? And why be inhospitable by not leaving your door open to welcome the chance visitor? He had completely misread the culture. Lesson number two – make no assumptions, listen to the locals and take nothing for granted.

A third lesson was learned soon afterwards: if you want to know what God intends humanity to be look at rural Southern Africans. As has already been mentioned I discovered that when people have nothing in material terms they may have everything that matters. When people are without the distractions which shield us from other people and the challenges of living – without money, television, private transport, myriad recreational facilities – and then the facts of life which really count are at the centre: family, friends, food, lodging, land, prayer, music, laughter. Consequently the Basotho struck me as a singularly intense and direct people, and initially I did feel an invasion of my personal space. As mentioned earlier, the most commonly asked questions were, "how much do you earn?" and "why are you not married?" in expectation of equally frank and pointed responses. What I came to realise was that this openness and sharing of vulnerability (and you are expected to be equally probing, within the limits of showing respect and attention, especially to elders) was an introduction to the extraordinary depth of African friendship, the like of which I had never experienced and from which I now feel in permanent exile. It is very difficult to explain to those who do not know Africa. It is felt in the gentle but firm way people will physically hold you, in the undefensive honesty of conversation, in a profound politeness that accepts and respects you, in the primary virtue of showing hospitality and particularly to strangers, in the ability to transcend supposed barriers of age and race, in a persistent patience and desire to understand, in a loyalty which means a friend is forever. To be told frequently "I love you", is a marvellously affirming and enriching experience, to realise you are not worthy of such deep affection and trust deeply moving and humbling, and to have permission to cry and be kissed when overcome by such overwhelming inclusiveness the most warming, healing and joyous times of life beyond all describing. But you need to be ready for this opening up or your reserve will be respected and you will miss the greatest experience of your life. Trusting myself to the people was, fortunately for me, an utter necessity as I did not live in an expatriate enclave and was faced by a completely new world: living where I did saved me from capture by my past and culture and exposed me to wonders undreamed of. This is the greatest lesson of all – let go of all that you know and walk hand in hand with the people in their world. Only then will you truly live, as distinct from survive, and only then can you be truly available to them.

After a time you are then trusted not only to be their confidante and advocate but also to be involved, if you are willing, in their more dire problems, though they will be extremely protective in danger and always open to your possible need to retreat. An example would be the involvement of my own seminary students in political activity. Lesotho was a nominally independent country but was totally surrounded by apartheid South Africa. South Africa had forced upon it a corrupt military government favourable to South African interest: this had been done merely by closing the borders so that no food or fuel could enter the country; the former government fell in less than two weeks. So there was a constant low level of unrest in the country. I have already told the story of the students of the National University of Lesotho, whose campus was adjacent to the seminary, calling for strike action against unjust policies from the administration occasioned by government pressure.

When Nelson Mandela was released from prison the Trades Union Council in the capital city, Maseru, decided to risk holding a procession along the main street in celebration. All public gatherings were illegal and this would be a test of the government's attitude and the new political climate. Again the seminarians were offered the huge honour of leading the march (and again I harboured my cynical thoughts!) so we met near the border, I and the seminarians in our cassocks, and the journey began. At first, support was small and timid. But people lined the sidewalks to watch, some cheering and many were in tears. Gradually more and more people joined in and by the time we reached the sports stadium for the rally we were a confident and happy throng of several hundreds. A great speech was given by Chris Hani, who was to become Minister of Youth and Culture in the new South African administration but who would be tragically assassinated a year later. This was one of the greatest days of my life, just to be a little part of ushering a new dispensation. It raises all sorts of issues about the engagement of the church in the political arena but the imperative of participating in the liberation of a crucified people swept all such moral hesitation aside in the exultation of the times. I had played my tiny role by learning to be so with the people that I had been invited into the agonies of their existence so that I might share with them in their resurrection and jubilation. It was a transforming experience.

Some considerations flow from this. Living with the people you are called to serve, listening humbly, sharing their joys and sorrows, always withholding judgement from your own perspectives and culture, learning their culture, letting go of your past to inhabit their present are all essential features of a ministry of presence. You do not "go native" or lose your own identity: you can never be fully one of them, and your identity is enriched and expanded by new experience. The problem can be that you find you really belong nowhere, incapable of becoming African but also adrift from your own moorings and roots. Vincent Donovan, in his *Christianity Rediscovered*,[9] reflecting on his work with the Masai on the borders of Kenya and Tanzania, describes the missionary as a "social martyr", sacrificing belonging for service. This may be the outcome though you will always be supported by those to whom you go. You may come to understand what it is to have "no-where to lay your head". Some find that, when they go to "the other side of the street" they cannot leave and come back. These are the heroes of selfless service in whatever context it is exercised. Implicit in this task of identifying with the forgotten and outcast, becoming "the voice of the voiceless", the one who stands for, the advocate, is the simple requirement of hard work. Being not merely the principal but the only resident, full-time member of staff at one of the poorest seminaries in the world meant having to struggle to teach most subject areas: to have done this badly would have been to seriously fail students who had struggled mightily to be there at all and who deserved every support and attention. It is hard work trying to learn a totally new language, to understand an unfamiliar culture, to become sensitive to social customs and practices, to accustom yourself to strange food, to live in a political climate of threat and uncertainty, to exist without creature comforts, to make time for writing letters which are the sole contact with the outside world in the absence of telephones and computers. How you need that love and friendship to survive, and how you appreciate those deep human realities, in which God is also found hidden, as never before.

I was at greater personal risk – thought negligible compared to those I was seeking to help – through my work for the African National Congress. I had been contacted by them upon the announcement of my appointment to the seminary and told I would be expected to co-operate with them or I would be "in the way" and would be advised not to go. This was certainly a starker challenge than I had anticipated. I was interviewed in London at a time when the ANC office there had been infiltrated by the South African security police so I was met at Finsbury Park Underground Station, shown to a car by three Africans I had never before met, blindfolded and driven off. I sat there thinking, "if this is not the ANC I am in serious trouble"! I was grilled by Reg September who seemed an old man then, back in 1987 but who still sits in the South African parliament. As everyone was, I was offered the choice of working for either the military or the political wing. As the ANC had been attempting change by peaceful means for most of the seventy-five years of its existence I had no qualms about supporting the limited campaign of aggression (mainly against installations) now being waged (it was an important tenet that violence came principally from the government and response to that was secondary and really needed another word to describe it). However, I did not feel I could agree to stash arms in a seminary without the students' agreement so I took the political option. The task assigned to me was the care of refugees.

Now Lesotho was, of course, a convenient place to which to flee, but not a permanent solution owing to the complexion of the government, so my job was to provide a safe house and to organise ongoing repatriation. My visitors would always arrive in the middle of the night and give me the name of Tito, my ANC contact. You were given only one contact person so that, where you to be detained by the South African security police you would be able to reveal only one name. Tito was Tito Mboweni, a distinguished academic resident in South Africa but with a lovely Mosotho wife. As he had not permission to enter Lesotho I had, on occasion, to smuggle him back over the border under cover of darkness. When he visited me he would also meet students and address clandestine meetings. He has certainly risen in the ranks since those days. He became Minister of Industry in the first Mandela administration and is now Governor of the Reserve Bank of South Africa. I would receive help obtaining passports and money from friendly embassies, especial the Swedes and the Russians. They also offered much vital advice. Money had to be hidden in case I was raided. I needed to check my vehicle each morning for possible interference or limpet mines. I must expect to be constantly detained at border crossings (my passport was always marked the letter K, for the Afrikaans "Klein", implying I was a small risk – but how did they know?). If my charges, usually young men, decided on reflection they would risk returning to South Africa I had to take them by night to porous stretches of the border where they could hike mountain passes or ford rivers. If they wished to fly out the snag was that all flights but one from Lesotho went through Johannesburg, where they could be easily apprehended. If they chose the flight to Maputo In Mozambique, which was in a state of civil war, they would probably end up in ANC guerrilla training camps in Zambia or Tanzania, which was acceptable for some but not for others.

When it became known that I made an annual visit to friends in Zimbabwe, on occasion I would meet in Harare an ANC agent from Lusaka in Zambia and be given documents or money to bring back. This involved serious risk but, for some unfathomable reason hand luggage, unlike large baggage, was rarely searched at checkpoints and I was never caught. Once Mandela was released and the apartheid system began to implode in advance of the general election my secret work quickly terminated and I ruefully felt a little out of things – and certainly missed the excitement!

I think what sustained me through this process was certainly the adrenalin rush of high adventure but mostly a deep commitment to the cause in the face of which my own safety and even survival seemed of minor significance. Most of my students had relatives or friends killed during the apartheid era. Desmond Tutu, our Archbishop, was our teacher. He raced to Lesotho the very day after our confrontation with the military, a typical hands-on response. He taught us that sometimes we must pray against as well as for our persecutors. He taught us that it is not heresy but blasphemy to abuse any person, for we are all made in the image of God, and to oppress or marginalise people is to "spit in the face of God". He taught us that if we wish to find Jesus present among us we had only to look into the eyes of the worshippers in the pews around us. He taught us that every forgotten, isolated and neglected person is a V.S.P, a very special person in the sight of God, and sometimes he would get congregations in the townships or Bantustans to chant this mantra. I grew into a deep love and reverence for these incredible people (not to mention for my Archbishop) who just went on loving and hoping, whatever they were expected to endure. The liberation of this people was sufficient cause for the offering of my life in my own small way, and my strength and endurance lay in the renewed faith I imbibed from their lives, examples and friendship.

I sought to respond to some needs by being an unashamed beggar, asking for money for all sorts of circumstances from health care and schooling for poor families to building a church in the mountains for a village with almost total unemployment, from meeting the needs of the seminary to supporting refugees. I was quite good at it, and my friends and institutions overseas were patiently responsive. But one of my biggest responsibilities became my sons! Two boys were abandoned by their mother on my doorstep just months after my arrival. They were in their teens and classic opposites: Sello was plain and dull, David (whose Sesotho name was Mabekebeke, which appropriately means lightning) beautiful and wicked. I built them a small house to encourage some independence, knowing that I would not be able to give them all the attention they would need with a seminary and a parish to run single handed, and I adopted them by local custom through the head man of the adjacent village. I fed and clothed them and sent them to school. I don't recall Sello ever passing an examination and David was too lazy to really try. As he grew older there were run-ins with the police and there was trouble with girls, in all of which I had constantly to intervene. The last straw was when, in my last year, he had sex with several girls in one day and then stole a bus which he proceeded to drive into a petrol pump at a garage. (I remember saying to him,

"David, why couldn't you have been satisfied with a car?"). He was arrested and incarcerated in a seedy juvenile detention centre. I could have had him released but the wise warden of the facility urged me to leave him there for a couple of weeks as he needed to learn some discipline. I complied. David was incredulous and, I think, never forgave me. I saw him little after that although, through thick and thin, we had always remained close. When I left Lesotho it proved impossible to keep in contact. With some difficulty they could both have written but were not so motivated. Sello turned up trumps and found a job in market gardening in Qwa-Qwa, a homeland bordering on Lesotho to the north. David sought out his mother in the mines of the Free State where I suspect she was earning her keep as a prostitute. They have both disappeared from view and nobody in Lesotho knows of their whereabouts. I fear David may be dead, from HIV/AIDS or a fateful, drunken knife fight, not quite smart enough to survive. I still do not know what to make of this experience which had its great moments but also acres of anxiety and frustration. I could not have refused them but clearly I was an ineffective parent, pulled in too many directions. Scarcely a day passes when I do not think of them.

My five years in Lesotho ended in illness and exhaustion because, as usual, I could not resist attempting the impossible. I was drawn increasingly to the pastoral care of the poor villagers of the area and the seminarians sometimes resented this. Of all the work I attempted in the seminary, in the parish, with the clergy and in committees of the Province of the Anglican Church of South Africa, the two accolades I most treasure are two short letters. One was from the head man of a remote mountain village: he wrote simply, saying, "Thank you for all your work with our youth in the Senongkong valley". The second was from my fellow principal of the nearby Catholic Seminary with whom I had cordial relations, and we had brought the two institutions to work ever more closely together. The local Christian population was predominately Catholic. He wrote, "Thank you for your assiduous care of the Catholic people of the Roma valley". Those letters meant so much and have sustained me since: the work of revealing God's love was recognised and reciprocated.

4. Deserted by the Church

I was the Pooh-Bah of the Diocese of Harare. I had one of the very few diocesan appointments, apart from the Bishop, and, as Canon Missioner, I was responsible for all aspects of training - Sunday school teachers, youth leaders, adult education, stewardship programmes, in-service training of the clergy, Mothers' Union, and more – and, in the few months I survived in Zimbabwe, I organised meetings around all these concerns all over the sprawling diocese. I was also a Canon of the Cathedral, and had pastoral responsibility for two of its outstations, Cranborne, the first Salisbury (Harare) suburb to become African, and Arcadia, a coloured (mixed race) area. As usual, I tried to tackle everything at once and quickly became tired and overburdened. I was sustained by the wise elders on my committees and the rich worship of churches, where the devotion of the congregations was palpable. I once had to drive down into the Zambezi valley and crossed the bush without a road to follow to visit a marvellous old priest who was sick; he told me that mine was the first car – and an ailing Mazda 323 at that – that had ever made it through. Further east along the valley, towards the border with Mozambique, were villages that had never seen a missionary. At times, in these remote areas, where an elephant could appear at any time, it felt more like 1890 than 1990. I spent a lot of time with vibrant youth fellowships which, with the women, often ran the churches. I loved the electric worship of the townships and would sometimes encourage the clergy of Glen Norah (where there was an excellent choir) to take a Sunday off so I could officiate.

My Bishop, Ralph Hatendi, was a troubled and perhaps unbalanced man. He had suffered in the War of Independence and had an ambivalent attitude towards whites. He hired foreign clergy because he had insufficient indigenous numbers but he also often fired them. However, I felt that we had a good relationship: we met weekly and occasionally I would perform some small task for him as I travelled the diocese.

One bright spring morning I drove to the Cathedral to be informed on arrival that the Department of Immigration wished to see me urgently. I thought nothing of this – perhaps there was a paper to sign – and went along. I was told that my work permit had been cancelled, that I had one week to leave the country and that they wanted my passport. I remained relaxed: I told them this was clearly a mistake; perhaps there was some other Corbett. But they persisted and, perplexed, eventually asked me whether my employer had informed me of all this. They were baffled by my negative response and I was ushered into the office of the head of the department. He could not believe I was ignorant. My employer had asked them to cancel my work permit three months ago and he apologised that they had taken so long to act on his instructions. Now light dawned: I could expect anything of my employer, the Bishop. I asked if I could go to see him before any action was taken and permission was granted.

22.3.11

I found him in his office. The following conversation ensued, so surreal that I remember it exactly.

"Good morning, Bishop"

"Good morning. How are you? Please sit down."

"Bishop, I have just come from Immigration".

"Oh yes".

"They tell me that you have asked them to cancel my work permit."

"Yes, that's right".

Shocked silence. We had been meeting and planning during these three months.

"Could you give me some reason for this decision?"

"I am not obliged to give you any reason".

Pause.

"But it would help me, in my future ministry, to know how I have erred and what reparation I can make".

"You can drag me through every court in the land but I will never give you an answer".

End of interview. And he never did.

I consulted a few senior clergy, resolved to appeal, but had no choice now but to surrender my work permit. I returned to the Head of Immigration who was, in fact, the one who ministered to me. Seeing me crestfallen he was very sympathetic, prayed for me and offered me two weeks grace to leave the country.

There are two views as to what happened. The one states that I was being too successful with the youth. We were planning a large diocesan youth camp, and a youth synod in Harare. The diocese was very conservative and these gatherings would have certainly been very critical of the church and diocesan policy. It is argued that the Bishop felt threatened, could not bring himself to cancel these events directly, and so decided on the simpler option of getting rid of me. This is not an impossible scenario for some African bishops. The second view is that he had somehow found out that I was gay. I did enjoy one of the great relationships of my life with a friend in the rural areas but I am confident that this was not known. I did have close friendships with some of the youth leaders that could have been misinterpreted. But it would have been enough for him merely to suspect a person of homosexual orientation whether or not there was any practical evidence: He had dismissed a former dean on such suspicion. The Archbishop of the Province of Central Africa was extremely supportive: the only word he could get out of Bishop Hatendi was "life-style", which does tend to support the second view, but then, he may equally have thought it inappropriate for me to have spent so much time with youth groups. We shall never know.

I had a right of appeal by canon law but he refused to recognise it. I went to stay with kind friends in South Africa, fully expecting something to be worked out and my returning to Mashonaland. I waited weeks, then months. He refused to co-operate with the Archbishop so the latter tried to convene his

Episcopal court, but no bishop would serve: I think that some feared, "it could be me next", considering the corruption in some dioceses. So, in the end, the Archbishop consulted with the Chancellor of the Province and issued a judgement almost as though the court had sat. It accused Bishop Hatendi of breaking both canon law and the Zimbabwe labour laws, pointed out that I had not been accused of anything and ruling that I was in "good standing" and worthy to be employed anywhere in the province. I could not have asked for more. I could have pursued Hatendi in the secular courts but there is no way you can effectively compel a bishop to employ you if he does not want you. So I had to face the fact that my work in Zimbabwe was over. I was torn from people I loved (leaving my two churches was heartbreaking) and, above all, from my lover, which I know would have been the special friendship I had been waiting for. Like all good Africans he has since married.

In my desolation Archbishop Makhulu offered me a similar position, created especially for me, in Botswana. What a marvellous man! To Botswana I went, the Archbishop's own diocese. However it was a very poor diocese and, though they could just about support me, there was no money to underwrite the huge amount of travel I really needed to do, for it is a huge country with a population around its edges, most of it being the Kalahari Desert. Again, I was a Canon of Gaborone Cathedral which, incredibly, had clergy in almost double figures, even if most were non-stipendiary (at the university or in other occupations). But, unable to travel far, I was sucked more and more into cathedral life, enabling the regular clergy to do less, and one of my chief pastoral assignments was Old Naledi, a deeply troubled squatter township that cried out for ministry with fluency in African languages. But I enjoyed grappling with it, and particularly with the pastoral care of HIV/AIDS victims, whose situation was desperate, but this was not the work I had been invited to do.

So when the Bishop of Kimberley and Kuruman, still in the Kalahari region but across the border in South Africa, approached me about the diocesan training post I was responsive. He assured me there were the funds to use me better and I could remain available to the Diocese of Botswana. I knew Bishop Njongonkulu Ndugane from his time as Chief Executive Officer to Archbishop Tutu, and had always been inspired by his zest, intelligence and enthusiasm. I moved across the border and again threw myself into a hugely demanding job in a characteristic manner. My chief support and soon to be close friends were Steve and

Marion de Gruchy, who ran the Moffat Mission at Kuruman, where I lived and looked after the parish there. The mission was the oldest and largest permanent ecclesiastical structure in South Africa and we grew a plan to develop it as a training centre for clergy and laity in the Northern Cape, South-West Botswana and South-East Namibia, situated as it was in the Kalahari Desert. They were an engaging couple of tremendous energy and were, and have remained, an enormous inspiration and encouragement to me.

However, matters soon took a turn for the worse. Bishop Njongo had changed since I had known him in Cape Town. He was heavier in body and spirit, dulled in intellect and without sparkle. He did not take easily to rural work, his new wife and children had remained in Cape Town, he was lonely and often ill-tempered. As I got on with my work I learnt that he was under some pressure from political activists who felt it had been a mistake for him to appoint a white ex-patriot to one of the few diocesan posts. He had been imprisoned on Robben Island for his active membership of the Pan-African Congress (PAC), a more radical group than the African National Congress (ANC) of Nelson Mandela. He made no secret in discussion, of his ambition to succeed Desmond Tutu as Archbishop of Cape Town, and he was being advised that promoting whites was no way to win support. I decided, eventually, to broach the issue, but he denied it: as a man who did not make mistakes he assured me that he was "happy with my appointments".

However, several months later, he convened a meeting of my Training Committee. This was in itself irregular and I could discover nothing of its agenda. When I arrived at the meeting I observed that those who would have certainly spoken for me had not been invited. He proceeded to dismantle my job before me, handing out different portions of it to different people, particularly young favourites who constituted his "kitchen cabinet" on whose advice he ran the diocese, avoiding customary channels. There was, in fact, nothing left for me except the work in Kuruman. I tried to speak but was rudely silenced. Clearly another authoritarian bishop had decided and had spoken. I decided all I could do was to accept the inevitable and reconcile myself to an easier pace in Kuruman.

But my health was already under serious threat and the trauma of this latest development pushed me over the edge. I simply could not function. I could not think. I could scarcely walk. My marvellous Afrikaaner doctor secured me and immediate appointment with a former professor of his in Bloemfontein. He diagnosed Myalgic Encephalomyelitis (ME), a viral infection of the immune system and the central nervous system, and recommended treatment in England where more was known about this recently recognised ailment. The Bishop seemed particularly eager to allow me three months leave. Three days after I arrived in London I received a letter unilaterally cancelling my contract.

I had to wait many months to get into the system requiring, as I did, specialist treatment at Kings College University Hospital. I had to drag myself back to South Africa, however, to deal with my belongings. Then I heard the rest of the news. My parish had been furious at the bishop's decision and the churchwardens had insisted on meeting him. He first of all gave them frivolous reasons, such as I was spending too much on travel (never mentioned to me). When they were clearly not going to be fobbed off he resorted to a tactic he knew would stop two Afrikaaner churchmen in their tracks: he asked them if they knew I was gay. They did not know how to handle this. Though it was not given as a reason for my dismissal it was an issue they were asked not to discuss further. Of course, they told the church council and they told me. This was a particularly viscous act as I had told the bishop in confidence and had been assured that it was not an issue. Again I cannot tell whether his young acolytes among the clergy gossiped to him about my involvement in youth work. The bishop may have known that, of all places, beyond Kuruman in the Kalahari was a group of Africans who actually describe themselves as gay and to whom I and a local Tswana priest ministered. But I was not accused of any impropriety nor were there any complaints. I know this because I asked a lot of questions on my return. The view of local Africans was that it did not matter who was bishop, white or black, they, the little ones, would always be neglected and their priests taken from them. I met my church council and, to save the wardens any further embarrassment, decided to "come out". I feared the worst as the council, representing the whole area, contained many conservative whites. I need not have feared. I think most of us were in tears, and the woman whose reaction I had most dreaded said "Father Ian, we don't care if you are gay or straight, we just want you back". Of course, the bishop was not going to respond to this extraordinary opening up of a right wing bastion. The African youth of the area, some of whom had fathomed me and were not bothered, were incredulous at my enforced removal.

Njongonkulu Ndungane succeeded Desmond Tutu as Archbishop of Cape Town. I hope he considered sacrificing me worth it. He had perpetual problems in his new role arising from his inability to establish mutual, equal relationships.

After six months in England, the missionary society who had sent me to Africa, The United Society for the Propagation of the Gospel, (USPG), also abandoned me and withdrew financial support. In my incapacity I was left to penetrate the intricate labyrinth of the Social Security System and exist, as the British say, "on the dole". I had nowhere to live but was blessed to be rescued by two parishes in turn that had accommodation available. The Diocese of London was of no assistance at all.

Being abandoned by two bishops and a missionary society is quite a record. What do you do when your faith family deserts you? In my small way I was sharing the crisis of John Henry Newman who, in the 1840's, was forced to ask himself (in his case over matters of doctrine), "What do you do when the bishops are not to be trusted?" In his case he departed to the Roman Catholic Church and became the Cardinal of beloved memory. My faith in the Anglican way of doing theology and being the church is too deeply rooted for that to be an option for me. But I have been deeply wounded, and the effect on me has been to move me further and further out to the edge of the church and to find my spiritual succour in what Alan Jones memorably calls "the antic outposts". My placement on remote native reservations has probably been what I most needed. The institution of the church I feel little love for or commitment to. The institution is likely to wane further so that Christianity becomes more of a movement and a presence in the Dark Ages that are approaching. I stay on the margins uncomplaining, waiting, with Alasdair McIntyre (in *After Virtue*) for the "new Saint Benedict".[10]

My meditation on this episode, written later in exile in South Africa, appears as Appendix 1.

5. Eire – Ruairi O'Conor and the Lambeth Conference

I had never heard of Tuam in the West of Ireland before I was considered for the post of Dean. It lies to the north-east of Galway and was the ancient capital of Ireland: its remains can still be seen. The last native High King of Ireland, Ruairi O'Conor, lived there and had indeed built the cathedral for which I was to be responsible. The part that survives, the sanctuary, contains the widest Romanesque arch in all of Christendom. The handsome thirteenth century addition to the east now served as a capacious meeting hall, and the grand Victorian extension to the west comprised the present nave. It would seat hundreds but had a congregation of about fifty and perpetual maintenance problems.

I arrived in Tuam after two years of being off work, undergoing treatment for the M.E. that had developed in Africa. I was not very strong and, while not expecting an easy passage, I was looking forward to what I assumed was the gentler pace of rural Ireland. I lived in a little village called Cong (Celtic Cunga, meaning isthmus, set as it was between two lochs) and also had a church there and another at Aasleagh, set on the only fjord in Ireland. It was an idyllic place.

I had a prehistoric stone circle in my garden, from where I could see two others. Nearly every field contained remains of a burial mound or a standing stone. The old Celtic religion could almost be felt in the air.

One day my sacristan, a good Catholic who attended mass at the Catholic cathedral before the Eucharist at the Anglican, Jarlath Canney by name, casually remarked, "Mr Dean, I thought you would want to know that it is the eight hundredth anniversary of the death of Ruairi O'Conor next year". He had a genius for saying just enough to be tantalising and encouraging further exploration. Not looking for extra work, I thought first about keeping silent and hoping nobody would notice. But Jarlath would not allow that to be, and inaction now might result in a call for celebrations at the eleventh hour and a frenetic flurry of activity. So I decided that we had better start planning. First, I had much reading to do. Secondly, this gave me a good excuse to visit all bodies in the very predominately Catholic city of Tuam and introduce myself. I thought of a long weekend of worship, exhibitions, concerts and lectures.

However, I had underestimated the enthusiasm of the Irish and the dedication of the political and business leaders of Tuam to raising its profile and improving its image, for it had certainly seen better times. We came to see that a festival could arouse civic pride and participation. A committee was formed with me as chairman, and any idea of a short festival quickly evaporated. The University of Dublin was keen to organise a major exhibition. Several of the most eminent medieval historians were prepared to lecture at a Summer School (a popular Irish institution). Many of the leading folk singers of the day came from the West and were eager to perform – the "Saw Doctors" insisting on playing in the Scout hut where they had practised as teenagers. Two medieval music groups wanted to attend so we actually heard music from the time of Ruairi O'Conor. The Chamber of Commerce would arrange a business exhibition, and a street fair would take place on the last day. At Cong, where Ruairi O'Conor died in the Abbey whose gracious ruins still adorn the river, the local people would mount an improvised play on his last days and send his funeral pyre down the river towards Ashford Castle (beautiful and dramatic if not historically accurate), a traditional storyteller would recite a memorial poem, and the music department of a local high school would compose and perform a special instrumental item. There was storytelling and music in the pubs, school art competitions, other concerts and a grand finale given by the visiting choir of Napa Valley High School from California, who left behind them not a few broken hearts. The festival eventually lasted for two weeks and was an enormous success. We invited the President of Ireland as the successor of the High Kings but the notice was too short for her to attend. I had never worked harder and was elated but exhausted.

Then we were informed that the President, Mary McAleese, would come to Tuam after all but the week after the festival. Panic! We had to reconvene some of the acts and stage an impromptu concert of some of the prominent features of the festival for her. I had to welcome her, introduce her to the civic dignitaries and escort her. She was a delight. Protocol soon collapsed into organised Irish chaos and she departed leaving us all in great high spirits – me particularly, especially as, by this time, I had developed close relationships with the Catholic Church and strengthened my own congregations. I regarded the Archbishop of Tuam as my bishop, during a long Anglican interregnum, and my fellow parish priest in Cong as my friend and confessor; we would concelebrate house masses together. The Archbishop and I developed a well honed double act going round the area blessing everything from supermarkets to water projects.

And then the magic spell was broken. Every ten years all the bishops of the world wide Anglican Communion meet in conference, latterly at the University of Kent in Canterbury. This meeting is known as the Lambeth Conference after the domestic residence of the Archbishop of Canterbury, the titular head of the communion. The next one was due in 1998, my first full year in Eire. At least eighteen months before I had been asked to write one of the briefing papers for the bishops submitted by the Lesbian and Gay Christian Movement (LGCM), for they were to debate the complex issue of human sexuality. Indeed this was to be the Lambeth Conference notorious for its handling of this matter owing to the ill advised insistence of the then Archbishop, George Carey, on calling for a vote. My article was very modest. I knew I was addressing very conservative bishops from the Americas, Africa and South East Asia so I did not touch on contentious topics such as gay marriage or gay ordination. I merely argued that it is possible to be both Christian and gay, quoting in support dangerous authorities like Desmond Tutu. I then quite forgot about this document until, just prior to Lambeth, I was telephoned by a diligent reporter from the Irish Sunday Times. He had been looking through the advance papers for the conference and had noticed my name. We had a brief discussion and I thought that, if my article merited any mention, it would be a brief paragraph on an inside page. Instead, the second page headlines of the next edition read, "Dean of Tuam says you can be Christian and Gay".

This caused a furore. The issue was not much discussed in Ireland at the time though I fraternised with a gay group in Galway. My own congregations were, of course, quite unprepared. Over the next two weeks I lost a third of the cathedral congregation and the senior warden at Aasleagh petitioned our newly arrived bishop for my removal. My bishop now was Richard Henderson, at thirty nine the youngest bishop on the bench. We used to call him the "boy bishop" as he looked much younger. He was supportive in principle but understandably worried by the ballyhoo. The Archbishop of Armagh was distinctly unsupportive and his press officer positively viperish. The irony of this was to be that he, Robin Eames, was to become chairman of the committee that produced the Windsor Report on homosexuality as an irenic discussion document for the Anglican Communion. But he had a distinguished record, in Irish politics, of waiting to see just how the tide was turning before issuing an archiepiscopal pronouncement, and he clearly thought I would have no support in the matter. That was sadly true in the Church of Ireland which, outside the large cities of the East, was very conservative. But it was not true of the rapidly changing intellectual environment of Ireland as a whole, fomented both by its membership of the European Economic Community and by the growing hopes for peace and reconciliation in the North.

I found myself the subject of much media attention, both on radio and in the press, and gave many interviews (I had to decline television appearances because of other duties). These gave me a great opportunity to argue a case for equal treatment for lesbian, gay, bisexual and transgendered people (LGBT), and generated considerable correspondence, particularly from isolated gay people in the West and parents of gay children, who were equally relieved to find that their issues could be discussed with a minister of the church. Members of the Dail and the Senate, and even the Office of the President, encouraged me to stand my ground and promote the debate in which, they argued, the country needed to engage. Most warming of all was the reaction of the Roman Catholic Church. I feared that all my work of bridge building would now be lost. But a senior

Catholic cleric took my breath away: I was not to worry, he told me; it was good that I had been put into this position as his church had, of necessity, to remain silent on contentious sexual matters. Everybody seemed to respect my courage even if they disagreed. As Jarlath Canney put it, "Well, Mr. Dean, I don't agree with what you have said but I defend to the death your right to say it". That, to my relief, was also the attitude of the festival committee.

However, I did not feel as though I could morally continue in Ireland, using the cathedral as a platform for civil rights that my own people clearly did not own, so I resolved to move on. My new bishop was visibly relieved. I had always intended to move from Africa to Canada. The Anglican Church of Canada had an impressive record of support for the anti-apartheid movement and had supported my work in Lesotho financially. While convalescing in London I had met my contact in Canada, John Rye, who was passing through. I was asking myself, "what do I do next which will build on the experience I have gained in Africa?" Responding that this probably meant working in an inner city area with great cultural and ethnic diversity. However, in such work you need to hit the ground running and I doubted if I would be sufficiently fit and resilient. John saw the issue quite differently. "You are used to working with indigenous people in remote rural areas", he said; "why not come to Canada and work with indigenous people in remote rural areas?" He seemed to answer the question and helped me to make enquiries. At the time there seemed to be no position available. (Many of the posts in native work in Canada are non-stipendiary, that is, clergy or Church Army officers have secular jobs and perform their religious duties in their free time). As I desperately needed to work again after many months surviving on social security I looked around locally and that is how I came to be in Ireland. I loved the Irish people, the splendour of the West coast, the mountains – and the Guinness (it never tastes the same outside Ireland). But it was again time for this tired pilgrim to move on.

Even as I arrived in Ireland offers of employment had begun to come from Canada. I responded one, and was eventually appointed to a large stretch of desolate territory in North Central Saskatchewan on the Manitoba border. It comprised two declining country towns, several smaller settlements and three First Nation reserves. It was to prove a better fit than the church establishment "across the pond" but there was beginning to grow in me a deep ache and hurt that would gnaw away at me until it produced a diagnosis of post-traumatic stress syndrome in years to come, the pain that I had again been rejected by my own church, which proclaimed itself to be the Body of Christ, for being myself. And I have, then or now, no answer as to how to cope with a reality so devastating. You just go on, like those travellers down endless roads in Beckett's novels. The Irish experience of surviving darkness, explicit in much of its literature, was certainly an encouragement, as is Samuel Beckett's wonderfully gentle letter to a bereaved friend:

> *"I know your sorrow and I know that for the likes of us there is no ease for the heart to be had from words of reason, and that in the very assurance of sorrow's fading there is more sorrow. So I offer you only my deeply affectionate and compassionate thoughts and wish for you only that the strange thing may never fail you, whatever it is, that gives us the strength to live on and on with our wounds."[11].*

6. Saskatchewan – Death Threats

I arrived in Eastern Saskatchewan in early spring: the land was grey and lifeless, awaiting warmth and new growth. It was forest and lake country, of distant horizons and large skies. It could be so cold that ice crystals were visible in the air. In winter you drove on ice, praying that you would be spared "white-outs" (total blizzards) or, perhaps worse, freezing rain (which also froze your windscreen wipers). Winds howled across the plains and drove the forests to frenzy. Black bears and moose were common, white tailed deer ubiquitous. The depressed weather found an echo in the people. Those in the two small towns I served were often farmers whose family livelihood was threatened by falling profit margins and the encroachment of agribusiness, large commercial farms. There was widespread resentment against "Indians" who were commonly regarded as lazy, feckless, drunk – and privileged: they lived off social security and enjoyed more generous hunting rights than whites. Indeed, the situation often recalled that of apartheid South Africa, the small reserves replacing the townships. Canada is a truly liberal society but in remote rural areas other values can be dominant. Tempers were not helped by the eagerly anticipated arrival of spring after a long, dark winter, for the thaw brought with it plagues of mosquito and black fly. The summer was always short, hints of autumn appearing as early as August.

The "Indians" (who accepted this designation) had little going for them. They were displaced Saulteaux people, originally from the Sault – St.-Marie area of the Great Lakes, who had been pushed far west and north by the expansion of empire and the displacement that was enforced on eastern tribes who, in turn, propelled the next tribe westwards in a domino effect. They had largely lost their traditional culture. The climate and land were inhospitable. There was widespread unemployment owing mainly to lack of opportunity. Substance abuse was prevalent and, especially at weekends, every sort of inner city problem appeared in the wilderness, including extreme violence. The reserves I served were not always safe places and the only way to survive was to put myself totally in the care of the local people. They were naturally suspicious but life was often so brutish that anyone who persisted in visiting became welcome. Here it was not so much a question of entering into a different culture but merely standing with and for people in situations of great extremity, stripped to your basic humanity.

A few vignettes of local life will set the scene. In my first year I came one night upon a street fight in the town where I lived and I recognised a young Indian being set upon by a gang of angry whites. I drove straight into the crowd and, with panache worthy of John Wayne, pulled the victim into my car and, tyres squealing, and headed off to the reserve. But his persecutors gave chase so we were skidding over the iced roads, travelling far too fast for safety, to shake off the pursuit, my not being helped by my inebriate friend's desire to share in steering the vehicle. They gave up once we entered the reserve, most whites being irrationally fearful of these places after dark. I delivered him home but on my way out was followed by another vehicle. This was particularly unnerving but, knowing the back roads, I took risks in using them in freezing weather and again lost my pursuers.

On another occasion some of the young men found me and asked me to accompany them. I learnt that someone had been killed in a gun fight and had been hastily buried, and now those involved were in a state of panic and uncertainty. The scene we arrived at was like one from a B horror film: out of the crudely dug grave a hand protruded. Where do you find resources to cope with an emergency like this? How can you be prepared for such eventualities? In retrospect I think I acted as well as I could, though I doubt whether any course would have been free of moral ambiguity. I said we must disinter the body and re-bury it in a recognised burial site. It did not take long to retrieve it when, to our horror, we realised it was still breathing – but not for long. Everyone was paralyzed. I got people to talk and we all agreed that nothing of this should be told to the victim's family: such news would be too terrible to bear. The correct course, it now seems to me, would have been to take the body to the parents because naturally the police would have needed it and news had already travelled of the killing. I asked not to be told who was responsible though clearly all my informants were implicated. That was a matter for the police and the community. My responsibility as a priest was to respect the confidentiality of those who had approached me. And I think nobody ever knew of that first burial.

Another night the wife and mother of a young family I knew well asked me to take her husband away as he was so drunk he was a danger to her and the children. I took him home with me where he proceeded to demonstrate, with me a victim, the various ways he knew to kill people. As the neck locks and other physical contortions went on – arguing with him at this stage would have been suicidal – I remember praying that he would not be too inebriated to realise that these were only demonstrations and not the real thing! I survived and next morning he had no memory of anything of the previous evening's activities.

On my very last night, before I removed to Navajoland, I didn't sleep at all because of dealing with two disasters. The young chief of one of the reserves, who, as a bright young lawyer in his late twenties, was one of the great hopes for the future, succumbed to alcohol and beat his wife. The police were summoned and he was incarcerated. I spent half the night with him in his cell as he raged and agonised. The other half I spent with the husband and father of a young family to whom I was particularly close. Holly had disappeared into the night taking their young children, to whom they were both devoted, with her. Jude was inconsolable, lost and fearful. I sat and held him. They were both alcoholics and drug addicts but very loveable. I myself was in a highly emotional state and almost felt I could not leave.

The death threats were, in contrast, relatively minor matters. I enjoyed telling people back in England about them because they always assumed that the perpetrators were Indians but the fact was that they were the whites. As I had experienced in South Africa, if you were seen to be friendly towards indigenous people then you must necessarily be anti-white. As there, I was sometimes the recipient of verbal abuse in the street if seen companionably with local Indians. The first threat was telephoned in the early hours by a drunken voice who told me that my house would be set on fire. I remember lying in bed wondering whether every nocturnal creak or sound was the house beginning to incinerate. A further threat was received in a bar, a third through a third party. Nothing happened but these instances were indicative of the state of race relations among the less educated and more redneck whites. Even the more educated and prosperous tended to have a patronising and judgemental attitude, and nobody had Indian friends, although this was often alleged; normally it implied nothing more than a few amicable conversations or backslapping in a bar. No white ever visited first peoples in their homes.

My willingness to be involved in their lives gradually gave me entree to many native homes. The elders were always welcoming and instructive to hear. But the closest bond grew with the young men and women who came to see me as a friend they could confide in, who would not judge them and who would offer whatever assistance was possible. In fact this was one of my primary sources of strength and support. I came to really love them and felt safe even when there were elements of danger. I would always be protected. Sometimes it could mean smoking or drinking with them so they would be at ease or so that conversation would flow. Often I cannot tell how I drove home in one piece. But their friendship was a great gift and it sustained me – at least for some of the time. The problem is that such relationships are never reliable: they cannot be for the people are often so tortured, depressed, unhappy, and sick or out of their minds that they cannot be consistent or dependable. Often when I needed them the most they were withdrawn, hostile, somnolent, pre-occupied – or just disappeared for days on end. Some days I would visit and be on the reserve till late, sometimes almost nobody would be around. Life was entirely unpredictable and unplanned for a people traumatised, distressed, fearful and lost. Yet they were my joy and the reason I persevered.

Another great inspiration was their rediscovery of their culture which I could participate in and so learn alongside them. The source of this rebuilding was partly some strong women who had returned to the reserves after a period away and who had preserved their traditions but mainly men out of prison who, with all passion spent, had rediscovered their roots there and were determined to follow their pilgrimage once out of jail. The Chief when I arrived was such a man, Campbell Papequash, who welcomed me cordially, held a feast in my honour, and taught me what he had learnt, especially about approaches to prayer. I found that learning to pray in another tradition greatly revivified and enlarged my own capacity for prayer. He introduced me to the sweat lodge, which has been a great blessing to me. And he took me seriously enough to start preparing me for my first Vision Quest, showing me how to build a sweat lodge and erect a tipi, and how I should be praying. It has been a permanent regret that I had to leave the area before this took place owing to the church's inability to pay me. His brother, Harold, unlike Campbell, walked "in both worlds" and was also a church member. Though his health was broken he was a man of gentle wisdom who also taught me much. Even Desmond Key, who was drunk most of the time, could be a compassionate and discerning guide. I was privileged to be invited annually to the Sun Dance, their most important ceremony, only recently re-established, and, like them, I learned to walk in two worlds, attending the ceremonies of both religions, traditional and Christian, and finding no essential conflict or discontinuity. I also tried to introduce some elements of traditional into Christian worship.

The church on Key Reserve was the second oldest in Canada. A simple rectangular wooden structure it stood like a beacon on top of the highest hill, surrounded by pine trees and far-flung vistas. It was appreciated widely as a holy place: it and its graveyard were used for private prayers and often for funerals. When one young man went missing I found him prostrate on the floor of the church in a cruciform position, waiting to die and go to Jesus. I saved him that time but not later when, inebriated, he fell into a lake and drowned. The church was unreachable in winter owing to deep snows but I recall struggling through the drifts on foot with a tribal member to feed a pair of bald eagles who, mysteriously, had decided to remain the entire winter. He provided for them until spring returned.

The winters could be hard to bear but there were compensations in the Northern Lights, the local sports of ice hockey and curling, deer running over icy wastes, little Ukrainian Orthodox churches in snowy forests. The wilderness was, at the start, huge and threatening, perhaps bigger that anything I had known in Africa. But, as always, walking in the wilderness became the greatest solace and salvation. The forest was endless but, at one higher point, it was possible to look due north over the trees and I would stand there incredulous that there was no further human settlement until the Pole had been traversed and Russia gained. It was always an awesome moment. It was out of the forests to the south that my first pow-wow Grand Entry emerged into the arena, a sight so overpowering in the sheer physical beauty of costume and dance in that epic setting, to the sound of the great drum echoing the heart beat of the earth, that I dissolved in tears. I came to love the great forests and the voices of the winds and spirits they harboured. In my second month I was joined on a hike by a lone wolf. It was a large animal but so benign and unthreatening that I felt not at all afraid. I kept to the track and the creature kept me company to my right. Wolves are very curious and intelligent and there is no known case of their having killed a human in North America. Once I reached a highway the wolf disappeared. It had been a strangely comforting experience but I did not grasp its significance until, on reporting this event to the elders, I was told this had been unusually propitious as the wolf is a protecting spirit. Maybe it had been a spirit wolf.

I felt deeply humbled to have been granted this grace, as I was when I received my vision at Wanuskewin, an ancient Cree gathering place near Saskatoon. As I ascended the hill to the prayer circle a voice insistently urged me to "tell my story", to share, as I understood it, my understanding of the Creator and his world with others. Then an extraordinary thing happened. The clouds overhead were forming and reforming and, at one point, suggested an arrow, but even more remarkably, moved to form the distinct head and body of an eagle. Nobody seemed to notice this but me. Was it there only for me? A few days later, on Seventy Mile Butte, I experienced a strong wind from the west being met, in unlikely fashion, by a gentle wind from the east. Remarkably, the soft wind prevailed and the rumbustious wind subsided. This seemed to me like an enacted parable, saying something about quiet faith and determination. I was momentarily shocked to realise the extent to which I was entering the Indian world, and that it was speaking to me. But I came to see that this is precisely what I should expect: God is always present and always speaks to us appropriately, according to context and culture. These experiences were as a rock to me in being my firm grounding from which I was able to face exposure to the tests and trials of reserve life. Any fears I may have entertained about losing my identity were very soon put to rest by the awareness that I was being immeasurably enriched by the wisdom of an ancient culture in which God had been active long before the birth of Christianity. I was participating in the "Old Testament" of another people who, I was convinced, God equally chose and loved.

7. Alone among the Navajo

After you descend the western slope of the Rocky Mountains around Grand Junction the landscape changes suddenly and dramatically. Alpine vistas give way to sparse vegetation, bare cliffs, and distant mountains – all rust red or grey blue depending on the time of day. It dawns on you that, for a people to determine to return to such stark and inhospitable territory after enforced exile, they would need great resources of character and resolution. Yet this was what the Navajo achieved. After being deported by the federal government to Basque Redondo, a concentration camp in New Mexico, as a punishment for raids in which others also took part, they aroused public opinion to demand their return and have struggled ever since to enlarge their territory so that, although smaller than it was originally (the Four Sacred Mountains of Dinetah are now all beyond the borders of Diné Bikéyah, the present reservation), it is the largest reservation in North America, bigger than some small states. The Navajo (or Diné, as they call themselves, meaning simply "the people") occupy parts of the states of Arizona, New Mexico and Utah in the Four Corners region. I was responsible for the

"Utah strip" (the land between the Arizona state line and the San Juan River) for the Episcopal Church.

You quickly realise how essential the land is to Navajo identity. They know how to survive in such an arid zone, subject to incessant droughts, and are moulded and defined by it. They see their creation story around them every day, the eerie rock formations telling of battles of the mythic past, the lava rock being the blood of the monsters slain by the Holy Twins and the high places the dwellings of the Holy People, the Yei. Their beliefs all derive from this complex saga and their ceremonies are all concerned with helping them live with the land and the spirits, and curing their maladies, whether physical or spiritual. It was challenging for me, coming from one sophisticated religious system, to enter into another so surprisingly complete, flourishing and equally nuanced. Their relative isolation has also helped render them the most different people I have ever worked with, even compared to rural Africans: they have unique modes of thought and language, social mores and organisation. And because of their recent experience, from the Long Walk onwards, of learning to walk in two worlds, theirs and the white man's, of keeping pace with accelerating change, of enduring the tyranny of the boarding schools, of accepting the enforced culling of their livestock and of suffering the scourges of illness and substance abuse, they are a traumatised people, often withdrawn and suspicious, not at all like the open, friendly folk encountered by early traders and missionaries. At my interview for the post of Vicar of the Utah region (based at St Christopher's historic Mission near Bluff) I experience hostile but pointed and discerning questioning from a Navajo church councillor.

I had discovered Navajoland a year before when, on my second vacation to the United States whilst working in Canada, I had made a point of visiting to meet Steven Plummer, one of the few native bishops in North America. The only other one I had met, having risked life and limb on atrocious roads to find him in northern Saskatchewan, had advised me to use only the old Prayer Book; I hoped Bishop Steven could help me rather more! However, I found out that he was suffering from cancer and had no clergy – a diocese, a bishop and no clergy, almost incredible! I immediately warmed to his charm and humility: when I sought advice he answered that he was in no position to respond as he had been a bishop for only ten years; would that more senior churchmen were as wise and as silent. So, when I knew I had to leave my position in Canada, I knew where a priest was needed and south I came.

On my first Sunday there were good congregations, curious to see the new man. On my second both congregations were in single figures. The second Sunday always provides the true impression! So I embarked on what was to become eight years of arduous and assiduous visitation. The People lived in isolated homesteads as, traditionally, they were sheepherders, and the land was so poor that even sheep and goats required much space in order to survive. It often seemed as though they hid in their houses nursing hurts, grievances and disappointments, though there were many warm welcomes and I was never turned away. This proved an ideal learning environment for me as I listened to their stories and heard something of their history, culture, politics and beliefs. Priests always need to visit, not so much for their people as themselves: you come to truly know people only when you meet them on their own turf on their own terms. The Navajo make you sweat to gain acceptance or, rather, they take their time in assessing and trusting you. I received very little direct appreciation but other people would tell me how, in certain areas, they were glad to see my vehicle around and have the first visiting priest in decades. They really welcomed being remembered, noticed and given attention. The language was a problem as many of the elderly spoke only Navajo and I often needed an interpreter (Diné bizaad is one of the most difficult languages and, though I could eventually use it in church, I could not preach in it or hold simple conversations easily as I could, say, with Setswana in Africa). A problem was that the person most willing to accompany me, who was extremely fluent in both languages, was more interested in his own conversations than with mine, or in what he thought I should be saying, so the interpreting was too often inaccurate. I also discovered that there were many family and clan feuds, sometimes going back generations, despite the fact that K'é clan relationships, are the basis of Navajo social life. Being an outsider could on occasion be useful in striving for peace and reconciliation but I was also constantly the butt of manufactured gossip as one family would vilify me for visiting another. Sadly, one of the worst culprits was Catherine, Bishop Steven's wife, a sad a disturbed woman who had alienated many of the families across the river from the mission. When it was clear to her that I was unwilling to play the part of a Plummer emissary or further her interests and agenda she mobilised most of her own many relatives against me, and this remained a constant handicap. It was a measure of the disruption of Navajo life, mentioned above, that the basic foundations of their society, K'é and Hózhó (walking in beauty, that is in peace and harmony), were often honoured more in the breach than in the observance.

St Christopher's Mission, on the register of National Historic Places, nestled between the reservation and the City of Bluff (population 277). Two thirds of the village were white, of very different and often colourful backgrounds, very friendly and supportive – indeed some really close friendships emerged more quickly than with the Navajo. But it was peripheral to the core of my ministry and I inherited an elderly and eccentric woman deacon who felt threatened by my presence so it was easier to leave the town to her (though I often needed to be involved as she had absolutely no concept of confidentiality!). The upshot was that the work was a solitary task and residence at the rather isolated mission could be lonely. Familiar resources had to come into play.

The first was the spirituality of walking. It was a great area for hiking – deep canyons in the winter and high mountains in the summer. It has been shown psychologically that walking calms the mind and raises the spirit and it has always proved my most significant safety-valve and inspiration, ever since I had scaled all the major peaks in England's Lake District. My favourite area for exploration was Cedar Mesa, a vast plateau to the north of the reservation. It was intersected by huge canyons, often requiring some tricky footwork, concentrating on which was the key needed to empty the mind of human unpleasantness, indeed of the sheer intractability of the human condition. In the massive Grand Gulch I even found ruins not mentioned in any book. For all these canyons were full of ancient remains – cliff dwellings, petro glyphs, pictographs, pottery shards, even desiccated corn kernels, all preserved in the dry climate – of the people who mysteriously disappeared from the region around AD 1300, when the population of the Bluff area was around twenty thousand people. In Road Canyon the ruins were on a high rock island in its midst. I spent weeks of visits finding different routes into Slickhorn Canyon and in a canyon I will not name (some of these places need some protection) I and a friend found a site where the rock ceiling of the dwelling had been painted with an astrological map and nearby was a kiva (a chamber for worship and gathering) with its wattle roof almost intact after all those centuries. There seemed to be a very thin veil between the past and the present, and a sense of presence was often to be experienced. At times I almost expected to see a figure emerge from a dwelling. I have certainly heard voices, once of children, as though their spirits were still at play. It was a magic world I could easily escape into, another time and civilization in which I nevertheless felt welcome. Anything seemed possible. On more than one occasion a blue jay has led me along a canyon. The interconnectedness of things is deeply sensed. Being absorbed in native life, even a past one, in Indian country, was a cleansing and renewing experience from which I always emerged more ready to face whatever the future held. And the natural settings were awe inspiring, stone cathedrals and castles, rock arches and windows, the smell of juniper and pinyon, the gay variety of wild flowers, the dark depths of the canyons.

The other feeder of my spiritual life was participation in Navajo worship. I was also kept mentally alive by the continuous challenge of inculturation – how to speak of your own faith when, in this case, the people have no word for God, religion or sin? The concepts obviously exist in some way but have to be approached in a manner comprehensible to the

Navajo world-view, which involves study of their beliefs and philosophy. Some of the ways of prayer I learnt I would try to incorporate in Christian liturgy, as also on occasion the use of smoke (incense) and corn pollen. I would always try to have parallels from Navajo stories in my preaching and teaching. I deeply appreciated the invitations to traditional ceremonies, to which you came and went as they often lasted several days. All ceremonies are, without exception, concerned with healing, and I have been blessed to witness the Fire Dance, the Enemy Way, the Blessing Way, the Kinalda (the coming of age ceremony for girls), and especially the winter Yeibichei ceremonies. The so called medicine man (Hataali) acts as priest and healer – his Diné name really means chanter or singer. I found the Yeibichei especially moving as, on the last night, when the dancers are masked, they represent the Yei, the Holy People, being actually present. It is the witnessing of a multiple incarnation, as arresting as when I saw a young girl in Nepal who was believed to be an incarnation of deity; it was like meeting Jesus. It was the highest privilege to sometimes share duties with a medicine man or woman in praying over a sick person, in a wedding or funeral, occasionally in a church service. I also regularly consulted them as a patient enduring, as I do, five chronic ailments. I have never come away the worse for the consultation, even when I could not begin to explain the treatment, such as when small arrowheads were sucked out of my neck. Herbal treatments have always been of benefit. I enjoyed each spring, blessing the animals, especially the new born, an office people could accept from either traditional healer or priest. My greatest ongoing experience was the Hooghan Mass at the home of Terrell and Alta Begay. The hooghan is the traditional home where all ceremonies must take place. I would offer a celebration of the Eucharist as the Christian Hataali. This might be preceded or followed by a sweat lodge, there would always be a sharing circle and, perhaps, if Lakota were visiting, a pipe ceremony. It could take several hours, and would culminate in a shared meal. It was a profound spiritual centring for me which kept me going in even the most trying times. The different traditions fed and illuminated one another.

This all strengthened me for the isolated work of priest for the Navajo. The founder of the mission, Father Baxter Liebler, had been a saint, working tirelessly for the pastoral care of the people right up to his death in his nineties, an impossible act to follow and an unattainable model. All clergy following him had been disappointments! When anyone compared me to him I knew I had done something right! Bishop Steven, as already mentioned, was a real source of enlightenment and a delight but he had been suspended early in his Episcopate for a sexual misdemeanour and was now dying of cancer. The effect of his indiscretion was a retreat into himself and his home, and this was now intensified by his illness. Instead of bravely going out to minister to his people and take whatever knocks might come his way he never visited, was entirely reactive in his ministry and was very cautious in decision. He was a disappointment to his people as they felt they had given him a second chance to which he had not responded, and had not assumed the leadership they desired of him. So here, following upon so many white clergy who had come and gone, we had only inadequate models of vocation which did not inspire Navajo to take up the reins. Bishop Steven had actually closed one church, the enticingly named St Mary of the Moonlight in the majestic Monument Valley. I reopened this and it provided me, as it were, with my own platform, unencumbered by the fraught relationships experienced by the other churches. A largely new congregation of previously unchurched people emerged. They proved to be great fun, quite crazy and we had a marvellous time. Of course, it could also be effortful, frustrating and exhausting keeping things together; motivating them and visiting them all but it gave me a community of my own where I could begin to build the church afresh according to my strategy of listening, responding, and creating a culturally sensitive liturgy.

There was much other work. As is the case wherever I have been I made a point of visiting the secular institutions – schools, chapters (local government units), businesses – to become known and available but this time spread over a huge geographical area, often on poor roads. Such agencies were often happy to use me in a pastoral capacity as their limited resources were always overstretched and the officials themselves needed affirmation and encouragement. At the suggestion of one them I started visiting the jails. Navajo inmates often did not receive visitors because of the distances and costs involved. As with African Americans a hugely disproportionate percentage of Original Americans are incarcerated. I had time to visit only really serious cases but many strong bonds developed and I came to deeply value a developing friendship with some of them. I treasure many of their letters. I also inaugurated the Bluff Arts Festival, as San Juan County in South-East Utah is one of the most impoverished in the country and no community, Navajo, Ute, Hispanic or Caucasian, was either exposed much to the arts or had a platform on which to showcase their own, often considerable, artistic abilities. I will long remember our regular evening for local poets and writers, the exhibition of the work of local graphic artists, the demonstrations of weaving and basketwork, and one particularly hilarious evening of Navajo story telling.

It has been said that some people learn from their experience by being able to reproduce all their mistakes exactly. That appears to be singularly true of me. After six years of hectic hyperactivity, and the concomitant anxiety, I was something of a burnt-out case. Post-Traumatic Stress Syndrome was diagnosed, not the result of one catastrophic experience but of several lesser ones, some of which I have mentioned, some going back to childhood, that cumulatively had produced a situation in which I was exhausted, unmotivated, angry, unpredictable and simply unable to cope. On the surface I staggered along much as normal but, behind the facade, I was depending very heavily on a dear friend in Bluff who just happened to be a retired psychiatrist with much experience of the church. Her patient – and free – counselling enabled me to survive but, now past retirement age, I tendered the Bishop my resignation for a year ahead.

What happened next I relate in the words of an article written for the local press but that I decided in the end not to offer for publication. It overlaps with some of the foregoing but I think usefully, in that it offers more detail in relevant places and in the context it gives, renders the denouement all the more shocking.

The Wild West, the Last Frontier, is alive and well. It is called Bluff, Utah, population 277, one store, a post office, a few motels and restaurants, and a cemetery where the presence of a tombstone does not necessarily guarantee a body underneath. The bars were closed years ago because of fighting between Navajo, Utes, and "Bilagaana" (whites, literally "the enemies"). Whenever a community issue arises the people splinter into myriad factions – we may be coming to the end of a forty year old bitter dispute about waste water facilities. People have disappeared here.

But it is also the centre of red rock country where by the end of the day the cliffs seem to defiantly move forward and combust in a fury of colours ranging from salmon pink to stormy magenta. It is the resting place of the Anasazi, the ancient ones, twenty thousand of whom used to populate the pueblos and cliff dwellings the ruins of which, together with prolific rock art, can be found in every canyon. It is also the home of St Christopher's Mission, founded by Father Baxter Liebler in 1943, to "serve", not to convert, the Navajo who, like all native peoples, call themselves simply the Diné, the People.

Liebler was unusual for his time in that he did not approve of Episcopal Church policies towards native peoples, which tended to support the assimilation programmes of the governments of the day. He felt that native language and customs should be encouraged lest cultural identity die, and it was the task of the church to "indigenise" or "inculturate" its own theology and mission to make it understood. Initially the Mission was independent of any diocesan structure. When you read his memoir of this time, "Boil my heart for me" (this being a translation back from Navajo to English of "Will you get my car engine going?" as the Navajo personalise every part of the mechanical process), you automatically think he is referring to 1842 rather than 1942, the year of his first exploration: there were no roads, no schools, no clinics – nothing but poor, isolated native families with their flocks of sheep and goats which require in this arid territory plenty of room to graze. Father Liebler learnt Navajo (Diné bizaad), built the first school and then the first clinic. Soon most babies were born there. Although his own model of ministry was inflexibly Anglo-Catholic (he sometimes celebrated the Mass in Latin) and his style was patriarchal and condescending. He loved the People and was tireless in his devotion to them, setting a pattern and standard of pastoral ministry that has never been surpassed – sacrificial is scarcely the word. He established other mission centres and travelled assiduously throughout the entire "Utah strip" of Navajoland. Bluff sits on the Northern edge of this and the reservation itself spreads widely into Arizona and New Mexico. When Liebler retired aged 73, he moved down to Monument Valley and started all over again, building a new church and serving it until his death twenty years later.

The Utah strip is the most remote and traditional part of Diné Bikéyah. It's arguable that it has little need of a new religion as the traditional is still very strong and all ceremonies, without exception, are concerned with healing in various ways. But it did, and does, need tender loving care and pastoral attention for people often were – and are – poor, sick and depressed, and today there are high rates of unemployment, poor nutrition, sickness and domestic violence. The People are traumatised, learning to walk in two worlds at a breakneck pace of change. Old certainties are breaking down. This is not to underestimate the valiant efforts of the tribal government in raising standards, and the huge strides that have been made in education and health care. But the United States seems content to let a third world exist in the middle of the first and the People are under considerable stress. There are few paved roads and many people have neither electricity nor running water in their homes. Yet the Navajo are a proud people, maintaining their ceremonies and their crafts and, in Utah, claiming an ancient heritage as they were not removed during the Long Walk of the 1860s and have always occupied their ancestral land.

However, since Father Liebler's time, standards of Christian service have declined. His successor left after endless disputes with a new bishop of Utah, and there followed twenty years or so of priests coming and going – and often none at all – generally unable to penetrate the protective wall of Diné introspection, or to withstand the climate, or to keep their families here. During this time several independent charismatic churches – and the Mormons – moved in to the Utah strip. The former are usually Navajo led and Navajo speaking but are fundamentalist in their approach, telling congregations that they must forego their traditional culture in order to be Christian. This is a pathetic double oppression, the Diné having first been oppressed by Bilagaana invasion and now by their own people using the white man's religion. The Mormons build churches in every sizeable community but generally are not very successful because their own church culture is not very adaptable and they often survive by bussing people in from other areas. So the churches were failing their constituencies. But then the Episcopal Church ordained its first Navajo priest, Steven Plummer, in the late eighties and he represented the great hope for revival and renewal.

I got on well with Steven at first. He had undergone some training as a medicine man (hataal'i) in his youth, was very knowledgeable about the culture, had some great stories and was an entertaining companion. His wife Catherine seemed always to hover somewhere near as a rather dark cloud. It soon became clear that he was distinctly unprepared for his role. Neither he nor Catherine were very fluent readers. He had not completed high school and his ordination course had to be tailored towards his abilities and his capacities. But he knew something of being a priest. He knew little about being a bishop, which he had become at the behest of politically correct but spiritually insensitive white bishops because he was the sole Navajo ordained. The Navajo generally are not too concerned about the ethnicity of their clergy as long as they are good and faithful but, of course, white liberals always know better. A very moving letter exists in which Steven asks the then Presiding Bishop not to insist as he feels inadequate to the task. This priceless piece of self-awareness was ignored and Steven became the first native bishop of Navajoland. Sometimes he tried hard but one of his recurrent refrains was, "I don't know how to be a bishop!" With most people this realisation would be a crucial step on their journey and they would then find help and support, but it was as though Steven went on to say, "so what?" and never made any serious attempt to overcome his diffidence. The Church had sentenced him to a role he could not fulfil and he lived a life of having to fail in the face of demands he could not meet and which often he could not understand.

This manifested itself in his inability to use a colleague. I would find him sweeping the church, preparing for services, filling the tea urn and I would say, "Steven, you don't have to do this, this is my job, you are free to be the bishop". But he did not know what that meant and he enjoyed the small tasks. I think he really wanted a curate who would go around with him. But I had come to a place where there had been no priest for ten years (just the bishop) and there was much to do. One church had been closed. Huge areas had been neglected. The buildings looked derelict and one, the former clinic, was full of garbage.

There was a further major problem. The bishop had been suspended a few years earlier for a sexual misdemeanour involving a young man. He had undergone a Navajo ceremony, accepted psychiatric counselling and been re-instated. But the experience, as much as the cancer, had broken him. He could not face visiting on the reservation and largely stayed at home, responding only to occasional callers (if he chose to answer the door). And when he urged me to visit I soon realised that this was almost exclusively to see his wife's relations across the river, none of whom attended church. Then this drew me into a deeper maelstrom, namely that Catherine Plummer, possibly feeling she was defending her husband, had, in her very aggressive and critical behaviour, alienated most local Navajo families, including many of her own relatives. Many people told me that they would never return to church while the Plummers, especially Catherine remained on site. Many others felt that they had given Steven a second chance by accepting him back as their bishop and had hoped that he would adopt a leadership role, but he had disappointed them a second time by his passivity and now they had given up on him. It also became clear that Catherine Plummer was prepared to be manipulative, deceitful and dishonest in her dealings with people and that I needed to operate quite independently of the Plummers. This naturally drove Steven and me further apart, though, to the end, he needed to confide in me when Catherine became too much.

My goal was to work in the spirit of Father Liebler but without the paternalism, and also to put into effect the sensible plans that Steven had for the future, often called his "vision" but this is a grand term for the practical policies that he envisaged, namely, reviving pastoral care, building up the congregations, using the Navajo language, re-establishing the community farm and promoting the Hooghan Learning Circle, an educational process by which the gospel would be expressed through Navajo thought forms and using Navajo story and mythology. I worked hard in all these areas, though the lack of willing lay leadership, understandable in the circumstances, made life difficult. But in the area where I could have offered the most, the Hogan Learning Circle, I encountered a further problem. I had been both a seminary principal in Lesotho and director of education in three other dioceses during my time in Africa and am well versed both in liberation theology and contextual theology. I was well placed to make a leading contribution to the Circle. However, it appeared that Bishop Steven was seriously threatened by competence and felt at a disadvantage – I was put down in meetings and never allowed to play any significant part in this strategy. The political and spiritual crisis of the Church among forgotten, marginalised peoples was becoming ever more evident. In the Province of Southern Africa Desmond Tutu argued that black clergy must aim not only to be as good as but better than their white counterparts if they were to win full acceptance: there was to be no diminishment of standards of training. Here in Navajoland there was becoming apparent the stark results of an inversion of that policy, with an inadequately trained native bishop being given carte blanche by his liberal but undiscerning white peers.

Bishop Steven eventually succumbed to cancer in 2005. I laboured on. Mrs Plummer, whom I sought to support in many ways, used her uncle to spread scurrilous gossip about me on the reservation. But whereas there appeared to be little change, in fact church life was deteriorating further.

Bishop Steven eventually died.

Our Interim Bishop was Rustin Kimsey, retired Bishop of Eastern Oregon, who knew Navajoland and had tried to guide Steven. For the first time it felt we actually had a Bishop. Things were demanded of us, and he would come and spend days at a time with us, travelling around, picking up drunks in my truck, visiting and getting to know the area and our work. This was repeated with my colleagues in the Arizona and New Mexico regions. But he was no longer young and at his first annual convocation announced that Mark MacDonald, the Bishop of Alaska, would become our Bishop if we so requested. This was apparently as much a surprise to Mark as to everyone else, and an unfortunate if spontaneous event, as it interrupted the new sense of stability and direction that was being found.

Mark MacDonald is ambitious, and came to us while remaining Bishop of Alaska and retaining residence in Fairbanks, which was scarcely helpful to Navajoland. A few months later, without any consultation, he accepted a new position as Bishop for all Native Communities in Canada. He would resign as Bishop of Alaska but remain Bishop of Navajoland. We clergy felt angry and betrayed, having been informed by telephone the day before the press conference, clearly to prevent any possibility of discussion or negotiation.

The pastoral care of a few hundred people in Navajoland, the "little people", anawi, of St Luke's Gospel, could easily be sacrificed in the grand designs of church leaders.

In press releases, and in conversations with the Episcopal Church in Navajoland, the Bishop's reasons for taking on this ridiculous appointment – covering the whole of Canada being utterly impossible with any discernment and depth, let alone the Navajo connection – became more forced and desperate. It gave native Canadians a voice, he said – as though they needed someone jumping on the bandwagon at a late stage when they had already, without any help, made their huge grievances heard and compelled the attention of government. He said his position made a point of not recognising colonial boundaries: this was one of the more bizarre claims, with Canada and Navajoland at opposite ends of the United States. If he had chosen to identify with one of the peoples who bestride the borders and who are actually arguing for a waiver of passport, and had engaged in their struggle, the point would have been better made. As for those of us in Navajoland, his living in Toronto (his choice) was closer to us than his living in Fairbanks: this provoked much mirth as, though it is undoubtedly true, it hardly makes any real difference. For he was an absentee Bishop – from both his constituencies: native needs in Canada are concentrated in the west and north where there are already native bishops. It is very strange for someone with native lineage to be at ease not living where their vocation takes them. Indeed, in the Church of England in the eighteenth century, it was made contrary to canon law for bishops to live outside their diocese, abuses having become legendary: one Bishop of St Asaph in Wales had entered his Cathedral for the first time in his coffin, and one Bishop of Norwich was so often absent that the diocese became known as the "dead see". We were told that the Bishop would visit regularly and he protested too much in repeating this: visits of two or three days, however regular, are of little help; less frequent visits of longer duration would have enabled him to know people better, examine work being done and grasp the many nettles that an absentee Bishop does not notice. So we were governed largely by telephone conferences and e-mails as though church business can be conducted from behind a desk. Navajoland could have become the first virtual diocese in the Episcopal Church.

The Episcopal Church in Navajoland was in a mess. We were experiencing abuse of church property, a lack of openness and honesty, financial irregularity, no pastoral care exercised over most of the reservation, a breakdown of the Hooghan Learning Circle, and a lack of vision and purpose. There was nobody to take this in hand. Aware of a deterioration I could do nothing about, and myself being what Graham Greene would have called a "burnt out case" after years of what a doctor had called "self-abuse" (one friend wrote and told me how lucky I was but the doctor had meant overwork), I informed the Bishop that I would resign the following year, giving him ample time to find a replacement.

It was little surprise, in the circumstances, that a disastrous turn of events was soon underway. The Bishop met with the church councils to discuss the future. He allowed this meeting to be hijacked by one Father Dick Snyder, who, in his short period as a late Ordinand, had left one parish after a year and now needed to move again as he had virtually shut down his present parish. He had been rejected as a candidate for the Arizona region some months previously but had a sentimental attraction to Indian ministry as many fatally do. But, as a cub reporter for the Episcopal Church press, he was well known to some in the hierarchy. The Bishop allowed him to meet the people but then let this develop into an interview. The people, feeling pressurised and unsure whether this would be the only candidate, appointed him. The search process had lasted two hours! Uncertainty was expressed as soon as the meeting was over. The councils had not been prepared. This was the first time that they had participated in the selection of a priest and the opportunity had been wasted – by a Bishop so mobile as to be almost inaccessible, who did not have time to weigh the issues involved. Alternatively was this a "done deal"? Did the hierarchy of the church collude in this appointment on a sort of old boys' network?

It was agreed that, as I needed to work until the summer of 2008 for pension purposes, and Father Snyder needed to flee Brigham City, Utah as soon as possible, I would step down early and overlap with him, easing him in and continuing responsibilities in fund raising and organising the volunteer groups who came to work over the summer. As soon as Father Snyder arrived (with a terrible mixture of fear and incompetence) he cancelled this agreement, saying he and not the Bishop was in charge (an interesting interpretation of canon law). He accused me of financial irregularities, which was ironic considering his record in Brigham. He proceeded to effectively shut the church down: there was no visiting, no care of prisoners and youth at risk, no freedom for the women's groups, no Navajo liturgy, no communication, no interest in the Hooghan Learning Circle, discouragement of partners – nothing but poorly prepared, hastily led Sunday services. All the problems that Brigham City had experienced resurfaced – no personal skills, outbursts of temper, unexplained absences, no hospitality, no response to need. Local leadership was insulted. In a word, seven years assiduous ministry had been destroyed in a matter of months. And the Bishop did nothing. It is no wonder that some of the people wondered whether Snyder had been sent to close the place down. Clearly no background checks, references or testimonials had been sought. I wrote at the time:-

"The lessons are plain. The Episcopal Church in Navajoland is experiencing diminishment and is losing its focus. The Presiding Bishop is directly responsible for Navajoland as the last mission area in the mainland United States. And she is well known for her concern for minorities. She is yet to visit Navajoland and will know of it mainly through Bishop Mark and his secretary who regularly overstate the achievements and possibilities of the Episcopal Church here to outside audiences. It seems as though, in the grand plans and great meetings of the Episcopal Church, while noble stands are taken en masse and in the abstract, the detailed, painstaking, sacrificial pastoral care of individual reservations is being sold short. It seems that even Bishops with native credentials cannot be relied upon. Totally inadequate clergy can still be dumped on unsuspecting reservations. The only hope of making a dent in the armour of the smooth talking bureaucrats is to raise these issues in the public forum because a body such as the Church, with its high calling and residual respect in society, needs to be challenged in its virtual collusion in the political and social exclusion of native people. This is part of a continuum in the refusal of the churches to take ministry to minorities seriously, whether it be with dispossessed youth of Lancashire where I began, with the sexually different, or with indigenous peoples. These are issues not merely of ecclesiastical but of public concern because many people still trust the churches to be responsible in ethical standards and because the churches themselves have developed ways of stifling internal criticism by their leaders bonding together in solidarity, right or wrong."

So my final year in full time paid ministry had, on the face of it, ended in disaster. I can only hope some seeds had been sown. I had sacrificed much for this position: the need to leave behind much intellectual and spiritual baggage in order to enter the strange new world of the Navajo; the bearing of much false gossip and misunderstanding; the deterioration of my health; the loneliness of the priest who becomes in Donovan's words "a social martyr", never belonging fully to the new but uprooted from his own society, stripped to the core of his being to be poured out in the service of the poor and outcast; standing with the excluded on "the other side of the street", not knowing whether one would survive or return. I have no complaints about all this. I chose my lot and I accept it, at best gladly. But I do not yet know how to cope adequately with a church, in the persons of corrupt officials, which has betrayed me and, much worse, those little ones to whom it is particularly commissioned to show the limitless love of God. I find it difficult to conceive how I can continue to serve in my retirement such a travesty of what the Body of Christ and the fellowship of the Holy Spirit should be. Maybe it is beyond reform, and has to decay and die so something new and better might arise from its ashes. Now, in my imagination, I walk along the canyon rims of the Utah wilderness, of arid and windy desolation but also of a terrifying beauty, mirroring the Navajo soul, shadowed by the silent presence of the Creator but unable to read his mind or purpose. I have fought a long defeat.[12]

My thoughts on mission upon leaving Navajoland may be found in Appendix 2.

Grays Peak, Rocky Mountains USA

Monument Valley, Colorado Plateau USA

SECTION 3

In the final part of this memoir I want to try to make some sense of the life I have sketched; to observe the factors that have promoted growth; to learn what growing up as a closeted homosexual has done to me; to measure the cost of having given the greater part of my life to an institution – the church – that has proved to be so uncaring and so self-absorbed; the price of having lasting intimate relationships denied and, above all, to see how an ecstatic vision of life and the close relationships I have indeed enjoyed have emerged from this pruning and the anxiety it has often produced. I want also to strongly assert that, if the church is really in the business of developing relationships, consequent upon its claims that God is Love, that it must not only allow but also encourage its officers to practise that reality in their own lives whatever their sexual orientation. Love cannot be proclaimed by the loveless.

I realise that little mention has been made of my family in this regard. That is because, until recently, it has mattered less in my life than other relationships. I was very close to my mother but she died as I finished university. For at least a year I daily relived her last, agonised hours in my mind. She had found herself with three children to look after, not only my brother and myself but also my father who was emotionally immature and dependent. I never felt close to him though I admired him for his achievement in running the family business – shop-fitting – with severely reduced eyesight (from birth), and was grateful for an economically stable childhood. But it was far from emotionally stable: my memory is of constant arguments between parents and, once, of my mother referring to their "failed marriage", words which seemed to drop the bottom out of my world. He was stubborn, very conservative in his views and verbally, occasionally physically, violent. I had little respect for him. I certainly could never disclose my sexuality. He remarried and was in fact wedded to his second wife for longer than his first, but they seemed to share most in each other's worst qualities, not least snobbery and I had little in common with her. As time passed my father and I had little to say to each other and, when I visited (as rarely as was decent), after half an hour the silences would lengthen and conversation was spent. After his sudden death, at eighty, I felt remorse for not having made more effort, while recognising that he, too, could have tried harder. While receiving psychotherapy years later I found it necessary to write him a letter, both apologising for myself and forgiving him. I hope we are now more reconciled. I had little in common either with my younger brother who, as a child, was far more adventurous and less academic than me and who I was to learn only in recent years, had deeply resented my being constantly praised by our parents and held up as a model to him. However, he got his revenge: he emerged fully-formed scholastically, as it were, with unexpectedly good O'level results and went on to read Spanish at the University of Bristol and, eventually, to become a distinguished head teacher of one of the largest and most difficult primary schools in the city. And since returning from America I have resided in the south west to be near the family, and my brother and I are now closer than we have ever been. I have great respect and affection for my sister in law and it has been deeply rewarding to deepen my contact with their children and grandchildren with whom I have previously had sketchy communication owing to my absence overseas for twenty years. So this aspect of my semi retirement has proved richly satisfying.

That experience of insecurity in childhood did help, I think, in making me more independent and self-reliant, though it also led me to find emotional fulfilment in friends rather than in relatives. I first caught a glimpse of the potential depth of friendship in the sixth form, and some people from that time are still very much with me and we have never lost touch. Few survive from university days as my first years at Cambridge were anxious ones, wondering whether I could survive in such a gifted environment. A marvellous personal tutor, Dick Gooderson, helped me through this time and convinced me I was a better academic than I had thought. I was offered a research option after my first degree, which I declined as ordination beckoned. But what I describe as my "second conversion" – to people – happened as a result of my decision to teach for a few years first. I chose to go to a comprehensive school, Great Barr[13], in my home city of Birmingham, which was situated on a huge council housing estate in the North West. It was there that I discovered and received, amidst so much deprivation and need, unquestioning love, care and affection from these young people. Because the school was the worst comprehensive in the city –

older pupils and younger staff were very much thrown together against the common enemy – senior staff – whose experience was solely in other types of school and ran the place as a failed grammar school. Friendships still survive from this period: indeed at the time of writing, I shall be baptising a grandchild of a pupil from that time, whose mother I have also baptised. You will notice that radical tendencies were starting to emerge as I responded to these young folk. Coming from a lower middle class background and being only a little older than they, I found myself drawn into a deep level of response. I came to believe that it is patronising to refer to "children": they are people, equal in status to me and, often, because of their wider experience and rapid maturing, wiser than me. I deeply resent the institutionalised ageism that is encouraged in our society as the "nanny state" takes root: there should be no close relationships between older and younger, no touch or affection, no friendship. No longer can an old man on a park bench safely talk to a lost child or respond to requests to play. We so impoverish our adult souls by disengaging with the young in this way. They need mentors, of course, and that needs to be kept in mind, but they also need experienced older friends to help them grow, and we need them to be kept alive and on fire with their youthful enthusiasm, hope and vision. But that partnership has been wrecked by our society. Little wonder that there are riots in our cities as I write. Friendship is the greatest of gifts: indeed, it must be the bedrock of all close relationships, including marriage. The medieval church used to prize it highly and write about it. But the more puritanical influences of the Reformation and, today, scandals over paedophilia in the church, have contributed to a neglect of this vital area of living and we are all the poorer for it. Ageism is a modern disease of the West, not prevalent, for instance, in Africa.

It is perhaps not surprising that I began to really come to terms with my sexuality at theological college! I had sensed that I was different from a very early age. I distinctly remember, at the age of five or so, finding excuses to sit on the knees of my two cousins in uniform, who were doing their National Service, because I was madly attracted to their dashing good looks. When, a year later, I was in hospital with mastoiditis, and was placed in a men's ward as the children's was full, the two people I remember are Joe and Harry, two handsome young men whom I befriended. I used to write to them afterwards. I found only one friend at school who I could be relaxed with, and, at university, one of the friends I "came out" to deliberately avoided me after that! But at Westcott House, Cambridge, I was in a more understanding environment, and two gay fellow students helped me to come to terms with myself. I shall forever be deeply grateful to them. My first sexual experience was there. It was a blessed time at every level, and I owe it all to Peter Walker, the Principal, later Bishop of Ely. Once I met him I was sure that this was the man under whom I wished to prepare for the priesthood. He was of immense wisdom and discernment. I shall always remember going to him with a problem: I talked, he listened; there were long silences. Eventually I thanked him and left, feeling greatly relieved, and it was only as I descended his staircase that I realised he had said nothing at all – a lesson in positive listening that has remained with me.

My new openness and acceptance of myself was cemented by my experience in my first parishes in Farnworth and Bolton in Lancashire. Most of my surviving friendships date from this period and my subsequent time in Manchester. All Lancastrians, whether native or adopted, know they are the salt of the earth! I particularly valued the characteristic blend of sturdy masculinity combined with a gentle sensitivity and keen intelligence to be found in the men; and they could accept difference. I was once told, as a compliment, that I was, like them, a man's man: little did they know the layers of meaning that phrase had for me! I was a great believer in visiting, not because it produces church attendance (it mostly doesn't) but because you only really get to know someone on their home turf where they are in control, and from this ministry of "wasting time constructively" or "loitering with intent", as I used to define it, there developed many lasting friendships to this day. They were usually with younger people for this was the era of hippiedom and "flower power", an age of optimism and experiment, and I was unresistingly drawn into this world of Leonard Cohen, progressive rock, denims, long hair, recreational drugs and scented deodorants. At that time I sported shoulder length hair, a beard and denims, looking rather like Rasputin from the neck upwards. I had carefully considered this and it did help my integration into student communities but only, of course, because my commitment and concern were genuine. I was a regular visitor to student communes, travelled with them to concerts and gigs, smoked and drank with them. It was one of the happiest and most fulfilling times of my life. Moreover, as a good correspondent I have been able to keep in touch with people from each of these various periods in my life and am therefore supported by a marvellous network of friends who really became my family. And I have continued to find that, if I have the courage to be myself and open to others, I discover friends wherever I go, who respond in like manner. I have never found it necessary to consider this personal agenda whenever I have moved because I am convinced I shall find friends wherever I go. Theologically, I suppose this is saying that God always precedes us in situations and that, as we are all made in his image, if we allow this to shine in us we shall discover ourselves strangely but wonderfully bound together. But it is only possible when we ARE ourselves, without apology or inhibition.

My only experience of having my own family in a traditional sense was in Lesotho. One evening I returned to my house to find two boys sitting on the doorstep. They had been abandoned by their mother who, having once worked at the seminary where I was now principal, had decided they would be looked after here. They were both teenagers. Our story I have told above. A day scarcely goes by when I do not think of them. They were certainly happy times, and it was probably better that they found me than not, though I failed them as a surrogate father not least because I could not give them all the attention they needed. I become ever more conscious that this was a big failure and it troubles me.

One crucial factor that has grown from the gift of friendship nourished in me by so many others is that I carry within me an expectation that the world is friendly. So many people seem to have a fear of unfamiliar locations and cultures. I go out eager to explore and confident that I will meet people who will be friendly and helpful – indeed, that most people are so disposed and not inclined to take advantage or pull you down whatever their economic status. I have found this to be true almost without exception from my beginnings in Lesotho when Dennis Koatsa, a teenager, was outside my door every morning because his mother told him the new man would be unfamiliar with the land and its people and may need assistance. To put yourself into the hands of local people is the most sensible option rather than to stay apart and try to survive like a colonial hangover: you learn from the people who, in turn, support you.

I am sure that this being at ease with both myself and the world around me must also, in some mysterious way, derive from my earliest childhood memories which were happy and secure, memories of tactile attention, music (some of which I still recall), the domestic daily round, classic Christmas celebrations. These, I feel, were not erased by later recollections of my mother's indifferent health and family dysfunction. Indeed, my sympathy for my mother's being overweight (from glandular causes) induced in me an immediate and emotional reaction to any large lady struggling with shopping or offspring which effects me even now and, I suspect, has led to a wider empathy for those suffering for any reason. The withdrawal into myself in my teens, in response both to domestic stress and sexual difference, and its concomitant sense of isolation, also enhanced my sensitivity to the trials and tribulations of others. A quiet confidence began to grow beneath a nervous and wary veneer, deepened by study in the humanities and a keen observance of human behaviour, a confidence in the absolute rightness of an obligation to see justice done and love vindicated to which I was becoming committed. And this growing ethical awareness was deepened by a nascent faith.

My parents had both been church goers but had fallen away since marrying and especially since the arrival of children. I was taught to pray by an elderly aunt who baby-sat for my parents once a month so they could have an evening out. These prayers were very simple and childlike but left their mark. Much later on, when I was praying alone as I continued to do, aged about thirteen, I was in tears because I had committed to the rubbish bin my ancient one armed teddy bear, convinced that grammar school pupils should not possess such childish things. I suddenly became aware that my petitions were not being sent out into the void but were being heard, received. It was a sense of presence akin to that experienced when, sitting with your back to the door you are aware that someone has entered the room silently by a scarcely perceptible change of atmosphere. That sense of being met by God, a silent listening presence, has never deserted me: even when at seminary my theological studies led me at one point to doubting everything that sense of presence remained and held me. I think that alone must have kept me in church, to which I started to go monthly with the youth club when a friend of mine, Peter Beck, known as Bunny for his exceptional fair hair and skin, persuaded me to attend as he felt I needed "bringing out of myself". I was not happy in either club or church (where the Vicar always addressed me as "boy") but I persevered until the arrival of a new incumbent. He was equally unlikely to attract youth, being a retired business man ordained late in life, but what impressed me was the fact that, upon my arrival in church, he was always already there, on his knees in prayer. I began to realise its depth and in my last year at school, was confirmed (my father, in one of his rages with me, refused to attend). A year later, at university, thoughts of ordination began to fly, perhaps typical, in Pauline fashion, for a young but late convert. When I confronted my discerning college chaplain, Alan Wilkinson, with this great offer the church could scarcely refuse, he wisely counselled me to concentrate on obtaining my degree. But it was during my education diploma year, following my graduation, that I was interviewed by Peter Walker and my course was set – to return to Cambridge after two years "out in the world" teaching.

1. Intellectual Foundations

Those years at Westcott House laid the foundations for my coming journey of theological exploration and for my reflections on growing experience of the world. These were grounded initially in the writings of contemporary English thinkers – Michael Ramsey, Harry Williams, Kenneth Leach, David Jenkins – but, above all, of three remarkable parish priests, Charles Browne (a predecessor of mine at St John Chrysostom, Victoria Park), Bill Vanstone (also of the Manchester diocese) and Alan Ecclestone (of Sheffield). This is a deeply incarnational tradition with an emphasis on social responsibility that grafted on naturally to my experience as a teacher. I produced a little book collecting some of the unpublished and unfinished work of Charlie Browne, but, for now, let Alan Ecclestone, with whom I used to talk in his retirement in the Lake District, speak for them all – quoted from his first, award winning book *Yes to God*.

> *Prayer...is not a rock pool but an ocean...those who pray must be inured to storms and tempered by great strains. Engagement without passion is a heartless hoax...for there is no real engagement of ourselves with others that is not costly. Passion without engagement is a display of fireworks, a*

waste of energy, a self-abuse...it knows and offers no guide to the worth of what it touches. Prayer strives to penetrate what (seems to be)...too hard to understand, too cruel to endure, too meaningless to use, in order to discern the lines of the emergent work, the future of humanity being shaped, and in order to engage the one who prays with what is being wrought...It is the job of praying to refuse to be disengaged. (People pray) to penetrate below and beyond the appearances of things. The pray because they are perplexed, disillusioned, frightened, because of the way of the world and of religion itself has become too sterile to endure. Exploration, geographical and spiritual exposes men and women to new ordeals, and their praying reflects their attempts to meet them. Such souls must face with courage the loss of all the guidelines of familiar features. They must accept the need to let go the things in which they have trusted and face the outlines of a strange, benumbing, terrifying void. They want to know how to live with contradictions, and how prayer can deal with fragmented lives...Our task is to find out what love means in the moment that lies before us now. We must mine and refine such love as we can from the tracts of experience we come upon at this time in our lives "we have not passed this way before" and we need not to be ashamed to confess that we need new help in setting about it. Prayer is our cry for such help, made in pain and joy, a cry to the Other in faith and help.[14]

This was a heady spirituality for one only recently exposed to the need of the world and who was to become ever more rigorously exposed. It has contributed to the development over the years of an essentially tragic view of life which I once made some notes on to this effect,

Christians have always been tempted to transform the tragedy of Jesus into comedy by supposing the resurrection gives to his story a "happy ending" but no story has an ending until it is fully told. The context that gives meaning (or fails to do so) to the history of each individual (including Jesus) is the history of the human race. And because that history continues the story has, as yet, no ending. The question of the meaning of history remains an open question. It is not closed by faith in Jesus' resurrection.

But this view of the lives of both us and Jesus being tragic, in the sense of Shakespearian tragedy, the cost of the witness to truth to Hamlet or Lear, for example, has been complemented by the sort of ecstatic French mysticism to be found in Peguy and Teilhard de Chardin, which finds a home in my mind, heart and soul with the Romantic era of classical music that often reflects it. Chardin writes as the theologian of evolution: the task assigned to us is the climb towards the light.

Once I had become more immersed in the world I became very influenced by Liberation Theology and Situation Ethics. The former, coming initially from Latin America, was an intoxicating mixture of rigorous Biblical study and Marxist social analysis, regarding the world, as it were, with a Bible in one hand and a newspaper in the other, seeking the relationship between salvation and liberation, the Kingdom of God and progress for the poor and marginalised – a Christian worldliness. The Church's task was one of "prophetic denunciation" and "conscientizing evangelisation" in the sort of disadvantaged situations in which I worked. We believed "since God has become man humanity, everyman, history, is the living Temple of God" and therefore what was needed was a new "conversion to the neighbour" – words of the great high priest of Liberation Theology, Gustavo Gutierrez. Without a real commitment against exploitation and alienation, and for a society of solidarity and justice, the Eucharistic celebration is an empty action. Further to deny the fact of class struggle is really to put oneself on the side of the dominant sectors – neutrality is impossible. In this area Situation Ethics taught that one of the most important factors to be taken into account in making moral decisions is the context of the agent, and that informed compassion should be the dominant determinant in resolving a problem. These disciplines were re-enforced by Conceptual Theology when I moved abroad, namely the study of how Christian motivation and conviction can be expressed in different cultures and philosophies whether African or American. It is all a question of holding together two mantras of one of my mentors, David Jenkins, formally Bishop of Durham (who himself exemplified these truths) – "God is as he is in Jesus" and "God is in reality" (not fantasy): The God we worship inhabits his Creation and demands justice for all humanity in which he is Love Incarnate. The so-called Social Gospel (a misnomer – there is only one Gospel, with social implications) I felt called to live was undergirded by the astonishing congruencies with

Celtic, African and Native American spirituality that I experienced, all aware of a God rooted in what he has made.

Perhaps I could draw these threads together in referring to the convictions driving the work of a remarkable doctor, Paul Farmer, in Haiti. He is convinced that God is to be found most distinctively in the suffering of the poor: indeed this is where the meaning of the Crucifixion is to be found. But he says, "God gives but doesn't share": it is our responsibility to be stewards of his bounty and to see it is justly shared. However, in this response we shall have to make sacrifices: most of the world is poor and we have to try to fix that but, in order to do that, we shall have to pay the cost of listening, committing and enduring in our task. We should come to feel anger at the state of the world for anger brings clarity. And we must be prepared to do unglamorous work for all lives are of equal value. It is this sort of vision to which I have attempted to give my life.

In recent years, while this ministry of care has not weakened, in exposure to other beliefs and philosophies that I must take seriously, I have come to believe less but to believe more fervently in what is left. At core that "ultimate reality is gracious", that the planet is a living organism to be cherished and nurtured, that we have a profound obligation of kindness to one another, that all life is holy and an expression of the life of the Creator. I have come to appreciate that all of us share transcendent experiences and a feel for absolute values of love and compassion, however conditioned by cultural context that I have been eager to explore. I find in these explorations a sort of implicit religion that can also be detected in those of a more agnostic disposition and which therefore enables conversation that crosses traditional boundaries. In this sharing I am always encouraged by the most frequent command of Jesus in the Gospels, "do not be afraid" (that is, plunge in!) and his concern that our "joy be full".

A real problem for me, therefore, has been the failure of the Church to consistently embody those truths by which I try to live, for its usually being far more an only too human institution rather than the Body of Christ in the world. I had a good training in the Diocese of Manchester under two deeply human bishops, Patrick Rodger and Stanley Booth-Clibborn, and under a distinguished cathedral chapter under two fine deans, Alfred Jowett and Robert Waddington. But I have to say that, in mission work abroad, in churches still then under white dominance or the dominance of indigenous clergy much influenced by their training in white institutions the perceptions of these clergy and the demands of the institutional life of the Church too often took precedence over the needs of the majority of impoverished people and, if I supported them, I was seen as a threat or a danger. I received minimal support in hugely demanding positions in Lesotho and Zimbabwe and, when I was expelled from Zimbabwe, hardly anyone in the diocese of Harare spoke up for me. In Botswana I was well mentored by the marvellous Archbishop who created a post for me, but in South Africa it was possible for a further Bishop to dismiss me on his personal whim. In Canada, the church at any level in the diocese cared nothing for the benighted lives of Indians on reserves and, in Navajoland, USA, I found myself in the most corrupt church of my experience. What I can say for the church is that it has given me the freedom to pursue the work to which I had been called, even when perhaps it has not understood me or my work; for that I am grateful. But for many clergy the church is still a career.

This was brought home to me when I left England for Africa. Shortly after the decision had been made I was summoned by the Suffragan Bishop Donald Tytler, for whom I worked in the Board of Ministry. I had not yet had time to tell him of my forthcoming move and it transpired I was to experience one of God's little jokes. He told me that my name was to be placed on a list that mysteriously circulated among diocesan bishops, in a very Anglican sort of way, of people who, it was thought by someone, would make good suffragan bishops. What a dilemma! I had just decided to go abroad on missionary work whereas, if I stayed put, I could perhaps become a bishop. Bishop Donald's reaction was instructive: he was very angry; I was presumably being unwise or ungrateful. I soon realised, however, that there was no contest between doing some useful work in Africa and waiting to see if I would become a sort of Episcopal curate. My name did not go on that list. Apparently, gaining a wide experience of mission is not a qualification for episcopacy – loyalty to the institution is. Going overseas in middle age was seen as not courageous but eccentric. Whereas I have to confess that I sometimes wonder what might have happened – I think I would have made a good suffragan bishop! I have to admit that I have been spared a life of service to the institution that I would have found limiting and stultifying. I think I am best placed as a coal face worker in pastoral situations. But I have to make a further confession: the lack of recognition in such work can be disheartening. You do it, of course, for the people and for no reward, but a little encouragement helps! I was surprised by how moved I was to receive from the state government of Utah through its Humanities Council a Humanities Award for my work with ethnic minorities in San Juan County. It meant more than I could possibly have thought. Some pain was felt in the acknowledgement that this came not from my Church but from a secular state influenced by the Mormon Church. Yet in the midst of such isolated and demanding work a little recognition came as a great blessing.

The Church's allowing me to serve in such situations certainly opened me up to being civilised by indigenous people, if not always by their churches. If I have anything to contribute in ministry today it is because I have been loved and mentored by rural Africans and Americans. In particular, I owe immense debts to my two Archbishops in Africa, Desmond Tutu of Southern Africa and Khotso Makhulu of Central Africa, who both, in their different ways, helped me to cope with my anger and learn to forgive. Africans have a genius for forgiveness. I am blessed to be still in contact with them. A long letter from Desmond at a critical time was, and remains, a life line for me, so full of love and acceptance. On a later occasion, when I was sick in Navajoland, he wrote recalling that I was "a ball of enthusiasm and energy" in Lesotho and added, "your people are fortunate to have you, for you are a dedicated and committed person – no half measures here". The humour and the affirmation, especially coming from one of my heroes, lifted me then and continues to do so when I bring the letter to mind. It is beside the point that he is being over-generous: what matters is that he believes in me, and suggests implicitly that perhaps God does too. For that is always what we need to remember about our faith: the crucial issue is not whether I believe in God but whether God believes in me. I learnt from them how the reality of the Church is its people, not least the poorest, who God loves and in whom he is incarnate. I learnt from them, and from the Navajo in America, how the church is the keeper of the holy signs, the mysteries, the sacraments which are the pledge and promise of God's love and dependability. I could lose the institution but not the mysteries, the sacraments; where they are celebrated the Church is there.

2. Music and Experience

I want next to reflect on the major forces that have shaped my life, namely, the arts, the natural world, personal relationships and prayer. Any of these could occupy a book on its own and, despite being an avid reader and a lover of the visual arts. I am going to let my first love, music, speak for them all. Its power is well illustrated in this graphic paragraph from Louise Erdrich's novel, "The Plague of Doves". She is describing here the playing of a native violinist, named Shamengwa, and its effect:

> *Here I come to some trouble with words. The inside became the outside when Shamengwa played music. Yet inside to outside does not half sum it up. The music was more than music – at least what we are used to hearing. The music was feeling itself. The sound connected instantly with something deep and joyous. Those powerful moments of true knowledge that we have to paper over with daily life. The music tapped the back of our terrors, too. Things we had lived through and didn't want to ever repeat. Shredded imaginings, unadmitted longings, fear and also surprising pleasures. No, we can't live at that pitch. But every so often something shatters like*

ice and we are in the river of our existence. We are aware. And this realisation was in the music, somehow, or in the way Shamengwa played it.[15]

Or compare the opening of Arthur O'Shaunnessy's poem so memorably set by Elgar in *The Music Makers,*

We are the music makers,
We are the dreamers of dreams,
Wandering by lone sea-breakers,
And sitting by desolate streams;
World- losers and world-forsakers,
On whom the pale moon gleams:
Yet we are the movers and shakers
Of the world for ever, it seems.[16]

God created the arts in order that life might be held together by them, so that we should not separate ourselves from spiritual things.
St John Chrysostom

The artist speaks to our capacity for delight and wonder, to the sense of mystery surrounding our lives. Author unknown

So what are the elements in life which encourage me to such passionate absorbance in it, a desire to explore every place and possibility to hand, to entwine myself with others, to sense the ecstasy of the breathtakingly beautiful world we inhabit-to live as recklessly as I have described and not to waste a moment? Music has certainly been one of the most vivid windows into experience, mainly Western classical music, because that is my background, tradition and first love, but increasingly so-called 'world music', and certainly much of what I have found can speak to people through whatever sort of seriously intentioned music appeals to them. I speak as a failed composer and pianist, but mainly as a listener so our understanding may be based on common ground.

My reveille occurred when I was but five or six years old. I used to creep into the sitting room where my father would be listening to his records and, on at least two occasions, was transfixed. Indeed, I am told I visibly and audibly responded to the slow movement of Dvorak's 'New World' Symphony in my cradle, so perhaps there was some innate quality within me primed to react. On one occasion, my father had on the turntable an LP of Moura Lympany, a British pianist of the post war years, playing Rachmaninov's First Piano Concerto. At the beginning of the development section of the first movement the orchestra is brought to a halt by strange, insistent, repeated chords. The chords in themselves, I now know, are not remarkable, but it is the way the composer uses them which makes the effect. It is as though the listener is summoned from beyond, from the unknown. It was my first intimation of a vast world out there which I now glimpsed, and which filled me with both curiosity and fear. That fear of the wider world persisted through childhood, imparting a disturbing sense of insecurity, but the curiosity was to prove unquenchable, released by those chords.

I am certain of the work cited by remembrance of the sleeve of the LP, as I am of two other works, Beethoven's 'Emperor' Piano Concerto and Tchaikovsky's First, the latter played by Solomon, another notable contemporary British pianist. These childhood encounters with two masterpieces brought a new depth of life, but this time of joy, a happiness of a depth not hitherto experienced. It is little short of a miracle that Beethoven can exalt so infectiously using almost entirely scales, arpeggio and chords in the piano part, and the stunning opening of the Tchaikovsky, with its broad melody and grand chords always seems to open the gates to new experiences of feeling and sensibility. Music can open a door to the heights and depths of human experience.

We are all familiar with how music can lift us out of depression, what Nietzsche called its 'tonic' effect. I am referring to what he termed its 'dynamic' effect, its capacity to awaken and stir creativity. Many years on, as a teenager, I recall borrowing a friend's ticket for the music section of the Public Library in the centre of my home city, Birmingham. I took out the famous recording of Wagner's 'Tristan und Isolde,' featuring Kirsten Flagstad and conducted by the great Wilhelm Furtwangler, simply because I knew no Wagner at the time. I listened to the entire work in one sitting, and was so electrified I started it all over again until my mother objected. The effect was volcanic. Wagner had, incredibly, constructed a whole new musical language for this work to express the ecstatic eroticism he wish to portray: it relies much on a quite novel use of the interrupted cadence, so progressions are not resolved and the aching yearning of romantic love is conjured from the notes. It was as though the great love duet released all the adolescent, unformed, unknown passion within: my world was changed in an instant. I did not know what to do. I had to walk. I could not sleep. The delirium of the score was infectious and I was reminded, as I was to be again upon reading Dostoyevsky's 'The Brothers Karamazov", 'that you approach some products of the human spirit with fear and trembling: you are never the same again.' It was Wagner as much as experience that alerted me to the possibilities of human relationship and has made me so passionate a friend and lover. I knew now that love can be so all encompassing and all embracing that even considerations of life or death may be of little account. Because music can be so seductive, ecstatic, erotic or enigmatic, it can never be relegated to the background because that is to demean and degrade it. It demands attention. It pierces the heart and un-dams the feelings.

A discerning example of this occurs in Shafer's play 'Amadeus,' about the life of Mozart. Salieri, an older composer who feels threatened by the young genius, hears the marvellous Wind Serenade (Grand Partita). He ridicules the opening of the slow movement, where the low winds, establishing an accompaniment figure, remind him of a barrel-organ. But then, high above, the oboe enters with a seraphic melody that seems to come from another world, and Salieri is smitten. Music that seems to objectively address us, like God Himself (and Bernard Shaw wrote that Sarastro's arias in Mozart's 'The Magic Flute' are the only music composed fit to proceed from the mouth of God), can either draw out of us emotional depths we never knew we possessed or open to us the possibilities of other worlds we never suspected could exist. Thomas Merton wrote:

> *The mind that responds to the intellectual and spiritual values that lie hidden in a poem, a painting or a piece of music, discovers a spiritual vitality that lifts it above itself, takes it out of itself, and makes it present to itself on a level of being that it did not know it could ever achieve.*[17]

The symphonies of Gustav Mahler illustrate perfectly both possibilities. His life, in both its angst and its vision, and work are inextricably linked. A man who knew deep suffering, he constantly sought spiritual transcendence. His Sixth symphony is a terrifying picture of utter catastrophe and annihilation. Trying to enter into and understand its meaning has helped me to empathise with the hopelessness I have encountered in the Western inner city or the African desert or slum. In the Ninth Symphony, the ironic second and vicious third movements seem to portray all that is dark and depressing, first in a rural and then in a city environment (an insight of the conductor Simon Rattle). But the first movement the composer Alban Berg described as 'an expression of an exceptional fondness for this Earth, the longing to live in peace on it, to enjoy nature to its depths,' a movement which another composer, Arnold Schoenberg, described as having a cool beauty. The last movement is quite extraordinary, poised on the very edge of what is possible to express in any form. Four great interpreters of the symphony have perceptive words to share:

> *I think some of it comes from the other side. This is music from an unknown region.* Simon Rattle

> *There is only the majesty of death...come as a friend, and not to punish.* Otto Klemperer

> *We are cleansed, when all is said and done, no person of sensibility can come away from the Ninth Symphony without being exhausted and purified. And that is the triumphant result of all this purgatory...we do ultimately encounter an apocalyptic radiance, a glimmer of what peace must be like. [The last page of the score]..."is the closest we have ever come, in any work of art, to experiencing the very act of dying.*
> Leonard Bernstein

> *The Sixth is for me one of the greatest symphonies-and so seldom played in the past! There we have complete catastrophe. It is there in the Ninth but in the Ninth there is great beauty*

*and a sense of harmony with death Coming to the
end of the symphony is one of the hardest tasks in
all conducting...I know I was madly, madly
involved with the symphony to the extent that
when it was done-and it is one of the few works I
say this of-I would not dare touch it again.*
Herbert von Karajan

Music can reveal the depths of ourselves and the
heights of heaven. It enables us both to find ourselves
and lose ourselves, a spiritual vitality that takes us
'out of ourselves,' as we say. That is why it is so
dangerous and subversive, and is to be approached
with awe and preparation. A concert can be a service
of worship, a spiritual epiphany. Music has enlarged
my mind and my feelings, my sense and sensibility. It
makes me alert to the unsettling clouds that often,
unnoticed by the casual hearer; pass across the
outwardly happy surfaces of Mozart and Shubert, and
to their import, as the former passingly reveals depths
of tragic sorrow and the latter bursts of intense rage
against the Light. Such music helps me to appreciate
the ambiguity of existence, gives me allies in the
struggle, and shares with me the wisdom of those who
have suffered and survived to tell us in their art.

As a gay man, music has been, too, a refuge. Many American composers of the twentieth century were homosexual, as in Britain were Britten, Berkeley and Tippett. It was still difficult in the fifties and sixties, in middle class England, to be relaxed or 'out of the closet.' Here was a group one could secretly identify with. Then, as Alex Ross points out in his seminal 'the Rest is Noise,' conservatories and concert halls were havens for introverted boys who had trouble 'fitting in'. And classical music appealed to some gay youngsters because of the free-floating power of its emotions. Instrumental works, especially, can 'give voice to unspoken passions.' Some composers, however, were quite explicit and works by the Polish composer Karol Szymanowski (especially 'The Love Songs of Hafiz,' the Third Symphony and the opera 'King Roger.') and the British Benjamin Britten (the operas 'The Turn of the Screw,' 'Billy Budd,' and 'Death in Venice) became, however tragic their tone in some cases, oases of identity for us. 'Do not sleep friend, through this night...' Furthermore, music such as the Sea Interludes from Britten's opera 'Peter Grimes,' like the tone poems of Sibelius, gave shape to what a wanderer feels as he walks along. That recognition, somewhere, however remote, that our condition was recognized and accepted, was balm and such experiences steeled us for the continuing fight for freedom and equality. Music could create an invisible web of identity and belonging.

In its capacity to illuminate and deepen story and myth, music has a unique role in the theatre. Wagner's late music dramas all deal with the deep tragedy of the human condition. The cycle of four operas comprising 'The Ring of the Nibelungs' can be interpreted as a scathing indictment of capitalist society in the nineteenth century and of the suffering it caused. Now it is one thing to study this in the writings of Karl Marx and suffer twenty pages of turgid prose for every brilliant idea, but quite another to be confronted by the issues in Mime's dark, slave operated factory or Wotan's grandiose schemes for Valhalla, and the manipulative processes of them both. On a smaller scale, in the very human plots of most of the operas of Strauss and Puccini; how the music transcends the libretti in say, the plight of the ageing Marschallin in 'Der Rosenkavalier,' or the tenderness and discovery of young love in 'La Boheme!' The music makes the characters and expresses their inner thoughts. Probably Mozart is supreme in commenting on both the mythic and human qualities in his subjects. In the great operas in which Lorenzo da Ponte was his librettist – 'The

Marriage of Figaro,' 'Don Giovanni' and 'Cosi fan tutte' – the music describes acutely observed personalities drawn with psychological insight while at the same time commenting philosophically on the human predicament in tones of deep compassion and piercing truthfulness.

There is something very mysterious about what music can unleash in us. It can also be enormously cathartic, a safety valve. I have listened to music in recent years mainly when driving huge distances across the American West. I find that certain composers, notably Mahler, Bruckner, Sibelius and Elgar, both comment on the outward scenery and on my own inner journey, but also, in their passionate emotive force, draw hidden feelings from me and help me to resolve, or come to terms with, current emotional problems and crises.

As Nick Clegg, Leader of the Liberal Democratic Party in Great Britain, recently observed "Music provides a crucial emotional outlet, but it also provides perspective. It travels across time and inspires emotions that everyone shares. That makes it a powerful unifying force." At its basest, this is completely understood by tyrants such as Stalin. But composers from Central Europe like Bartok and

Janacek had in mind, when collecting folk songs, the significance of this exercise in affirming the working classes from whom such material comes. On rare occasions the benediction of a corporate enlightenment can happen through music. I remember the first performance in Manchester, England, of the completion of Mahler's Tenth Symphony by Deryck Cooke, conducted by the hugely talented Bryden Thomson. This glorious, affirmative music had only recently been revealed to the world and at one point in the last movement there occurred a moment out of time when upon the audience, utterly silent and transfixed, and the performers, there seemed to descend the peace from above. Similarly, in the great Jascha Horenstein's last appearances, conducting Wagner's 'Parsifal' at Covent Garden, during the final Eucharistic scene, the same deep quiet enveloped the audience as the orchestral timbres acquired an opalescent glow and a spirit of deep joy welled up from the depths. He had no need to live beyond that performance and died later in the run.

Anthony Storr, in 'Music and the Mind,' says that the primary function of music is, in fact, collective and communal, bringing and binding people together by its power to represent emotions, events and stories.

Music, in fact, can for some prove the sole antidote to depression. It seems nothing else can pierce the melancholy and provide, at least for a while, pleasurable feelings and a sense of life stirring again. The experience can be the more effective for being unexpected: a well loved piece, or a work totally unknown that resonates with the feelings at the time, suddenly heard on the radio or a distant cassette or CD player, can pierce the heart and release a flood of emotion after a phase of numb unresponsiveness. I am a workaholic, have suffered 'burnout' and also post-traumatic stress disorder. In my worst states the emotions are deadened. Not even the kindest personal contacts can enliven them. In every case, it has been music which has been the release. Once it was Schubert's last piano sonata. This is always a surprise as, at its start, it steals quietly upon the listener as though this exquisitely beautiful music has started long previously and someone has just opened a door. Then the grief-laden slow movement articulates all one's anguish while at the same time offering healing and consolation. The climatic phrase of the principal melody has a rhythm recalling Dido's lament in Purcell's 'Dido and Aeneas,' when she sings 'remember me.' It sounds as a deep plea from the composer which finds echoes in the abyss of the depressed. The gift of tears can now flow. A warmth arises. Music is one of the glorious mysteries of our life. Its inexpressible depth is due to the fact that it reproduces all the emotions of our innermost being. Its power, whether joyous or cathartic, comes as a blessing or a grace. Music can pierce the heart directly; it needs to mediation. And while such music makes one experience pain and grief more intensely, it brings solace and consolation at the same time.

So the ability of music to enlarge our souls, minds and hearts is a creative experience for us, and, as we recall great music we have heard, and let it grow in us, it develops our capacity for wonder and our yearning for adventure.

The music of the twentieth century has had a deep effect on my personal formation. The symphonies of Gustav Mahler – especially as experienced in searing, live performances by Bernstein, von Karajan, Solti, Haitink and Tennstedt – have enlarged my sense of wonder at the world and deepened my awareness of the tragedy that being human entails. The French (musical) Impressionists, such as Debussy, have opened up new vistas of delight and exploration. The Stravinsky of the 'Rite of Spring,' much jazz and some 'progressive pop,' have shocked me into a realization of the violence, instability and visceral excitement that underlies the placid surface of social conventions. Sibelius has introduced new perspectives to solitude and the solitary life, the perfect companion to a wanderer through life seeking to experience it in all its variety and strangeness. Schoenberg and his disciples, especially in his unfinished opera 'Moses und Aaron' and in Berg's operas, challenge me intellectually, philosophically and emotionally. Shostakovich, seeking to preserve his individuality under persecution, gives expression to the many levels of depression that haunt me. Britten helps me face my dark side and remains a distant companion, with his friend Shostakovich, in the battle for authenticity and self expression. Messiaen expresses what I dimly feel but cannot articulate about the overwhelming beauty of the universe, not least in his great orchestral masterpieces such as the Turangalila Symphony, 'The Transfiguration of Our Lord Jesus Christ' and 'From the Canyons to the Stars,' where supernovas of consonance and brilliance are blasted out of dissonant ground, in Alex Ross' happy image, in overpowering displays of transformation.

Music is a way of exploring the cosmos – not, be it noted, primarily religious music. In the Christian tradition it seems as though the God of such composers is too small. An early Mozart Mass or the contemporary musings of a John Rutter cannot do what my musical heroes do. When an apparently religious work breaks through the ceiling of decorum and respectability it is usually by a composer whose faith was either uncertain or more questioning, as in the cases of the Requiem Masses of Berlioz and Verdi. Of course, Gregorian chant can disclose wells of stillness or centuries of the great English choral tradition can still nourish the soul in our great cathedrals or Oxbridge chapels. But for my spiritual growth and succour, the wild ones, those who cross boundaries, who are not limited by questions of taste and appropriateness, who discover new regions and resolve to go into the unknown, who are willing to risk challenging deity and tradition, these are the prophets I need as companions in my exploration into God and life, who will sustain my profound sense of the beauty and ecstasy of Creation. Wittgenstein claimed that 'ethics and aesthetics are one.' I think he meant that an appreciation of beauty, of the sensual world of appetite and feeling is as good a guide to how we should react to and behave in the world as is the intellect with its rules and regulations that arise more often from fear than openness to possibilities. Schopenhauer pleaded that the feelings needed the same attention in our educational systems as is given to the mind: both require training and development. But organized religion is suspicious of such approaches because they are very difficult to control. This is why many of us, even those who are priests, find we need increasingly to move away from the churches to connect with and develop our own spirituality. The salvation model on which they operate increasingly seems artificial and limiting, shaped to the needs of the institution rather than to those of many-faceted human beings.

I am inclined to stress original goodness rather than original sin in humankind, made as we are in the image of God, however flawed. This would be the emphasis of the Eastern Orthodox Churches and Native American belief. We need rather than to be shackled to the Church and its prescriptive programs to be free to explore the world and one another while finding our roots in the Great Spirit, The Holy Spirit, whose liberating and compassionate outpouring we see modelled in Jesus of Nazareth, first son of God, and, above all, Son of Man, the pledge to us that our vocation is to be engodded, to share directly in the life of God and rejoice in all God's works. Music, and indeed all the arts, provides almost a parallel entry into the glories of Creation without the debts claimed by religious systems. But without the support that they can provide, it means that our journey is more reckless, risky and death-defying. Yet surely that is to walk in the footsteps of the God who gambled everything in calling us into existence.

Music has this revelatory, even revolutionary, capacity to open us up both to the depths of our own existence and the endless wonder of the universe beyond. In Mahler's Third Symphony the soloist sings lines of Nietzsche describing how profound is the woe of the world, but how much more profound is the joy to be discovered in it, so deep it craves eternity for its expression.

The Danish composer Carl Nielsen's motto was: "music is life and, like life, inextinguishable".

3. Wilderness

I now want to turn to considerations of the natural world, which has been a critical source of sustenance. I write out of my experience of living in the American southwest.

> *Nothing in all creation is so like God as stillness.*
> Meister Eckhart[18]

> *O burning mountain,*
> *O chosen son,*
> *O perfect moon,*
> *O fathomless well,*
> *O unobtainable light,*
> *O clearness beyond all measure,*
> *O wisdom without end,*
> *O mercy without all limit,*
> *O strength beyond resistance,*
> *O crown of all majesty,*
> *All creation humbly sings your praise:*
> *Bright stars, high mountains,*
> *Depths of the seas, rushing waters,*
> *All these break into song at heaven's*
> *proclamation:*
> *This is my Son, my beloved,*
> *My chosen one.*

Alleluia, Alleluia, Alleluia!"
Mechthild of Magdeburg[19]

Learning to relate to the land, disenfranchised city dweller that I was, has been a deeply re-formative experience for me, learnt from the people in Southern Africa and North America who have been moulded by the land, among whom I have been privileged to live. To reawaken in you a sense of the overwhelming beauty of the world, the world as a place of epiphany, and a sense of belonging to the earth, a kinship with it and all creation ("we are all related"), I want to quote some vivid passages from writers whom you might not otherwise encounter. First from Mary Sojourner, a passionate, feisty and dedicated eco-warrior who used to live in Flagstaff, Arizona, where she waged a lifetime's defence of the San Francisco Peaks, sacred to both the Navajo and Hopi peoples – she now lives in the heart of the great Mojave Desert. Two passages from *Bonelight*[20]

> *I sit on the edge of a slickrock point a little north of Muley Point (in South East Utah). Hundreds of feet below, the San Juan River coils through grey walls. In this dying September light the water is bronze. The far horizon turns scarlet. Small pools in the rock are silver. The wind rises, the waves*

move across them, and they are mirrors of motion and twilight. I cry softly. Love seems to be all around, holding me in radiance, rock and silence, in glowing red sand and pinyon, juniper, ephedra and sage. For a moment, what chatters inside is quiet. Thank you, I say.

Again, after referring to health problems, Mary Sojourner writes:

The horizon burns rose-gold...Light fades, goes salmon, shell pink, seawater blue. The forest is, in an instant, dark...I will watch till long after midnight, alone, joyful in the presence of my most faithful companions. Fear. And wild beauty.

These two passages are, central to what follows, and I have learnt much from Mary Sojourner. I too have sat at Muley Point, gazing into the depths of the San Juan canyon, and to Monument Valley and beyond. I, too, know that only in the wild places do I find solace and some answer to pain, suffering and even sickness. And yet part of the experience is the fear and risk of entering such wilderness, being alone with the Creator in his most fantastic and fearsome handiwork. Wilderness is vital for a true sense of human perspective.

That is why in our time it needs to be defended and protected; why Peter Matthiesen, another great ecologist, laments, in "Indian Country", the tragedy of the despoliation of this very area, the Four Corners region of the Colorado Plateau, by uranium mining, surface coal mining, the two existing coal fired power plants and the possibility of two more, polluting the air so the great citadel of Shiprock is now seen through a permanent haze; while Barry Lopez grieves over the ignorance of the centrality of land to original peoples by successive waves of European conquerors. Their interest in the land was only to possess it and exploit it, whereas all environmentalists would argue that being in a place means taking up residence and paying attention to the land as one would to a person. The land speaks to the one who listens and, to one with imagination; it will teach him how to make it home.

Barry Lopez[21] argues that we all need to discover 'querencia', a Spanish word indicating a place on the ground where we feel secure. For this we need to love the land with a passion. Furthermore, for me, the high places are those where we "touch the void", where the presence of God is close and transparent.

But let me return to some original, unknown writers to guide our voyage of understanding. First a pupil of Rebecca Reppart, who used to teach English at Red Mesa High School in Navajoland:

The creek runs past
A fallen grandmother
Bay tree

Over stones
smoothed
by the centuries

The ripples
seem to be
everlasting

A buckeye leaf
floats down
the creek

While the wrentit sings
and the sword fern
stands guard

Five-finger ferns
peek

The love of this place
is like
A child's heart.
Tobi Earnheart-Gold

Now let me introduce you to two of the Simpson brothers, Barry and Steve. These are extracts from weekly articles they produce both for a local newspaper and for availability on-line. Their family established Twin Rocks Trading Post in Bluff Utah[22], and they encourage local Navajo basket makers, carpet weavers and jewellery artists to not only produce high class traditional ware but also to experiment with new colours and designs. The trading post is a treasure trove. Barry and Steve show a Navajo love and appreciation of the land, as these passages show:-

> As we cruised along the relatively vacant blacktop, I kept an eye on the landscape and began to gain a new appreciation for the charm of this lonely valley. The precious morning light was beginning to illuminate our surroundings with an effeminate apricot glow. The curvaceous valley floor entranced my senses as

it seemed to ebb and flow like gentle waves on a body of water. Rare clumps of stunted vegetation were but brief glimpses of smudged rouge with sage green highlights. The usually coarse cliff faces and jumble of broken boulders at their base were softened and smoothed by shadow and refracted early morning light. Undulating lines of sediment, frozen in time, flowed delicately across their surfaces like sheets of ruffled silk.

Just before the sun broke over the horizon, Laurie and I were graced with a vision of the snow covered flanks of the LaSal Mountains, situated behind, and rising abruptly above, the now lighter and passionately pink valley. The contrast between the brilliant uprising and the subtly demure valley easily took our breath away. The mountain peaks shown with a blue/white neon glow that was frosty and inviting at the same time. A faint peach aura enveloped the mountain and rose to a swirling, twisting crown surrounding the highest peak. A small number of twinkling morning stars were still visible like droplets of dew clinging to the heavens.

It did not take long before the sun exploded onto the scene and the vision began to dissipate into the bright winter sunlight. The gentle spell of dawn was broken, only to be replaced by a more realistic interpretation of the countryside through less romantic eyes. Dawn and dusk seem to me to belong to the more feminine aspects of our world, while day and night are more masculine. The ever changing face of nature never ceases to inspire my mind and imagination.

Recently I found myself standing on a small mesa rim overlooking an area of undulating, under-vegetated hillocks that tapered off into the rough and tumble canyon country a few miles below. As I marvelled at the scene unfolding within my field of view, a glorious morning sun began its heavenly ascent behind me. The landscape seemed to be moving and shifting right before my eyes. The play of light, shadow and earthy colour had a mystical effect on my imagination as I watched the scene evolve on the terrestrial canvas.

****

I left the house before dawn in order to be on time for one of Steve's early morning strategy sessions. While driving to Bluff, I noticed it had rained on the desert the night before. I rolled down the window and breathed deeply in order to truly appreciate the heightened aroma of the stunted vegetation and rich red earth. About five miles north of Bluff, the sun made its appearance on the eastern horizon. I quickly pulled to the side of the road and stepped out of the car to witness the birth of a new day.

The remaining wisps of storm clouds were being hurried along by an upper air flow unfelt at ground level. The slanted rays of light emitted by the uplifting orb backlit the lofty formations and fired up the surrounding countryside with a soft, rich, golden glow. I glanced off to the west where the land falls away to Cottonwood Wash and is framed along the skyline by the waves of sandstone making up Comb Ridge, and caught my breath. The entire area seemed to be moving in an extraordinary ebb and flow to which I was totally unaccustomed.

My spirit was drawn towards the spectacle, and I wondered how this occurrence was possible. I came to the tightly stretched range fence bordering the highway and nearly high-centered myself on the prickly barbed wire. I made my way across the saturated sand to the high, rocky point previously mentioned. Focusing on the heavenly phenomenon, I realized the cloud formations were drifting across the face of the Sun, causing shadows to traverse horizontally across the landscape. This, along with the natural contrast of early morning light and shadow, caused a visually intoxicating sensation.

What at one moment was darkened by shadow was, at the next moment standing out in sharp contrast. It was like watching waves roll across the desert. A disconcerting feeling of being out of place and time enveloped my earthly perception. Sandstone, sagebrush and red earth flowed in and out of focus, stimulating my sense of wonder. It was so overwhelming I had to sit down on a large weathered boulder to keep my balance.

It did not take long for the mirage to dissipate into the reality of "post sunrise depression," or a PSD as I like to refer to it. This is an emotional let-down that affects me to the very core of my being. To my knowledge there is no medication or therapy available that will cure, or even soften, the blow of this mortal encumbrance. I am deeply moved after witnessing a spectacular sunrise or sunset and having to suffer through the realization that it is now gone, only to be found in the confused recesses of my befuddled memory.

When I finally arrived at the trading post, I found Steve frustrated with my tardiness. His comment was, "How can we expect our employees to attend these meetings on a regular basis when you are consistently sidetracked by bright, shiny objects and occurrences?" "Good question", said I. 'I will try harder, I assure you!" Later that day, Chris Johnson, one of the best Navajo basket weavers ever to walk into the trading post came in with the most spectacular basket I have ever seen, and began to explain its origins to Steve and me.

It seems Chris had arisen early the other morning to welcome the day. He said that he had witnessed the most amazing sunrise he had ever seen. The problem, he said, was that he gets depressed whenever something like that happens and then fades away. The basket was his attempt to keep the image of that wondrous morning light fresh in his memory. I looked at Chris and then Steve, with a smile of satisfaction, and said "PSD. There is a cure!"

******

On a recent morning, I was focused on the warm air emanating from my truck's heating system as I approached the downward descent of White Mesa Hill. It was cold outside, the sunlight bright and crystal clear, as most winter days are in San Juan County. As I motored along, anticipating the view from the top of White Mesa, I knew the morning vision would not be disappointing.

Although I expected a beautiful vista, I could not have predicted what unfolded before me. In the valley below, a blanket of fog wrapped around the winter landscape; a shroud of mist covering the low ground and filling the canyons. The vision reminded me of a picture postcard of Lake Powell; with white clouds substituting for the lake's dark blue waters.

The hazy white lather wrapped itself around mesas and boulder strewn hillsides, turning them into floating islands. As I descended into this land of mystery, I noticed the sparse plant life covered in crystalline droplets. Sunlight filtered through the mist, backlighting the sagebrush and juniper trees, making the water crystals sparkle like diamonds.

As I drove deeper into the fog, I had the sensation of floating through the swirling mist and filtered sunlight as if I had entered a bubble. I viewed the outside world through an opaque, slightly smudged portal. The experience was sensuous, surreal and spiritual all at the same time, like a moment shared with the most intimate partner.

As I grow older I have realized that such moments of discovery, happiness and pleasure are extremely rare, and transcendent. Clouds affect me in strange ways. Those instances that sneak up and surprise me with their inexplicable beauty are sublime. May we always remain open to the world of mystery and imagination; the world of clouds.

And, finally, full circle to Mary Sojourner again,[23]

> Buffalo Park Trail curves in a figure eight through a meadow below the San Francisco Peaks just west of Flagstaff Arizona. In a wet spring, peepers sing from a little ephemeral wetland. In a generous monsoon summer, evening primrose, sego lilies and purple lupine lie in the deep grass like fallen stars. In October, the grasses have gone gold and silver; evening is the heart of a tourmaline. No matter what season, the moon traces time across the vast Northern Arizona sky. And I hunt the moon.
>
> I track the lunar arc. I watch what drifts across the pale stony face: monsoon clouds and jet trails and snow. I pursue the shape-shifting radiance for comfort, for beauty, for medicine and for the reminder of the nature of my own existence.
>
> Once, when I believed I was a pioneer in this high desert, still carrying city time in me as parcelled out by clocks and calendars, I walked Buffalo Park just past sunset. I raised my arms to banners of scarlet and purple. I said, "Thank you for this day." The light seemed to alchemize

forever. When only a ribbon of pale green stretched across the horizon I turned and began to follow the eastern curve back to the trailhead.

I was stopped by an impossible vision. The edge of what seemed to be a huge searchlight burned just above the lower slope of Mount Elden. I stood transfixed. And, as I imagined a plane crash, a night-time logging operation, a celestial visitor from who-knew-where, the full moon lifted steadily above the dark mountain. I stood in its light as though I were held in a great prayer.

Years later, I would watch a desert moonset from my sleeping bag on a Mohave playa and I would understand that it was not the moon that rose or set. It was the earth beneath me that fell toward radiance, and fell away. But then, on the trail at Buffalo Park, I was six months new to Arizona. I was a woman who knew little of lunar cycles and less of her own. I was forty-five years old.

Now I am sixty-seven. The forest between the meadow and the mountain is pocked with big houses. Flagstaff is no longer 35,000 people.

There are now over 55,000 of us living here. I am one of them. I am no longer a woman who believes she is a pioneer.

I am a settler. I have walked Buffalo Park over 5,600 times. I have walked with friends. I have walked alone. I have walked through seasons - racing monsoon clouds back to the trailhead; pushing hard into ferocious November winds; moving silently toward a red-tail hawk dancing on the carcass of a rabbit; going terrified and delighted into the impossible brilliance of lightning in a snowstorm white-out.

I have never stopped hunting. Once a month for 258 months I have walked at Full Moon sunset. Never again have I found myself gloriously paralyzed by a mysterious light rising from the flank of the mountain. Never again has the miracle repeated. Miracles cannot repeat themselves. Knowing that is the knowledge of the settler; it is the wisdom of the faithful witness; it is a great loss. And it is the unwelcome gift to one who is willing to grow old.

I will never again occupy the innocence that contained me twenty-two years ago. The West will never again be the echo of a frontier it was that miraculous evening. And still, I am held in a great prayer. To worship in this New West is to pray with a rosary strung with beads that are Black Holes. Lacunae slip through our fingers.

Where a wetland once gleamed, there is dust. Where a persimmon canyon curved back to its shadowed beginning, there is a golf course. Where ironwood and creosote once wove their shifting leaves, there is a badlands of red tile roofs.

We go to touch the beads and feel nothing in our fingers. There is an emptiness far more complete and dreadful than the "Nothing" new-comers tell us is "out there in the desert."

To be aware and bearing witness in the New West for the last twenty-two years is to look into a mirror. Beauty. Attrition. Weathering and scars. There is no miracle that will stop what is happening. There are only the gifts of hard witness - and hard prayer.

An old woman takes herself to a little ponderosa pine in Buffalo Park. She and the west wind have been walking into the hope of the moon. The sky is empty azure. "Where are You?" she asks and imagines writing a fable based on the failure of the moon to rise.

She decides to wait out her radiant prey. She settles into the pine needles at the eastern side of the young tree. The sun drops behind her. She stretches her arms toward the East and sees the shadow of a tree with arms. The shadow shrinks and is gone. She presses her hands into the dark earth.

When she looks up, she sees the moon floating above a long low bank of wood-stove smoke. She knows she will never again see the shadow of a tree with arms or a silver miracle surfing a violet haze.

"Thank you" she says. She rises to her feet and begins the long walk home.

If these "snapshots" are inspirational they also begin to demonstrate how an awareness of the land produces effects in art and people. For the moment, I want to dwell on how the capacity to really see, to pay attention to, the wonders of the natural world, especially in its pristine wilderness areas, is to begin to discern the veiled presence of the Creator thinly hidden in his own creation. When I am desperate for a sense of the closeness, the intimacy of God, then I will climb a mountain rather than attend a church service, where human artifice can often make Him seem more distant.

Golden, snow dusted peaks, tawny foothills, wide open spaces, high alpine valleys, dense evergreens, livid autumnal colours, abundant wildlife – the rugged beauty of the Rocky Mountains – first in Canada and later in Colorado, affected me deeply. There is something sacred about these high places and the benediction of a deep peace. Despite the aforementioned fear and risk sometimes involved in exploration they felt like home even at first acquaintance. I felt I belonged there. I always know deep feelings of stillness, authenticity and acceptance when I come. The vast mountains and the high, starry skies in their massiveness make me small, so there is room for me. Mountains and skies are home.

Someone wrote: "Home is where a person's soul and a place's soul intersect in time and space and have room to roam". Rock, sky and light. Ribbons of brown, blue or green rivers. The heavens, an inverted cobalt bowl, scarcely able to hold it all in. Skies so packed with stars it is as though a goddess has draped a sequinned robe over the night world in protection. The inky, indigo shadows of sunset.

But my more immediate home while working with the Navajo people has been the high desert of the Colorado Plateau. It can be very beautiful when the eye learns to see beyond the barrenness and aridity to the myriad pastel hues and huge variety of small flora and fauna. Yet it is also a harsh, challenging and pitiless environment that refuses to allow for sloth, cowardice or evasion. A mistake in orientation, for example, can cost you your life, and deaths are recorded in the Utah canyons every year. It is rock, thorns, heat, cold and scant water, and generally no footprints at all. Here you are left to yourself and that is a hard discipline. And yet the desert offers space and silence to find yourself and reach your dreams. The presence of death is never far away – bleached bones, reptile skins, skeletal vegetation – and, as for the hermits in the fifth century Egyptian desert, to live stripped to the essentials, in the shadow of death and the last things, is to rediscover the core and essence of our being, to "centre down", as the Quakers put it. The starkness and limitless horizons of the desert unsettle and disturb us and so drive us into our inmost centre. It can be the rock and hard place of renewal.

The desert imposes a slow pace, what Henry David Thoreau called "sauntering", deriving the term from the French "a la Sainte Terre", meaning those who go on pilgrimage. Walk slowly and look, not casually but closely. The desert bestows gifts – ghost animals in the darkness, the moon rising above ridges, flowers along the trail, sweet bird song – but you must be watching, listening, walking and gradually it dawns that we are an integral part of this wider, magical world. Thoreau wrote "In wildness is the preservation of the world".

Images of the desert – pink dawns, canyon rims falling away into a choppy sea of cream-coloured sandstone benches and domes, sandy bottoms, groves of cottonwoods and willows, small oases towering ramparts of smooth beige stone, rust-red blocks of sandstone, deep canyons in shadow and high buttes absorbing the sun, ravens circling above, the smell of juniper, natural bridges and arches, sage and cactus – a place of emptiness and solitude where we drop out of the human created order, a place of inevitable death (the vultures and hawks hover overhead) and abundant, stubborn life. The earth lives and renews itself in the midst of death, a parable of resurrection, rebirth in the wasteland. The desert seeks to teach us that we can live with the land rather than dominating and exploiting it, and that is why I often need to escape into the wilderness to repeatedly ingest the lesson. It is a place of pain and challenge: you are offered not only panoramas but a more profound understanding of life; you may be changed and your imagination will be stretched. Alien, remote, threatening – all these words can be used of the desert – and yet it is also mysterious and exquisite, as Barry Lopez writes of his wilderness, the Arctic, "full of eternity, humming with endurance, radiating completeness". We need to learn an intimacy with it and wait for it to speak. It offers freedom: there are no frontiers there but only the unmapped territories inside the self; it is here you can discover your own personal wilderness, your inner mystery, and begin to find healing.

Landscape is the culture that contains all human cultures. There are silences so deep you can hear the journeys of the soul.

One of the most persuasive arguments for preservation of the original landscape may be its spiritual value as a great reservoir of silence. We cannot afford to let such words become elegies for places that have disappeared in the brutal onward march of commercial interests.

One feature of the desert landscape of South East Utah has always transfixed me, namely the agonized contortions of the rock strata in the sandstone and limestone cliffs, sometimes crazily angled, sometimes twisted in folds, sometimes bent in great waving lines like petrified billows. And the colouring – the greens of the stunted vegetation, the yellow, green, red, black and grey rock, the cobalt dome above. It is the agony rather than the beauty which holds me: it speaks to me of a Creator who has had to wrestle, at great cost with the sheer intractability of matter, to wrest some order out of chaos. And it leads me to contemplate how even harder it must be for Him to tackle the even greater intractability of human nature in his ongoing struggle to evolve us. These thoughts are always with me in the terrifying, rocky emptiness of the great peaks and it is to these I am led to return. But let me preface my remarks with this glorious account by Baden Powell of similar climbs in the Andes, as he says much of what I wish to share.

I started out alone before dawn one morning, in the Andes of South America, to climb a mountain-side. The chill gloom of the early morning was deepened by the depth of the canyon in which I started and the heights loomed round one against the sky, and in the darkness it was difficult to judge of their heights or distance.

As I climbed the ascent before me, the light gradually opened out and cliffs and rock masses stood up more clearly defined. The air was very cold and clear and still, and the great tense silence around seemed to press itself upon me. Not a murmur of a brook, not a chirp of birds, not a whisper of a breeze. Stillness everywhere. Yet it did not seem altogether a dead stillness: it seemed rather as if everything – the mountains and the valleys, the peaks and the boulders – were all standing at attention – waiting – looking for the coming of day. It seemed almost sacrilegious to break that silence with the clicking of one's footsteps among the stones.

Immediately around me the mountain-side was bare. A short distance above me in front was the horizon to which I kept climbing as it continually kept receding. Looking backward behind me, a similar horizon was only a few yards below, leading down into the gloom I had left. One writer, describing the same climb, has compared the climber to an ant going up a water-butt. And that's what I felt like.

Then, above the shoulders of the cliffs that surrounded me, there began to arise the crests of higher crags and mountain-tops, like giants standing clearer in the morning light, but all cold and hard, peering at me over the shoulders of their lower neighbours. I was the only moving object in all that immensity of rigid rock and peak. I felt an intruder and so puny in that solemn domain.

Here the strata and variegated rocks spoke of thousands up thousands of years, from the time when our earth was being fashioned in the melting pot.

I was but as a short-lived insect among them.

I climbed higher and higher and breathing became more difficult; while the sense of loneliness and smallness grew upon me in that intense silence and among those vast gables of the roof of the world.

Suddenly above one of them I saw a great greenish-white peak of eternal snow, stark and clear cut against the sky; and soon another and yet another, on the different sides. It seemed as though the greater giants of the range, on whose steep facets the foot of Man had never trod, were standing up to overlook me, cold, stern and pitiless. The stupendous heights and the ghastly silence, and the loneliness and immensity of it all seemed to appal me. I was scarcely myself. There came upon me almost a desire to scream aloud to break the spell.

Yet the loudest human voice would have sounded there as feeble an effort as the piping of a wren as I once heard it among the vast ruins of the Colosseum at Rome.

I tried to shut my eyes to it, when suddenly a strange glow seemed to come into the air above me.

Looking back over my shoulder, I saw that which made me gasp.

One of the great peaks which a moment before had been almost grey-blue now suddenly gleamed at its topmost points a dazzling orange-pink mass, with its lower parts in opalescent shadows of violet and blue and tinted green, the whole mass standing out with startling distinctness of outline and detail against the darkened sky behind it. And as one looked around peak after peak took up the rosy radiance of the dawn.

One felt it was too much for one little mortal mind to grasp – one who was a trespasser in a holy place. It was something uncanny and beyond one's ken to be here watching the morning toilet of Nature herself. There was nothing to connect the divine scene with the life of men that I had left down below there in the gloom.

I stumbled on, awed almost to horror by it all, when, at the moment just when I needed some touch with the human world, over the next rise there stood up before me a figure – the figure of "Christ the Redeemer".

It was not the usual pathetic body hanging on the Cross, but a big generous Being with wide flowing robes and with welcoming protective arms outspread.

A fine statue, happily placed for its purpose of marking the boundary and a sign of perpetual peace between the States of Argentine and Chile, but even more happily placed that its sculptor had designed, in giving at that spot a tangible link between the human and the divine–the link which Christ in His time had come on earth to give.[24]

I have climbed probably a little less than one fifth of Colorado's "fourteeners", mountains over fourteen thousand feet. One must stand for them all as I seek to describe why they are so significant for me and, inevitably, the first I tackled, Grey's Peak in the Central Rockies, stands out especially. I approached it in June, not realizing that, while it was summer in the lovely valley of Georgetown, with its attractive old quarter, where I stayed, it was still early spring at fourteen thousand feet, as I was about to discover.

Often one of the hardest parts of the day is driving the precipitous tracks to the trailhead. The standard guide book declared this track to be suitable for two wheel drive vehicles but I soon became aware that this meant trucks and not passenger cars. I nevertheless threaded my way gingerly round horrendous potholes and rocks, and rose steeply through thick forest. This part of the day is always a test of stamina, nerve and determination, willing oneself into the heavens, as it were, a crucial element of prayer. I arrived at the parking space to find that I was the only passenger car foolish enough to have made it. But the greater shock was that what had been rain down in the valley the previous day had been snow up here, and it was quite deep. Indeed, if one or two people had not set out before me I could not have found the route.

As I begin, the effort of walking about ten thousand feet in thinner air becomes apparent. Frequent pauses are the order of the day. Yet I am constantly encouraged by the miracles of the natural world – spring flowers emerging where the snow has not covered them, little carpets of yellow, blue and crimson; or cliffs reflected in the still waters of a lake where the ice has parted. Soon I am well above tree level in a harsh world of barren rock, screed, snow and wind, though the sun smiles on me. The physical effort parallels the mental effort required in prayer, and reminds me of the conviction of Native Americans that attaining deep spiritual insight require perseverance that produced suffering, as in the Sun Dance, Vision Quest or even the Sweat Lodge – one's sacrifice to the Creator. He is certainly demanding that here. At one point I turn and catch my breath. Vistas of near hills and receding ranges are opening up behind me. The trail crosses a deep snow field, almost a glacier, and attains a ridge where the twin peaks of Greys and Torreys dominate the skyline. This is always a thrilling and sometimes terrifying moment, akin to Gerontius, in Cardinal Henry Newman's poem, begging to be allowed into the presence of God but then realizing that he is not worthy of being there. "I am not worthy" is inevitably the spontaneous prayer that escapes me at this moment, accompanied by a mixture of wonder, tears and terror. I press on but the elevation becomes steeper now and the effort gruelling. The eye tends to telescope high vertical distances so the peak is always further ahead than it appears, even supposing that what you are seeing is indeed the actual summit and not a false one. Then as I almost feel I cannot go on I am there, and fall to the ground in exhaustion, only to nearly disappear over the other side of what turns out to be quite a narrow ridge. I move gingerly to the left and stand aloft on the summit itself.

At this point all feelings of stress and strain evaporate. I can see for over fifty miles in all directions. Nearest to me is the twin peak of Torries, covered in ice, a destination many would want to add but it is too risky for a novice like me on a day like this. Yet, most stunning of all, in every direction receding snow capped peaks. The sky is now more clouded and magical patterns of light and shadow dapple them. The scene is impossibly beautiful and, at the same time, terrifying. Rilke wrote that "beauty is nothing but the beginning of terror..."[25] It is like meeting God. Terry Tempest Williams once said that "we are defined by what we choose to sacrifice"[26] – here, my comfort, ease and security to encounter the new, the unknown, a pilgrimage to the high places and a journey into God. It is surely no accident that many of the most significant spiritual encounters in the bible occur in such places. I never tarry long at the top. The beauty is too much to bear and the location too sacred to risk offense to the holy people, the Navajo yei, who inhabit such places. I mainly ignore my few fellow hikers, pray silently, and begin the decent, for the journey is but half done. There must be no lapse of concentration as I know what it is to suffer from careless footings, and there is still the horrific drive to face. Despite the tiredness a mysterious sense of benediction always envelops me, a deep peace, a gift of awareness of the presence of God who, while showing faces of beauty, majesty and terror is also now showing one of compassion as He protects my journey.

I encounter these landscapes with a passion and even adoration: they induce states of ecstasy and wonder as I gaze at the unending and timeless glory of what I never dreamed the world possessed. Every time I emerge through the tree line and on to a pass or ridge affording views of high peaks falling away to deep glacial valleys I feel the truth of what someone wrote, "the view from the summit is too awful to afford pleasure". It is a terrible beauty that its lofty majesty somehow points to the hidden Creator. Yet in the relief of the cautious descent a deep peace seems to fall and I wonder whether in the beauty of the world there exists the power to unify people, to bring them together around an all- encompassing appreciation of life and its infinite potential. A common appreciation of the wonder that surrounds all life could, perhaps, offer a way to tolerance and peace? I feel part of this indescribable beauty and I feel humble before it, a quality Tenzing Norgay, the first known Sherpa to summit Everest in 1953 has said is essential for those who would appreciate the high places, the homes of the gods. With this in mind, the mountaineer's maxim, "when in doubt, go higher", does something to explain the insatiable drive that some of us experience to access these sacred places whenever possible. In times like ours, which W H Auden described as *The*

Age of Anxiety[27], finding and creating beauty can be a way back to wholeness. The beauty of place, sometimes more than that of people, can pierce the heart and inspire us to care the more for one another and for the world we destroy. Love of place grounds us in reality, and the visions and dreams it can arouse in us may be our hope. To save our world, and ourselves, we need dreamers who will encourage us to walk on the edge, explore the margins, to build bridges, to explore the depths of spirit. And people who walk – who climb, explore, venture out, whose outward journey mirrors an inner quest – may be those people. They can teach us that there must be a dialogue between personal narrative and the landscapes we inhabit and discover, a dialogue between humanity and the planet. This is why wilderness must be preserved, not least because its remoteness offers the space and silence in which to rediscover our kinship with the land and learn a veneration for it – the wilderness as saviour, as healer.

I began to discover the significance of land in Africa and I have felt in exile from Africa and the Africans ever since. Being Warden of Lelapa la Jesu Seminary in the tiny land-locked Kingdom of Lesotho in Southern Africa, changed me. I discovered the spirituality of poverty. I learnt that if you have nothing in Western terms the things that really matter in life are at the centre of your existence – family, friends, home, land, prayer, song, humour, food – and this centrality makes for an intense, aware and rooted people, distinguished above all by a deep compassion and generous hospitality. It became a constant wonder to me how people who lived without distractions were so centred, outgoing, kind and outrageously giving. I have known nothing like African friendship – but more of that anon. The point here is that the people would claim it is the land that has shaped them: They are part of it, not lords of it, part of a living organism to which they are deeply devoted. They have fought to remain in their mountain wilderness, a potentially hostile environment, because it is home and where they belong. As I learnt to love this land I found I was driven to express this affection for it. My natural way of doing this would have been through music, but I need a piano at which to compose and so, in its absence, I turned to poetry. The first piece speaks of the Kalahari Desert in Botswana, the second of Mashonaland in Zimbabwe, countries where I worked after my time in Lesotho.

LITTLE LORATONG

Scattered azure hills like sleeping giants ring
the horizon,
misted and suffused with evening light
That points up dying colours in the nearer
koppies
of ochre, mauve and gold
While decking the grasses at my feet
in luminous yellow-greens.
From all around my rocky vantage point
innumerable birds dart flashes of vivid hue
and render their evening serenade.
Not to be outdone, a thousand insects voice
praises
that will outlast the feathered song
As the rose sky darkens into night
And a myriad stars, in turn, dance their own
paean.

MAKUTI

Naked trees like stick insects
Silhouetted against the glare,
Lifeless saffron grass,
Elephant grey bush
Retreating over slumbering hills,
Distant, rolling mountains

Recumbent in blue haze.
All dry, parched, waiting.
And everywhere, the silence,
Pressing heavily in the heat,
Broken only by the sad cry
Of lonely, fleeting birds.
Yet, beneath the deathly pallor
An awakening stirs:
Green shoots already struggle upwards,
Bougainvillea blushes its pastel shades,
The scent of blossom infuses the air
And a thousand little signs and voices
Hymn the coming annual miracle
Of rain and resurrection.

It was learning in Africa how the land points to its Creator, and nurtures and moulds its inhabitants, that enabled me to appreciate the high desert of the Navajo nation and similarly sing its praises:

BLUFF

Poised between heaven and hell,
The cobalt vault of the sky and the emerald rut
of the valley,
I cling to the rim of the abyss,
A human predator,
Waiting to devour not passing prey

but the entire forthcoming drama,
to possess and be possessed by the
transfiguration of day into night.
Stirred from the torpor of the heavy heat,
from the silence of sad birds,
I feel a ripple of movement in the oppressive air
as the colours begin their transformation.
First comes the gentle, sun- drenched
luminosity
of cliffs and grasses, growing golden
as the noonday tires.
Next, imperceptibly, the battlement tops
burn with an angry, threatening iridescence,
rusting into defiant splendour.
Then, the heart stopping miracle of red rock
burning a deep vermillion,
Entire escarpments pulsating with a fiery,
primitive energy,
only relaxing, as the sun falls to its daily death,
into richest mauves, lilac, magenta, purples,
And the depths below disappear into vaunting,
organ
sounding blackness.
For a moment, I am suspended, floating
between earth and
heaven

as the brooding darkness erases
corporeality of the ground beneath me
And I reach out involuntarily for –
the stars,
my dreams,
you?
Soon I am enveloped in the kindly shroud of
night
swallowing the light as it also
hides my grieving face and
buries my heavy heart.
I have shared in the daily transfiguration of the
natural
world,
and bathed in its brilliance and its glory.
Now I am left with darker realities
As I descend the mesa into
the gloom of the valley
the past
the future
myself
And the aching absence
of the light
that is you.

I wrote of Lesotho on returning to England from America:-

"I have been in exile for over ten years from what surprisingly and overwhelmingly became home, though I had never been there before, and, having discovered place for the first time, and people who belong to place, I am diminished by lack of it. I am losing identity and purpose, and are consumed and devoured by an insatiable longing and yearning to be in that place again, to rediscover the earth and the people of the earth, and the divine comedy of the convoluted connections between ourselves and the planet. I am also in despair at what we are doing to destroy the living organism of Planet Earth that succours us, by being so out of touch with poets, history, tradition and the very fabric of the dirt from which we came. We have to move back to the future".

In an age when reckless exploitation of the environment threatens the very future of life on the planet a renewed and lasting commitment to the fundamental significance of place – and particularly wilderness – may prove to be our most powerful tool of survival. We need to relate our personal narrative to increasing environmental awareness, the ways in which both the land and its peoples have endured.

Ultimately this is to look into our own souls and consciences.

Thomas Merton began our thinking here. I will let him finish it.

> *To deliver oneself up, to hand oneself over, entrust oneself completely to the silence of a wide landscape of woods and hills, or sea, or desert; to sit still while the sun comes up over that land and fills its silences with light. To pray and work in the morning, and to labour and rest in the afternoon, and to sit still again in meditation in the evening, when night falls upon that land and when the silence fills itself with darkness and with stars.*
>
> *This is a true and special vocation. There are few who are willing to belong completely to such silence, to let it soak into their bones, to breathe nothing but silence, to feed on silence, and to turn the very substance of their life into a living and vigilant silence.*[28]

4. Love

Next I turn to personal relationships as the third vital factor in my life.

> *Many waters cannot quench love,*
> *Neither can floods drown it.*
> The Song of Solomon 8:7

> *Love demands a complete inner transformation for without this we cannot possibly come to identify ourselves with our brother. We have to become, in some sense, the person we love. And this involves a kind of death of our own being, our own self. No matter how hard we try we resist this death: we fight back with anger, with recriminations, with demands, with ultimatums. We seek any convenient excuse to break off and give up the difficult task.*
> Thomas Merton, The Wisdom of the Desert[29]

> *Next to the Blessed Sacrifice itself your neighbour is the highest object presented to your senses...He is holy in almost the same way for in him also Christ...the Glorifier and the Glorified, Glory Himself, is truly hidden.*
> C. S. Lewis, The Weight of Glory[30]

Love is the most powerful and still the most unknown energy of the world.
Teilhard de Chardin, Le Milieu Divin[31]

I have experienced two conversions. The first was the revelation of a personal God. I had been brought up to say simple prayers by an elderly aunt who minded my brother and me once a month to give our parents a little time to themselves. They were mainly prayers of thanksgiving, together with some basic requests. Often my brother and I would fool around during this bedtime ritual but the observance subconsciously took root and a seed had been sown. When later I moved to secondary school I forced myself to do a difficult thing: I had owned a toy bear, a teddy bear, since infancy but I thought that high school kids should not have such childish possessions so I pushed Rupert, now minus and eye and an arm, into the dustbin, shedding a few tears. Rupert had been my confidant, especially in times of distress. I was now bereft. However, a few weeks later, while saying my childish prayers in bed, I was suddenly aware that they were really being heard, received. A warm, reassuring sense of presence filled the room, and that new confidence and trust in God, born that night, has never left me, even in times of extremity. To remember that "He is faithful who calls us"[32] has always been as a hand to hold, even in dark times. Sometimes, when the wells of emotion have dried up, it is helpful just to recall what we know even if we cannot feel it at the time. Though the cynical could say that God to me is a teddy bear substitute I would rather say that I needed to sacrifice Rupert to give God a chance to speak, to come through.

My second conversion was to people. I had been brought up in a conventional lower middle class home, not allowed to play with other children in the street as they were "beneath" us, and educated at elitist institutions – a private primary school, a selective grammar school and the University of Cambridge. My experience of people, especially the opposite sex, was severely limited. I was not truly exposed to the world until my post-graduate teaching practice and my first post as an assistant teacher, and it was a revelation. The "lower" classes, whom I had been taught to beware of if not despise, as represented in two very tough city schools, were a miracle of warmth and vitality, excitement and aspiration, challenge and love. At no time in my life have I risen so eagerly in the morning with a desire to get to work and immerse myself in this welcoming sea of humanity. The sheer zest for life of the younger pupils, the willingness to share hopes and dreams of the older and, it seemed the very presence of God shining out of those bright, eager eyes. It was like being enveloped in love in a totally new and amazing way. I can truly say that, throughout my life, my pupils have taught me to love and know the indescribable joys of deep human relationships. And the intensity of the experience has often been such that it has seemed that this love was nourished by a hidden presence far greater than the individual acts of affection and concern being proffered, in fact by the unseen participation of God himself loving us through others – or so it seemed to me. About this time I began to see halos around people – not necessarily those I knew, indeed once around a baby in a pram on the street. These experiences lasted only a few months and they have never been repeated, but it was though the Creator wanted to confirm my growing conviction that he is to be found most characteristically in his creature, seeking to share his love for us through them and desiring a response both to him and to one another. This is always the greatest solace and consolation in hard times that he is so easily to be found in us ourselves and is often waiting for us to hear his addressing us through others. As Charles Williams put it in *Descent into Hell*[33] "salvation lay everywhere in interchange".

There used to be a great Christian tradition of the sanctity of friendship, expressed most notably by St. Anselm in his Letters of Friendship.[34] This tended to be forgotten in the debates of the Reformation era, and later submerged in the newly emerging consensus that the only relational situations acceptable in the church were marriage or celibacy. Yet friendship is the most profound and passionate liaison, essential even as the basis of marriage itself. The closing down of the mind of the church on relationships during the Reformation has seriously impoverished an appreciation of the rich variety of human interaction and the possible range of committed unions. We need rites to bless engagements, "living together" (often undertaken because the couple conscientiously feel they are called to be partners but are not yet ready for marriage vows), homosexual relationships (of more anon), coming of age, business partnerships, animals and pets – the list is endless. And we also need to recognise that many relationships cross categories – friend and lover, for instance, a truth known in Africa, but we will confront that later as well. Close friendships may often require physical expression – and it is often impossible to draw a clear line between what is physical and what is sexual. But, of all the gifts of God, our sexuality is the one we have been taught to fear, and moral issues concerning it seen to occupy in the minds of many a greater space than those of world poverty, environmental destruction and nuclear war – perhaps a legacy of centuries of authoritarian patriarchy. As a young teacher and, thankfully, before ordination, I had discovered the glory and ecstasy of human bonding, and the thrills and insights it could engender. To share some of this joy let me refer to a few of the great poets and bards of love:-

The friend is your needs answered.

And let there be no purpose in friendship save the deepening of the spirit. For love that seeks aught but the disclosure of its own mystery is not love but a net cast forth: and only the unprofitable is caught. And let your best be for your friend. If he must know the ebb of your tide, let him know its flood also. For what is your friend that you should seek him with hours to kill? Seek him always with hours to live.

For it is his to fill your need but not your emptiness.

And it the sweetness of friendship let there be laughter and sharing of pleasures. For in the dew

of little things the heart finds it morning and is
refreshed.
Kahlil Gibran, The Prophet[35]

We were alone
And then we were alone together.
Oh gentle heart, would we again were drifting
Far from this world of waking,
Lulled by the peace of your arms,
Borne on the ocean swell of deep slow-breathing
sleep.
Christopher Hassall for William Walton's opera
Troilus and Cressida[36]

If the whole world were only capable of grasping
this principal that true happiness consists only in
the freedom of disinterested love – the ability to
get away from ourselves, and our own limited
sphere of interests and appetites and needs, and
rejoice in the good that is in others.
Thomas Merton, The Seven Storey Mountain[37]

Merton also says that we are to make no difference
between neighbour and alien in our reaching out to
others: "classifications are without significance in this
matter of love".

The lover is a friend inspired by God.
Plato

I am frightened
Of being misunderstood
And yet I know that
I must tell you
How much you mean to me.
It's as if
Your being here
Is
God's gift
To me.
To help me grow
Through
The partings
The changes
The pain
Of leaving
And
Into new things.
Thank you
For being
My friend.
To Ian from Brenda Meakins[38]

Love is the promise of so many things:
The end of loneliness, and richer days.
Other eyes, ears and joys come with these rings;
And the knowledge we are loved, and the praise
Of love to soothe self doubt. Shall we wed then?
Shall we come to life through one another?
Shall we have done with singleness? Then, when
You bare your heart, trust me not to smother
The tenderness of my own, or forget
What we glimpsed of love's alternatives.
Love that answers love with love will not regret
Love's costs, love's hurts or love's imperatives.
Let's love then, as God loved us in Christ, and ask,
In love, for love sufficient for the task.
Albert Radcliffe[39]

On such a scene as this
Angels in their flight must have gazed.
A greater wonder here than Livingstone's Falls,
A form honey gold with sculpted head,
Small intricate ears,
Deep eyes lidded by graceful lashes,
The mouth firm, lips half open, inviting,
The chest gently pulsing under its large, proud nipples,
The naval in its muscled setting

Spilling its trail of down towards the soft, moist
mound,
Hardening, growing at the approach of dawn,
The grace yet strength of hand and foot
Intertwined with mine,
The miracle of such a body,
Such African perfection of form,
of body fused with soul,
Such a young temple for such an ancient spirit.
No angel would pass this sight
But rather pause and worship
And behold the glory of Africa.
Ian D Corbett

A faithful friend is a sure shelter,
whoever finds one has found a rare treasure.
A faithful friend is something beyond price,
there is no measuring his worth.
A faithful friend is the elixir of life,
and those who fear the Lord will find one.
Whoever fears the Lord makes true friends,
for as a man is, so is his friend.
Ecclesiasticus 6.14-17

"There are no strangers, only friends". That has been a
conviction in which I have grown as I have taken a
risk of opening myself to widening circles of people I

have met and among whom I have worked. Of course, there is always the possibility of discovering indifference or even hostility, and therefore being hurt and wounded, but much more often the discovery is of welcome, hospitality and acceptance. The Christ in us meets the Christ in the other, a fact we celebrate in the Kiss of Peace in the Eucharist. As Desmond Tutu would say, if you wish to find Christ look into the eyes of your neighbour. It is this conviction that has enabled me to enter, alone, a host of different situations and cultures. The way not only to survive but to understand and flourish is to trust ourselves to the people we are among, listen, learn, and be guided: accept their openness to us and seek to live on their terms. We will not lose our identity or our roots, but we will grow in maturity and stretch our hearts and imaginations a little further. It is only when we love and receive love that the life of the Spirit can really grow in us, and Eros and agape flow into and out of each other.

Love involves paying attention to another in an act of gracious self-forgetting. The ability to be still and centred is a disposition I learnt from rural Africans. It produced a yearning for the other, and a generosity of spirit towards the lives of others as we contemplate the wonder and uniqueness of their being. A friend is

someone who wishes the fullest good of the other –
"Shalom", which is much more than merely peace but
"all the best", what God wishes for him. A soul friend
(the lovely Irish term) is one who is intimately close
but also manages to preserve a certain distance and
perspective so the other person sees you whole in a
desire to enable the best possible outcome for you.
Friendship is one of the fundamentals of survival for,
even if the friend is absent in your adversity, the
relationship is still there. A soul friend is rarer but
when found is the rock on which you build and the
anchor of your life.

You give all to your friend. That is why when a
relationship fails the hurt and the cost are
devastating. All your barriers are down so the pain is
the greater. This is the risk and price to be gambled
(Kierkegaard called life a wager with God) for the
prize of the friendship maturing, for when it succeeds
two souls are twinned. Friends, especially soul
friends, share everything and their bond dictates its
own appropriate terms and expression, overriding all
conventions and brooking no interference. Love
accepts us as we are – it understands. Friendship is
the greatest gift of God. Jesus said, "I call you friends".
This love is not sentimental, though it includes
affection and play, but is realistic, creative and

ultimately sacred as it draws us ever nearer to the heart of love, which is God. The Christian doctrine of the Trinity expresses God in terms of relationship, and a rare Russian icon of the Holy Trinity shows the three persons of the Trinity enveloping the world in their embrace and focussing on the Eucharist, the sacred meal in which Christians find God present among them as a pledge of his faithfulness and commitment to us. Love dissolves reserve and enables us to become childlike again, and by so doing also renders us more God-like. It helps us to see ourselves, and to realise that to profoundly love one another we need to accept and love ourselves.

Some of us find this very difficult and I shall return to this later. St. Augustine, in his "Confessions", tells us that in his youth his best friend died. This was such a personal catastrophe that he resolved never to open himself to such intimacy again as its loss was too powerful. He decided to wrap his heart in a sort of psychological protective covering, to insulate himself from such pain. He was not loving but pitying himself. However, he found that, in his desire to protect himself, his heart began to suffocate for lack of the air of relationship, and he realised that to live necessarily implies being exposed to the possibility of hurt.

It will be controversial in some circles to argue that close friendships may have a physical, even sexual, expression, but we are not disembodied spirits and bodies express us as do our minds and spirits. Physical affection has sustained me through many times of deep emotional stress, anxiety and fear – it often expresses care and support more eloquently than words. The body is much sinned against in Christian (unlike, say, Hindu) tradition, yet it has a sacred nature conferred upon it not least by the Christian myth of God-with-us (Emmanuel), Jesus, taking a human body in the Incarnation and subsuming it into Heaven in his Ascension. The completed circle of Jesus' revelation, the descent and ascent, makes a powerful statement about the body as the locus of the love of the Father towards us.

It is celebrated in the Bible in the Song of Songs and in the many sensuous portraits of the saints from the Middle Ages at least until the Pre-Raphaelites of the nineteenth century. After all, the body is a mirror of the soul, "the temple of the Holy Spirit", suffused with divinity. It is, in a word, a sacrament. The messages of the body are very truthful and do not try to deceive or manipulate us as the mind can. Moreover, it is through the senses that we discern so much of God in the world around us, by seeing, hearing, touching and tasting. Physical contact between friends, sexually tinged or not, can be the greatest reassurance in crisis.

I also find inspiration in reading about marvellous people from afar whom I might wish could be my friends, for regularly meditating on wonderful human lives can encourage hope and, in dark times, can be a reminder that great forces of good are working against great forces of evil. I think of Craig Kielburger, who was only fifteen when I first read about him in 1998, who at that tender age had founded "Free the Children", an organisation that campaign against child labour worldwide: he radiates care and compassion. I think of Patrick Cox, the shoe designer, who is just so full of life, humour, ingenuity and delight, a genius who is fun. They are both Canadian. Or I think of how Georg Solti, the great conductor and something of a martinet, would call his daughters daily, wherever in the world he was, or how Sister Helen Prejean dedicated her life to ministry on death row, assiduously bringing love and beauty into the lives of the poor and condemned. Such people lift the spirits and, hopefully, we all know less famous individuals in our own lives who act as exemplars and mentors, enlarging our vision of the possible.

Here is a picture of one of the happiest times of my life, my first year in Lesotho:

I grow more in love with the Basotho! I read recently, "if you look at whites you find despair, if you look at blacks you find hope" – this about the future of Southern Africa. I find this to be profoundly true. How moving it is to discover that colour prejudice (in reverse) scarcely exists, that you are so universally welcomed and accepted. There is a saying here, "a person is only a person through other persons". Values often seem so much truer here than in the northern/ western worlds. It has been said that one of the saddest things about apartheid is that whites deny themselves the privilege and richness of black friendship. I certainly rely very much on such hospitality and affection. I think that this extraordinary black capacity for relationship arises from the centrality of suffering in the black experience; when you have suffered so much, perhaps lesser sufferings, such as the day to day struggle to make ends meet in Lesotho, can be endured, and you can even open yourself to the needs of others, confident in your experience and self knowledge. One of the remarkable things about African life in this context is the capacity for humour. At first it seems as though serious matters are treated lightly until you realise that laughter can be a way of life and a means of coping.

The African experience also teaches people to quickly see through pretence or insincerity; it is good to learn to be always open and honest in one's attitudes and dealings. There is, too, a touching childlikeness – not, I think, the sentimental observation of the missionaries but a responsive spontaneity, a warmth and eagerness, often (I am glad to say) physically expressed; but this means also that, as the other side of the coin, violence can easily erupt and, particularly under the influence of alcohol (an enormous problem here) knife fights are common and serious. The Basotho are a very beautiful people and entrance me by their unselfconscious grace and dignity, even amidst their poverty. I am so "into" the Basotho that I even love their smell - mainly a mixture of smoke and Sunlight soap!

Within this general context the small community of the seminary, in which I am based, is a special joy. We are trying to operate on a very modified Benedictine Rule, giving time to study, worship and manual work, in a broadly democratic system. It sort of works, though most of the students expect a much more autocratic style from me and, inevitably we have our occasional misunderstandings. But they are marvellously supportive and I feel very attached to them. From the point of view of spiritual and human growth, living in such a community, surrounded by a stunning mountain wilderness, is a most conducive setting. Such marvellous air and often real silence too! I feel quite reinvigorated and deeply grateful for being here. The community broadens out into the small university campus next door where I have some very happy friendships with students and staff alike, and our little chapel is packed to overflowing on Sundays – and full of the most vibrant singing that I have ever heard. I am really enjoying teaching again. Then again, my community widens into the villages round about and, when time permits, I love visiting them (sometimes on horseback or on foot) and entering into real Basotho village life – as much as my poor Sesotho permits. I managed my first funeral last week – quite an experience and it took all day! I have also gained a family – two sons by local adoption, David and Sello, whose mother has abandoned them; though sometimes a headache, and a continual expense, they are my pride and joy, as, to a lesser extent, are many other boys from the villages (often in conditions of acute distress) who are frequent visitors. The house is always open and scarcely ever empty. It is refreshing, too, not to be dashing around at nights as in Manchester (few people go far at night here – the darkness is very dark and people tend to sleep and wake early) but to be in my house and available to people.

I now want to turn to the issue of same-sex relationships and to talk of the pain that is involved in living out such lives honestly and authentically.

I have known myself to be gay since I was a child: I was deeply attracted to my older cousins. So much for theories of dominant mothers, teenage phases and learned patterns of sexual behaviour! During that time, and throughout the teenage years, I was carefully closeted, realizing that openness was not an option. The only comfort came from friends who were open to some small degree of physical affection, but, of course, that had to be handled with extreme caution. I went through even my undergraduate years at Cambridge with the ache and yearning of unexpressed desire. As a teacher I came close to confessing to older pupils to whom I was close but naturally never acting: they were marvellously kind and accepting of what little I did reveal. I had no sexual experience until I was at seminary when a discerning friend, with extraordinary sensitivity and delicacy, helped me into my first sexual encounter with him – just once, to free me from my shackles. Imagine the explosion that was – the wonderful release of all that suppressed desire. That bolstered my confidence though it took me to my second parish appointment to become more open, relaxed and experienced, mainly through working in a college environment and discovering the gay bar scene. But I was leading a double life, open to those I could trust but closed within the church. It was a great relief to be able, a few years later, to "come out" to an understanding bishop who came to dine with me and my then lover and who allowed me to perform services of blessing for gay partners. Yet it was still a life lived in the shadows as there was enormous ignorance and prejudice about sexual minorities in the church, and I felt I could not risk frankness with my family and relatives. It was removing to Lesotho that finally liberated me. The high degree of physical expression in Basotho society and the almost bisexual status of many men offered me a healing, integration and freedom that I had never known. Many men saw physical or sexual expressions of affection not as affronting their masculine perception of themselves and their sexuality but as particularly intimate explorations of friendship, so a married man might have such a relationship with another one but it would not be considered sexual and not a threat to his marriage. I had several lovers. This, of course, is scarcely normative behaviour for a priest, and there were obvious risks. I was principal of a seminary but those students who detected anything were quiet, non-judgemental and even supportive. African culture tends to handle sexual issues in a more relaxed way than we do in the West. But I really needed to give and receive love as much as I needed air to breathe, and I feel the opportunity actually released me to be a more effective teacher and pastor. How does the church expect its leaders to pronounce on love if they are forbidden to taste its revelations and pleasures? Such intimate encounters have provided immense joy and solace and have enabled me to give and receive love in a way so many clergy never experience.

I think it is necessary to set out my own convictions about homosexuality and to show how the usual misunderstandings can countered. So I begin by reproducing an article I wrote for the Irish press when Dean of Tuam as it is succinct and continues to move me after all these years.

Christianity and Homosexuality:
a time for decision
Ian D. Corbett

I have followed with interest the discussion in Eire on Christianity and Homosexuality, not least because I wrote a paper on the issue to brief all the Anglican bishops gathered for the Lambeth Conference this summer. To those of us who have long been working to bring about a more compassionate and understanding approach within the Church the resolution from the Conference was a bitter disappointment. It included the phrases:

'...abstinence is right for those who are not called to marriage...'

'...rejecting homosexual practice as incompatible with Scripture...'

'...cannot advise legitimising or blessing of same sex unions or ordaining of those involved in same sex unions...'

'...notes the significance of the Kuala Lumpur statement' (of S.E. Asian bishops, which was stridently homophobic).

My paper merely asked the bishops:-

(a) to establish, from among your number, together with other theologians, representatives of relevant disciplines, and respected members of the gay community in the Church, an International Commission to search for greater clarity on the entire spectrum of the theology of human sexuality, including the ordination and consecration of lesbians and gay men:

(b) to call upon all governments to decriminalise homosexual acts and work for the guaranteeing of equal rights for sexual minorities.

We pray that we may then all be able to say together the Statement of Conviction of the Lesbian and Gay Christian Movement:

> *Human sexuality in all its richness is a gift of God gladly to be accepted, enjoyed and honoured as a way of both expressing and growing in love, in accordance with the life and teaching of Jesus Christ...It is therefore entirely compatible with the Christian faith, not only to love another person of the same sex, but also to express that love fully in a personal sexual relationship.*

Neither of these mild requests was acted upon. It appals me that Church leaders can be so wilfully blind to the vast mass of evidence that faces them:-

1. Theology None of the Biblical texts purporting to deal with this subject are without ambiguity. For example, the story of Sodom in Genesis 19 was not interpreted with a homosexual connotation until at least the sixth century – the sin is lack of hospitality to angels. Legal rulings as in Leviticus 20 seem to apply to basically heterosexual men having gay sex for kicks. The Pauline correspondence, as in Romans 1, appears to refer to the commercial exploitation of gay sex that he would have encountered in Rome, and nowhere shows awareness of the possibility of reciprocal, caring single sex relationships. In any case, the verses which appear to refer to the topic can be counted almost on the fingers of one hand, and nobody would dream of building a case on such flimsy foundations on any other subject.

2. Social Sciences It would be hard to find any researcher in the fields of medicine, anthropology, psychology, sociology and related disciplines who would claim any other than that homosexuality is part of the normal sexual spectrum of humanity. In the West, evidence suggests that between 1 in 4 and 1 in

20 people are partly or wholly homosexual, and many more have known homosexual experiences. Homosexuality is no threat to marriage, which is eroding itself quite effectively, without any outside help! Indeed, stable gay relationships are a strength to society, and gay parents are as effective as any other.

3. Ethics If theology must come to terms with modern knowledge, and social sciences are a very new field, then there are moral consequences. The quality of a homosexual relationship and the morality of any physical expression of homosexual attraction are thus to be assessed by the same basic criteria which are applied to heterosexual relationships. This has long been the stance adopted by the Methodist Church and the Society of Friends in the United Kingdom. Furthermore, it is a matter of simple justice that the Church should not persecute its own members. Of the categories of people harassed by the Church in the Middle Ages; usurers, witches, Jews, Muslims, Travellers and homosexuals, only homosexuals are still marginalised and denied. If the Judaeo-Christian understanding of marriage is that it is the human relationship that most nearly mirrors the covenant relationship of God with His people, then surely any relationship that demonstrates these divine attributes of faithfulness and loving-kindness, even a gay one, is as surely blessed?

4. Politics A particular area of concern is that the issue of homosexuality is rarely treated purely as a theological, social and moral matter. It is often politically manipulated. For example, examination has recently been given to the oft repeated assertion that homosexuality is a European importation into African, Asian and South American countries. It has been shown that, when the early colonists and missionaries wanted to discredit and humiliate the peoples they conquered, they would refer to homosexual practices by these indigenous peoples as evidence of depravity and inferiority. However, when they wished to ingratiate themselves with local peoples, such practices were never mentioned in letters home.

There is no space to develop the issue of gay history here, though the Church was silent on the issue in its formative early centuries, and openly tolerated it in the great heyday of Christendom in the thirteenth century. So often attitudes that we think are ancient and normative are in fact much more recent and relative. Homosexuality is present in all cultures worldwide, though bishops claiming to speak for those cultures are often strangely selective.

The real tragedy of the Lambeth 'motion' is, however, not only its inadequate scholarship but in the personal behaviour of those bishops to whom homosexuality is an overwhelmingly emotive issue. Some bishops were so vociferous in shouting down the prepared presentation of the issue, that it never took place: this is little known, but the Anglican bishops made their decision after a brief debate with no input. The 'motion', passed by an overwhelming majority of bishops, was, as one Archbishop put it, the result of a 'tyranny'. It is now well documented that there took place an unholy collusion between evangelical North American and 'Southern World' bishops: in return for Northern support calling for the cancellation of Third World debt, the Southern bishops agreed to support the Americans in their crusade against homosexuality. The Lambeth ruling was not the outcome of informed, prayerful debate but of sinister backstairs politicking. A further irony was that a far greater number of bishops than those who had opposed this conservative position signed an open letter affirming their support for homosexual Christians. Clearly, many had voted with the majority for reasons, presumably, of maintaining a spurious unity. But unity can never be at the expense of truth. I am glad that several of our Irish bishops signed that letter. I should say that, in fairness, Lambeth did commit itself to continued 'listening' to homosexuals, but it set up no machinery to ensure that this happens. Yet out of this sordid episode has come, of course, new strength and inspiration for the struggle.

Richard Holloway, Bishop of Edinburgh, a highly respected pastor and theologian (and, I might add, happily married), had planned to retire so as to enter the politics of the new Scotland – now he has decided to stay to fight this issue within the Church. He finds the Lambeth ruling (which, fortunately, has no legislative force) 'offensive', and warns of the danger of 'simply identifying God with a previous social dispensation'. A great champion has emerged in the person of Archbishop Desmond Tutu, who writes[40]:

> The Church has joined the world in committing what I consider to be the ultimate blasphemy – making the children of God doubt that they are children of God. Lesbians and gays have been made to reject God and, in their rejection of the Church, they have been made to question why God created them as they were. I have found this official position of the Church illogical, irrational, frankly un-Christlike, totally untenable... If the Church, after the victory over apartheid, is

looking for a worthy moral crusade, then this is it: the fight against homophobia and hetero-sexism.

Again he writes:

It is only of homosexual people that we require universal celibacy, whereas for others we teach that celibacy is a special vocation. We say that sexual orientation is a matter of indifference but what is culpable are homosexual acts. But then we claim that sexuality is a divine gift, which, used properly, helps us to become more fully human and akin to God, because it is this part of our humanity that makes us more gentle and caring, more self-giving and concerned for others than we would be without that gift. Why should we want all homosexual people not to give expression to their sexuality in loving acts? Why do we not use the same criteria to judge same-sex relationships that we use to judge whether heterosexual relationships are wholesome or not? I am left deeply disturbed by these inconsistencies and know that the Lord of the Church would not be where his Church is in this matter. Can we act quickly to let the gospel imperatives prevail as we remember our baptism and theirs, and be thankful?

As a result of my paper, I was interviewed by the media. The response sustained me in my thinking and continued resolve to fight for inclusiveness in the Church. There were touching telephone calls from isolated gay men, and moving letters from parents who had had to come to terms with their sons' homosexuality with no help from the Church. My own diocese has reacted rather nervously.

But my friends in the Catholic Church, some of them senior clergy, have encouraged me, saying that, whereas they do not necessarily agree with all I say, they defend my right to speak the truth as I discern it, and acknowledge that homosexuality is a major social issue which has to be faced, discussed and which will not go away. I hope that this article will encourage you to promote debate within your congregations and communities, and to open your hearts to the pain and hopes of your gay brothers and sisters. (I am available as a resource person if needed.) Let us all help the Church to overcome the violence it has perpetrated against them, by its emotional response arising not from sound theological argument but from 'the unconscious absorption of centuries of non-scriptural and essentially un-Christian dread'.

That is the context in which I am writing, basically the need to assert that homosexuality is normal if not normative, that it is part of the sexual spectrum of humanity as it is in the animal world and that gay, lesbian, bisexual and transgendered people should be treated equally before the law and in every other circumstance of life. Yet this, sadly, is where the Church is the enemy, lagging well behind public opinion. The gospel has been used in the past to subjugate slaves, Jews, usurers, alleged witches, women generally, other races and sexual minorities. The Church has learned the error of its ways and repented in all cases except the last. Churches are dividing over the issue as though it is more important than poverty, hunger or war. The Primates of the Anglican Communion, meeting in Tanzania in 2007 seemed to try to make homophobia official Anglican policy. This certainly tends to be the trend for the sake of achieving some spurious sort of unity within the Communion. It is frustrating that, within the Church, we are still locked in arguments that have been fought and won elsewhere, and so are unable to move on to other and more complex issues that need resolution. The Church should be offering its blessing for a whole range of relationships – marriage certainly but also betrothal (engagement), coming of age, a first job or change of job, business partnerships, gay unions, and even "living together" (not least because many do so out of deep convictions and either feel not yet ready for marriage or have problems with some understandings of it). And there is the delicate issue of relationships across age barriers which are too easily characterized as paedophile, which in turn is too often confused with homosexuality. Yet these are all instances of the immense variety of relationship experienced by the human race in which we should rejoice.

It is sad that the current polarity over sexual issues in the Church can inhibit discussion. Indeed, rather alarmingly, some people have come to think that religion promotes intolerance towards minorities, especially gay people. Gene Robinson, the only openly gay Bishop in a partnership in the Anglican Communion, frankly but disturbingly said in an interview with Gay Times in 2008: "I totally understand why people leave the church. I think encouraging gay and lesbian people to return to the church is not unlike telling an abused wife to go back to her husband. I am very sympathetic to that reluctance".

I wrote this poem upon being deported from Zimbabwe.

THE SCREAM

Why will my heart not break?
My love was killed within me there,
My mourning was in my leaving.
Now, after mute and sorry wanderings,
I come here,
Invited out of pity
but not with understanding,
Politely received with warm hands
but cooler hearts.
I scream. I can scream now
But it is a silent scream
So deep within it is not heard.
The agony.
No longer anaesthetized by shock
I bear the pain
But the tears cannot come,
The heart will not break,
The body does not obey the spirit,
The planes of being are out of joint,
alien to each other,
And I do not recognize myself.
Yet I dimly perceive my need of you is desperate,

Yours just being there,
A word,
A gesture.
And when you embrace me so
I sometimes think I feel
The tremor of response.
I know I love you.
I cannot feel I love you.
Can you be patient
And hold me fast till my heart breaks?
Then I may be made whole again
And find you as you are
And myself in you.

This poem about pain is the first I ever wrote, on being deported from Zimbabwe and so exiled from many friends. But its truth underlies my entire relational life as lasting union with a lover has eluded me. My first erotic friendships, shall we say, were with students in Bolton, Lancashire, all of us exploring the possibilities of relationships of any depth for the first time. But it was a little later in Manchester, that I met the first great love of my life - a chef - who described himself as Anglo-Indian but who was really a glorious mix of these backgrounds as well as Portuguese and African. Warm, striking, intelligent – he seemed to be everything I needed. He came to live with me, with the knowledge of my Bishop, and we enjoyed two of the happiest years of my life. But Gordon was bisexual and, as with many such, his sexual preferences rocked to and fro, and he became increasingly attracted to women. I felt very threatened when he began to bring them home and our relationship gradually cooled over four years until I had to ask him to leave to preserve my own sanity. I continued to love him dearly but have long lost touch.

Yet it was also in Bolton and Manchester that two tragedies occurred. I knew Michael, an art student, intimately and he often stayed. But he was found to be schizophrenic and eventually had to be hospitalized. However, he was allowed to stay with me some weekends. After one particularly happy, close weekend I never saw him again. He had thrown himself under a train. I was beside myself with a grief I could not share with anyone. I had been too insensitive to see even the possibility of this happening. About three years later, in Manchester, I was regularly visiting a student commune. Among the residents was Martin, a handsome and delightful person, rather withdrawn and apparently with a girlfriend. I always tried to spend time with him. Again the news was brought to me that he had committed suicide by consuming a bottle of whisky and lying on a beach while the tide came in. He had tried to contact me three times by telephone but I was never at home, too busy out and about. His friends told me he had wanted a much closer relationship with me. I was devastated. Gordon, Michael, Martin, all lost. What was happening to me?

In Lesotho I knew several friends intimately in the context of the tactile relationships of Basotho society but one in particular stands out. He was much younger than me and impossibly beautiful, the sort of person older men envy but realize are unattainable. However, he worked for his uncle, a farmer and builder, who was then building me a mission church in the mountains and he often stayed, to be away from demanding relatives, and soon we were sleeping together. But, like all good Africans, he wanted to marry and he met an equally lovely girl – I had the bitter-sweet pleasure of being asked to be his best man! A fortnight later he was around to see me, thanking me that our experience together had helped him relate to his wife, and asking to stay the night as usual. When this happened a second time I had to refuse. I could not handle this, and felt awful for his wife, of whom I was very fond. To him our relationship, though physical, was not sexual but a particularly intimate friendship which did not affect his relationship with his wife. I understood but, for her sake, had to let him go.

In Zimbabwe there were two promising beginnings in the year I was there: Ndlovu – of whom I spoke earlier, and another, whom I will not name as we still correspond and he would not favour any publicity. But tragedy struck again. Ndlovu later died mysteriously in Johannesburg, as already related, and my being deported from Zimbabwe deprived me of what I am sure would have been the great relationship of my life had I been able to remain.

In Botswana and South Africa there were several passing affairs as I tried desperately to fill the aching and lonely void inside me. Shame complicates matters now as I realize I may sometimes have used people to satisfy my own longings, though there was always genuine feeling and my lovers were willing. My periods in England, recovering from M.E., and in Ireland, as Dean of Tuam, were barren, though I had marvellous friends to see me through – David Melling (a distinguished classics scholar, now prematurely deceased) and Tom Ormond in England, Roy O'Ghislain in Ireland (he once wrote to me, "Ian, give what you lack", meaning, I think, if you go on loving even when you think you can't, love seems to renew itself – a wise young man!).

Unbelievably, the young artist I started to draw close to in Phoenix, Arizona, also committed suicide, certain he would not fully recover from a serious road accident. By now I was in such a fragile and needy emotional state that I have to confess I resorted to escorts (once called prostitutes). You'll be shocked by this but it was my salvation. In Dublin I had found an utterly delightful psychology student who had restored my faith in myself somewhat and, emboldened by this experience, I tried again in Salt Lake City of all places (it is actually less than fifty per cent Mormon in population) and met two marvellous people who became good friends, especially Ranald, who ran a business consultancy and was a considerable painter and sculptor. They really nurtured me and helped me towards a new healing and wholeness. So don't knock prostitutes! As I stated earlier, even one night stands can have a relational value, in depth if not in length.

Now, in old age, I have no-one. It sometimes seems as though God does not wish me to be in relationship but can that be true, for all the reasons adduced above? Does he really want me to be the classic celibate priest who, by denying his own relational needs, makes himself more available to others? Does that really work? We have all known desiccated, tortured, angry and unhappy old priests who have never been loved. For me to be sentenced to celibacy is a tragedy and torment.

Postscript: last week I spent a lovely day with a potential lover. It turns out he is emigrating to the Canaries! Is it me? If "love is proved in the letting go"[41] then I am a veteran at it! I can only pray that "the faith and the love and the hope are all in the waiting."[42] So I wait. But I often feel with George Herbert that "I wept when I was born, and every day shows why".[43]

Perhaps it is a little sharing in the suffering of God in becoming one of us and opening up new life for us: if only a "suffering God can help"[44] then perhaps that is also true of people. I hover between faith and doubt. I know God comes unannounced and without clamour, and I could miss him. Becket's Malone in "Malone Dies" well defines me, between hopelessness and hope:

> *Where I am, I don't know, I'll never know, in the silence you don't know, you must go on, I can't go on, I'll go on.*[45]

To live in this world
you must be able
to do three things:
to love what is mortal;
to hold it
against your bones knowing
your own life depends on it;
and, when the time comes to let it go,
to let it go.
Mary Oliver[46]

But my experience and even that of sexual minorities in general in the West, is as nothing compared to the oppression of the native peoples with whom I have worked. Thomas Merton wrote that "Western civilization is now in full decline into barbarism".[47] It has failed to notice that, by the Incarnation, God is in **all** human beings, so it has failed to appreciate, and has indeed destroyed indigenous cultures. "Where it failed was in its inability to encounter Christ already potentially present in the Indians, the Hindus and the Chinese...God speaks, and God is to be heard, not only on Sinai, not only in my own heart, but in the voice of the stranger"[48]. That is why all first peoples make so much of the virtue of hospitality. "the tourist never meets anyone, never encounters anyone, never finds the brother in the stranger: this is his tragedy"[49]. And the colonists came to exploit not to cherish the land and its inhabitants.

Barry Lopez, in his "The Rediscovery of North America"[50], writes that the Spanish invaders were concerned only with appropriation, and "what followed for decades upon their discovery were the acts of criminals". He chronicles the extraordinary cruelty of the usurpers, "a continuous recreational slaughter", a time of terror. The colonizing movement was but "a ruthless, angry search for wealth", a quest for possessions, a profound abuse of place. In their lust for gold the Spaniards destroyed communities, languages, ceremonies, traditional wisdom, plants and animals, "a long, hideous carnage. The Spanish impose, they do not propose...The Spanish wanted no communion with America, the place or its people...America was not to be a home or what a home implied" but an arena of pillage and depredation. There was no sensitivity to the inviolate relationship between people and place, no awareness that the true wealth of the Americas was to be found in a richness of cultures and biodiversity. This has become a common pattern in all Western colonization around the globe. This is why today the Western world itself experiences a crisis of culture, a crisis of character, as it seeks to come to terms with its legacy of incursion and ruthless exploitation.

Yet this racism is still to be found in the ethnic ghettoes of our cities, in the inequality of education for inner city children, the lack of affordable housing for the poor, the lack of jobs that offer a living wage for low skilled labourers, the tragic abandonment of single mothers, factories moving to the Third World under pressure of globalization leaving thousands unemployed, and the lack of concern for the poor. These realities are not only distortions of our democracy but also grave distortions of the Kingdom of God.

A member of "The Simple Way", a Christian commune in inner city Philadelphia, wrote:

> I had a dream, a dream of heaven. I almost didn't recognize it. There were no streets of gold. These were streets of dirt. The mansions with many rooms looked more like makeshift tents down by the river. But there was dancing. I could hear the people dancing on the wreckage of the old world.

This is to begin to readdress the balance of the apocalypse inflicted by our death-dealing civilization on the new holy innocents in the so-called developing world – to dream dreams, discern new vision, to trust the people, enter their world, learn their wisdom, sit with them in their place and listen with respect.

I would like to reflect more on my experience of living amongst the indigenous people of Canada and the United States by sharing with you two articles and a poem I wrote about them.

A LESSON IN COLONIAL HISTORY (2004)[51]

This week Omnibus is devoted to a reflection on colonial history which was elucidated by the former Dean of St. Mary's Cathedral Tuam, Rev. Ian Corbett, when he opened the Tuam Summer School at the end of June. Ian had worked in Africa before he came to Tuam, where he became in a short time one of the best loved pastors the town has known, and on his departure he went to work among the Native Americans in Canada. He is now working with the same group of people in the U.S.A.

The Summer School this year had as its theme "A Vision of Connacht in the 16th century" and Ian's speech was a thoughtful reflection on the impact of this great age of colonialism on the New World.

Perhaps the most apposite observations I might make to launch this summer school, from my present vantage point, would be to point to the astonishing similarities in the attitude of my own people, the English, to both the Gaelic Irish and the native inhabitants of the New World, at this outset of the period of growing colonization. In these remarks I draw heavily on the writings of Nicholas Canny, which I have been privileged to encounter recently, and from whom we are to hear later in our programme.

Both peoples were regarded as backward and barbarous and in need of Christian civilising. Although in both early phases of contact the British co-operated with, and were even dependent on, native peoples, as settlement increased, and the demands of new immigrants for new land grew, indigenous peoples, whether here or America, were dispossessed. They were driven to retaliate in rebellion and war: severe punishments followed, including further dispossession. An innate sense of racial superiority in the British bred a missionary fervour to civilise the barbarous, and indeed, the peoples of the Shetlands, Orkneys, Isle of Man, the Scottish borders – and the Irish – were often seen as more depraved than Native Americans, 'barbarous people' with 'primitive habits', 'living like beasts', a lower form of humanity.

Questionable though Livingstone's motives may have been in Africa centuries later in his mission to establish 'commerce, civilisation and Christianity' – in that order – England in the sixteenth century seemed mainly concerned with 'commerce' notwithstanding the veil of 'civilisation' already alluded to. This accounts for the eventual imposition of English law, which was cheaper than maintaining a dual system. Most of the early settlers were greedy and aggressive adventurers, many moving west from Ireland to the New World in search of further fortunes. In fact it could be said that some served their colonial apprenticeship here before moving on to apply these lessons ever more ruthlessly in North America.

It was in Ireland that the British first identified the native language as a cause of barbarity, and began its suppression with the Ireland Act of 1537, a practice later to be introduced to North America with great cruelty. As part of the assimilationist policies, the most coercive measures of appropriation and plantation were introduced, on both sides of the Atlantic. It amounted to a policy of transplanting English life abroad without regard for local sensibilities. Colonisation proceeded faster in Ireland than across the ocean, but patterns were similar: planters registered their 'right' to the land, assuming, conveniently, the land to be empty or 'terra incognita', and very soon their economic monopoly and prowess damaged the interests of indigenous people. However, as already noted, there seems to be, at least initially, more respect for Native Americans, especially for their social organisation, moral codes and religious beliefs. In fact, land was purchased rather than plundered from the Indians to begin with: in particular, in Virginia a real attempt was made to respect the political integrity of native society and to effect change by persuasion and gradual assimilation rather than through conflict. Even cross-cultural marriages were encouraged to promote this policy. But it was not to last.

Many of the disasters of colonial policies are attributed to ignorance. Ireland was as unknown to most Englishmen as Virginia. The 'uncivilised' habits of both Irish and Indian were thought to be similar. If, however, the real reason for 'civilising' was to open up new lands for 'commerce', it was inevitable that the rise of capitalism would, in the end, justify extermination if civilising failed or was resisted, as happened in Ireland in the 1560s and 1570s, and in Virginia in the 1620s. As with the Irish, the English alleged that the Indians (and later Black Americans) were an unsettled people who did not make proper use of their land, and could therefore be justly deprived of it. All were idle, lazy, dirty and licentious. It is hard to resist the conclusion that the proud English had a preconceived idea of barbarism, which they imposed on Irish and Indian alike. The nonsense of it was not perceived in the Irish situation and it was then imposed with ever more relish on the New World. They saw only a false vision of tyrants and serfs constituting indigenous society in both Ireland and America, a myth necessary to justify the English crusade.

So both sides of the Atlantic were forced into the same conceptual straitjacket to justify the English colonial enterprise, the need to convert the heathen, to civilise the barbarian, and to promote the enrichment of England. Indigenous people must be persuaded to change and assimilate, but, if needs be, must be coerced. And, in the end, private profit was pursued at the expense of concern for social and religious reform. To the local people what was called by the invaders 'settlement' could be seen only as conquest. The only redeeming feature from my side of the Atlantic is that there were always more visitors who found something to admire in Indian culture than there were in Ireland.

The forceful propagation of this policy was certainly buttressed by the Reformation in Europe because a Protestant predestination theology, which took a radically pessimistic view of human nature, concluded that people who lived in a primitive condition might be reformed in manners and religion only after they had been subjected by force. So schemes of colonisation were increasingly favoured by Government. Dr. Canny is more generous than I, and would find positive arguments in favour of the policy, but I find only that the economic needs of England were ultimately always paramount. Autocratic exercise of authority, military action, dispossession of local populations and the neglect of manifest injustices, both the Irish and the Indian, were commonplace on a scale that would never have been tolerated in England. The 'uncivilised' Indians could not grasp the Englishman's insatiable greed for land and his capacity for cruel retribution. The telling point is that there was no body of law to protect the Indians from exploitation or deliberate extermination. The joint stock company was law.

I worked in Canada before moving to the States. The same pattern can be seen further North. Jacques Cartier, one of the first serious European explorers in 1534, fired unprovoked on the Micmac and abducted

Iroquois, all of whom had welcomed him with great civility. European arrogance and disdain is almost beyond belief. However, the complex and civilised society of the Iroquois was recognised, and Indians were seen as astute and demanding traders, who initially controlled and dominated commercial transactions. Yet they were still also seen as barbaric and degraded, forced into the preconceived colonialist mind set. By 1800, 90 per cent of Canadian Indians had fallen victim to diseases, drug abuse and starvation, all introduced by the European invaders and their economic policies. Native economies, such as the Fur trade, were ruined by overseas demands, and the trade in alcohol led to widespread demoralisation. Increasingly, Europeans monopolised trade, and the epidemic diseases they introduced – measles, typhus, scarlet fever – swept through all communities from the Iroquois to the Inuit, decimating them all. Only when Indians were needed as allies did they enjoy European support: otherwise, the invaders were more interested in the agricultural potential and timber on native land than in the welfare of the people.

I was given a marvellous book by the Old Tuam Society when I left Ireland. It is Elemire Zolla's *The Writer and the Shaman: a Morphology of the American*

Indian. He demonstrates unequivocally the stylistic means by which a programme of genocide can be facilitated. The actual agent of slaughter is the very idea of progress, which by its very nature demands the elimination of everything that it decrees old and obsolete – and then removes this sacrifice from our consciousness. At best the American Indian was seen as a representative of a lost, Arcadian golden age, at worst as a savage to be civilised, as a young person needing to mature: in either case he had to be changed, (reformed was a contemporary word) to fit in with European literary and mythical expectations. The same was true of the English view of the Irish. Religious reformation was but a small part of the Imperialist project to make all life march with Western notions of progress. If native populations refused to co-operate, whether in Ireland or the New World, they could be exterminated. The colonial enterprise was a Renaissance revival of a vision of Roman Imperialism, to 'civilise' the world. It was also a way of purging the home country of the desperate, the debtors, the vagrants, the unemployed – and of Puritan ministers guilty of indiscreet and subversive zeal.

I first learned in Africa what my own nation was capable of. I discovered in Lesotho that the British had destroyed a thriving agricultural economy (now impossible to revive owing to massive soil erosion) to release cheap labour for the South African mines. They had also undermined an effective chieftainship network with guns and alcohol to enhance the authority of the colonial governor. I discovered in the West of Ireland that there still lingered Anglo-Irish attitudes to the Gaelic Irish, rather like an unspoken apartheid. Apartheid was alive and flourishing in Canada, where the white towns were surrounded by Indian reservations rather than African townships, but the attitudes were the same.

In all the places I have worked, I have received death threats only from my own people. I am ashamed to be an Englishman, as I stand before you now, and I am only too grateful for the deeper humanity I have learned from my African, Irish and Native American friends. We experienced '9-11' in America last year. With all the rhetoric about the 'war against terrorism', we who are white and European have still not heard the once colonised world telling us 'we will not tolerate your exploitation and arrogance any longer'. Perhaps they are telling us, 'we have learned from you: if you cannot get your way by persuasion, use force, and that is just what we are doing to you'. I wish we could learn from history. I fear we do not.

NATIVE AFFAIRS

AN OUTSIDER'S VIEW (2000)

I arrived in Canada last year to become the Rector of Whitesand parish in the Anglican Church. It includes Kamsack and Canora in Saskatchewan. I am from England, but had worked for nearly ten years in various parts of Southern Africa and more briefly in Ireland, before coming here. A major factor in my move was the opportunity to continue working with aboriginal peoples, whom, I am convinced, have insights into the nature both of our humanity and our world which are essential to our well-being on this planet: Indeed some of the Hopi people in Arizona see sharing these insights as an integral part of their identity and vocation.

We are all aware of the disastrous history of native and white interaction in the United States, which still continues, but I had succumbed to the Canadian myth that matters were different here. I have now come of age in my pilgrimage and discovered otherwise. I have the temerity to 'go public' as a newcomer and a foreigner, because I see the situation of First Nations People and their relationship to wider Canadian society to be at a critical point. Sometimes a newcomer can see more clearly than those who have long been immersed in a situation, though he will certainly lack their experience and then, if he is wrong, it is easy for local people to dismiss him on grounds of ignorance or arrogance. So, if I speak, I have nothing to lose, and nobody need feel hurt.

The crisis, as I see it, is both the inability and the unwillingness of the dominant white population to understand the immensity and gravity of First Nations issues. It begins with an imperfect knowledge of Canadian History, because some aspects were never taught and the worst of it contemporary Canadians do not want to believe. They cling to the rumour that life was not as bad for the original peoples of this country as it was for their relatives in the United States. This is the first myth that has to be dispelled. Canadian society is built on a fundamental injustice which diminishes us all. Let me refer to some significant events and examples.

When the first Europeans came to Canada, they found it inhabited by people of considerable culture and sophistication. In the east, the Iroquois Confederacy had been practising settled farming, democratic government and a degree of sexual equality from the fifteenth century. In the west, the Haida and Nisga'a produced a great visual culture and a complex social organisation. Yet Jacques Cartier, the first significant European visitor in 1557 fired unprovoked on the Mi'kmaq and abducted Iroquois, despite their welcome and assistance. This set the pattern for future contact. It seemed to be beyond the white man's comprehension (and still largely is) that any other people could have a comparable, let alone a superior, religion and culture.

The first phase of this ongoing contact was characterised by unscrupulous corruption on the part of the white traders. The bartering of fur for guns not only led to the over-killing of the wildlife on which the trade depended, but led also, as was intended, to aboriginals putting pressure on other tribes as they extended their traditional hunting areas to find game. Such catastrophes as the war in which the Iroquois destroyed the Huron Nation, and as the forced movement of Cree and Saulteaux people west (to whom I now seek to minister) displaced other tribes who were themselves the victims of Anglo-French rivalry, were directly the result of colonial pressure and not, as so many whites today want to believe, the pattern of natural 'Indian' behaviour. More native people died, in support of the British and 'Canadians' in the war of 1812, including the great Tecumseh, than all the white combatants on both sides added together; so much for native hostility to the white man. But, most disastrously, 90% of all native Canadians died in the seventeenth century of European diseases to which they had no immunity, namely typhoid, diphtheria, plague, influenza, measles, tuberculosis, venereal disease, scarlet fever and small pox. This is genocide – not intentional genocide, certainly, but the process could have been foreseen from the earlier colonial experience in Central America. The legacy of the white man to the native in Canada has been death.

The second phase of European infiltration was characterized by oppression, often brutal. Between 1763 and 1800, 24 treaties were ratified with the intention of abolishing First Nation's titles to land in return for cash and the reserve system, without any conception of how separating aboriginal peoples from their ancestral lands destroys them. As a result of these treaties, many natives were forced father north, where game was scarce. Both the Hudson's Bay Company and the North West Company traded manufactured goods, firearms and alcohol, thereby creating dependency.

The buffalo were recklessly slaughtered, often with the intended consequence of eliminating native food supplies. By the close of the eighteenth century, the white man's illnesses, smallpox and venereal disease, had reduced the plains Indians and the West Coast Indians respectively by one third. White cultivation further depleted hunting grounds. In the middle of the nineteenth century, without any attempt to understand aboriginal culture, the policies of 'assimilation' and 'gradual civilization' began, as did the strategy to force the surrender of further land rights in response for white greed for gold and other minerals.

The treaties we now know came into being after the creation of Canada in 1867. Only 25,000 aboriginal people now remained, yet these treaties were for the annexation of yet further land to appease the insatiable greed of the white settlers. Again cash and reserves were the reward, but with little provision for health and education. Treaties 1, 2 and 5 surrendered most of Manitoba, Treaties 3 and 10 of Saskatchewan, Treaties 6, 7 and 8 of Alberta and 11 of the North West Territories. The infamous Indian Act of 1876 with its vicious amendment of 1889 reinforced the genocide policies of assimilation and dependency.

With the pass system and residential schools, it is salutary to remember that the system of Apartheid in South Africa, universally condemned, was modelled on the reserve system in Canada, easier to study for a member of the British Commonwealth that the Reservation System in the United States. Veterans of the Second World Ward were treated shabbily in comparison to their white counterparts.

It was not until the resurgence of 'Indian Nationalism' in the 1940s that the tide began to turn and concessions were wrung from reluctant governments. Even so, native peoples had to beware official duplicity, as in the case of the 1969 White Paper which purported to be magnanimously abolishing the Indian Act while in fact seeking to slough off all responsibility for native peoples.

It is necessary to spend so much time on the historical overview because I believe that most white Canadians are either unaware or do not want to face the enormity of the crime their forbears perpetrated on the original inhabitants of this country. Adolf Hitler, Pol Pot and Saddam Hussein could have all learned their lessons in genocide in this bastion of liberal democracy. Later achievements, won by the peoples themselves, such as the modified Indian Act of 1951, the Assembly of First Nations, the recognition of Aboriginal Land Rights, success in local self-government and native businesses, and the pressure which secured the 1982 Constitution Act, the 1992 Charlottetown Accord and the Royal Commission of 1996, cannot deny the gross injustice, humiliation and degradation heaped upon those who welcomed white people to their lands until very recent times – our lifetime. Is this what young people learn in schools? Is that what whites accept their people did?

The burden is too dreadful to bear. Hence, the reaction of most white Canadians, even those who can face the truth, is to say 'but it is not our responsibility: we cannot be held to ransom for what our forefathers did'. Not so, for our affluence has been purchased with blood money. The judgement of history falls upon this generation. If not from us, from whom can Native Canadians seek justice and reparation? We are not talking only of wrongs committed centuries ago, but of those perpetrated in our times. Where we do see despondency, despair and hopelessness on our reserves, we are not looking at the native people of this land in their natural nobility, as Jacques Cartier met them, but as we have made them. It will take generations to undo what we have done. But our generation must begin to make amends. It is not so long since the last survivors of Wounded Knee died. The children who are suffering from Foetal Alcohol Syndrome, AIDS and abuse are the offspring of parents we, or our people, have abused. They are still with us. Of course, we must take responsibility for we are the ones here faced with this appalling tragedy. Perhaps this is what the Bible means when it refers to the sins of the fathers being visited on subsequent generations, both for the victim and the oppressor.

On the reserve I serve in central Saskatchewan, Key Anishinabe First Nation, levels of alcoholism, drug abuse and violence have significantly reduced owing to effective rehabilitation programmes. The population is small because most of the Band are away in the cities seeking work. Far from their luxuriating in welfare handouts, they are paid no more than whites in comparable circumstances, and in fact, Federal spending on First Nations communities over the past seven years has not kept pace with the on-reserve population growth, according to the Ministry of Indian and Northern Affairs.

Although there have been financial irregularities in the past, the present wave of younger chiefs and councillors, more at ease in both worlds, red and white, have an impressive list of achievements to their credit: In Saskatchewan alone, one could note the hundreds of jobs and opportunities created by The Meadow Lake Tribal Council, the La Ronge Indian Band's Kitsaki Development Corporation, Muskeg Lake's commercial development in Saskatoon and the Saskatchewan Indian Gaming Corporation (source, Indian and Northern Affairs Canada). Even greater achievements can be recorded for the larger bands in the west and east of the country, particularly in the logging and recreational industries.

Another attitude of white people is to deny the physical, moral and cultural abuses perpetrated by the Residential Schools: we simply cannot believe the extent of them. But most of these cases are true. The first Anglican diocese to complete its process of litigation, that of the Cariboo in the Rockies, has had most of the cases against it sustained, and now faces bankruptcy. So we then take refuge in asserting that we personally were not involved and so seek to evade responsibility. It is a measure of the sickness of our society and the rampancy of unbridled individualism in white culture that we are blind to what all aboriginal societies know and experience that we are called to be in community, in solidarity with one another, if only in sin, and that we bear one another's burdens, including those of our forefathers and those of the marginalised amongst us today. One might add that the remarkable response of Bishop Jim Cruickshank and his Kamloops-based church to the charges against them, seeking above all forgiveness, justice, healing and reconciliation despite the alarming crisis for the survival of the diocese, could be a model for white responsibility in a wider context.

The response of white people in the face of their corporate guilt is to deny any achievement to native people. Oh yes, we say, in the past perhaps they had significant cultures, but today they are a shadow of their former selves and are carried by the rest of us. It is instructive that, at the resolution of the Mi'kmaq fishing dispute in 1999, little credit was given in the media to their remarkable chiefs, Deborah Robinson and Wilbur Dedam, who persuaded heir people not to exercise their rights, recently agreed by the Supreme Court, for the sake of peace. Listening to interviews on the radio at the time, there was no comparison between the restrained and statesmanlike comment of the Mi'kmaq and the inflated and aggressive rhetoric of the white fishermen. The dispute was solved by native maturity and generosity.

Imagine the media reaction if it had been a case of natives seeking to curb the legal rights of whites! The best reporting was to be found in the native newspapers.

The political progress of the First Nations has been formidable, particularly in terms of local self-government in the areas of health, education, housing and the economy, of land management agreements and the gradual dismantling of the Department of Indian and Northern Development in Manitoba as the Bands take over.

The time has surely come for recognition of the Native American as an equal, a partner and a friend but in my part of Saskatchewan, in the Parkland, it is clear how far we still have to go. Scarcely any white people have native friends. When they say they do, it usually means that they might occasionally share a drink in a bar, that the white man sees himself as a good employer, that the white lady has polite conversation. But conversation between whites themselves reveals the truth, the patronizing attitudes, the perpetuation of the stereotypes presented above, and the unshakable sense of white superiority. My positive comments on reserve life in the *Kamsack Times* have been interpreted as being anti-white and dismissed as the ignorant ramblings of a newcomer: to be pro-Indian means to be anti-white, them or us. We are far from committed, passionate friendship across the colour divide. It saddens me to confess that the native friendships I now have took time to ripen because there were those who could not believe that a white man would want their love and affection.

While my instincts tell me we should resist pessimism, the one thing of which I am personally absolutely convinced is the perfidy of my own people. Having worked in Africa and Ireland before arriving here, I have seen how they have brought death and destruction wherever they have gone. In Lesotho, the British Colonial Government ran down farming to release labour for the South African mines and undermined the chieftain system to consolidate their power. The result today is that Lesotho is a dust bowl and the people amongst the poorest in the world. The atrocities of the settlers in the prolonged war of independence for Zimbabwe are well documented, and Ian Smith would have introduced apartheid if his regime had not been toppled.

The British treatment of the Irish was if anything worse. So deeply etched in the Irish psyche is the carnage and brutality of Cromwell's army, and the later long years of the famines and the 'rock masses', that virulently anti-English songs from these times can still be heard in Irish bars.

Many Canadians have British backgrounds. I am ashamed of my British past and feel, at least spiritually, stateless. I find myself in the strange position of sitting here on the dusty and windy northern edge of the world, alongside aboriginal communities who have not invited me, as lost as some of them, in a sort of desperate, impotent gesture of solidarity, daring to hope that the love of the Creator, the Great Spirit, for us all is not yet spent. As Jasper Friendly Bear in Radio One's 'Dead Dog Cafe' enjoins us, I 'wait for the sign'.

Reverend Ian D. Corbett
Rector, Whitesand Anglican Parish

The Medicine Man

He sits,
An entire world, with a still centre,
Contained in so compact a frame
Ancient, focused, still,
A universe of wisdom, healing and hozhoo,
His completeness a challenge I cannot
understand.

He averts his eyes
As I gaze in intrusive inquiry.
He talks in few words and measured tones
As I babble effusively with my
questions, my anxiety,
My lack of a still centre,
Not realizing that his experience
Is not to be grasped by the
superficiality of the western intellect,
But only apprehended in a willingness
to sacrifice my identity in entering his world,
in a quest to be more like him,
a sacrifice of which I am scared
and for which I am not prepared.
So I fill the silence between us
With the noise of my uncertainty,
While the worlds of ancient wisdom
and contemporary arrogance
again fail to connect.

The point of this lengthy discourse on original peoples is to draw our attention to the sad fact that many of those to whom we might go to draw from their wells of ancient wisdom have, in fact, been polluted and oppressed by us, and part of our remaking of ourselves as truly liberated people is to be repentant for our past aggression and to seek to learn what we can from those who have suffered so much and yet preserved so much. Then we are all free together. To recognise what we have done to others is part of our healing. To find the humility to then learn from them and accept them as friends is part of our maturing.

Jean Vanier wrote: "it's not just doing things for people but discovering we are changed when we come close to them. If we enter into a friendship with them, they change us. Here we touch a mystery that the person we reject because of prejudice is the one who heals us."[52]

The former President of Ireland, Mary McAleese, has written:

> *Practising the Gospel of love means different things to each of us, as we go about our own lives and reach for our own ambitions. It means that we have to accept that there are others beside ourselves that share the same piece of God's earth. It means that all of us are shaped to some extent by our heritage and culture. It means that the actions of others are largely determined by their constructs of the likely outcomes – and by the reactions of others to their actions. It should force us all to think of others before ourselves – to accept that there are hates, apprehensions and*

fears – and that these can blind people to what is right. It also means that we must accept others for what they are – we must accept that it is not possible to homogenize humanity – and that we must embrace the world in all its diversity.[53]

It was Thomas a Kempis who said, "It is no great matter to associate with the good and gentle for this is naturally pleasing to all.....But to be able to live peaceably with the disorderly, or with such as go contrary to us, is a grace, and most commendable..." Aristotle said, "Society comes into existence in order than men may live; it persists that they may live well". This I take to be a definition of the caring society. It has wealth, and it has warmth, and it is willing to share it according to need and not entitlement. It recognises that even the most impotent have a right to be protected from the loneliness of their own isolation. [54]

I wish I could say that I embark on my old age with calm and contentment but in so many ways life has made a pessimist of me. I look at the world and see no reasonable hope of "the peace of Jerusalem" in the

Middle and Further East. I see the continuing economic colonialism of Africa which denies the most soulful peoples in the world growing to their full stature and playing their rightful part in world affairs. I notice the increasing marginalization of indigenous peoples and, indeed, the renewed spread of human slavery in our time. I see Western nations refusing to modify their excessive lifestyles and ignoring the perils of global warming and species depletion. The very future of the planet is at stake and I am not optimistic. The only way through lies in the incipient decline of the West, which the current recession and banking crisis signals, and the perhaps forlorn hope that the nations of the East will be more prescient and responsible.

If I look to the communities of faith I am no more hopeful. The expanding churches of the South are evangelical, pietistic and blinkered. The old churches of the North and West are in institutional decline and locked in internal battles over issues such as human sexuality while the earth burns. They have outlived their usefulness and relevance. People now go to their doctors for pastoral support. The world of Islam is repeating all the mistakes of the colonial churches, from whom it so cruelly suffered, in seeking to enforce belief in defiance of all the lessons of history. Every faith, even Hinduism, has its mindless, fundamentalist factions, offering cheap reassurance in an Age of Anxiety. Judaism, after centuries of persecution, is too small to affect the issues. Faith communities have become largely inward looking, therefore turning their backs on the world.

5. Spirituality

Having lived on other people's edges of existence I now feel I face an abyss of my own, a deep sense of insecurity and danger. I find, too, that as I grow older I do not reflect on achievements to be pleasurably remembered but more on projects that could have been better done, people who could have been better served. I am very aware of lost loves and lost opportunities – those times when indolence or cowardice prevented my saying "yes" to life's challenges. "Only connect" is the motto of E M Forster's novel, "Howards End". If you don't respond to invitations they may never be repeated. I see a too ordinary life that has not realized its full potential, has not grown to the "fullness of the stature of Christ". I do not like what I see and I do not like myself. I would not want to be my own best friend. So, in these last years, it is not hard to let go of things, including the church, for me the greyness of the outside world reflecting the greyness within – a not very noble failure. Yet I rage inwardly against the failing of the light, the loss of the connection with the Greek ideals of youth and beauty that I treasure, the deaths of lovers, the inaccessibility of wilderness and wildness to the elderly. I shall grow old disgracefully, protesting against the evils that envelop us that are made worse by the lies and inaccuracies that the powerful spread around.

However, when all is said, "Old men ought to be explorers" (T S Eliot in *East Coker*). I try to hold on to what elements of vision and, certainly, a sense of wonder that are left. I try to believe and cling to these spiritual insights which are left to me.

I try to maintain a faithfulness to the old monastic rules, whether Franciscan (poverty, humility, simplicity, prayer, joy) or Benedictine (poverty, stability, and the "conversion of manners"). I take the basic monastic requirements of poverty, chastity and obedience to translate for me into simplicity, solitude and silence. But I make a poor novice. I continue to be inspired by favourite writers:-

> *I have spoken to you, so that my joy may be in you, and your joy complete. This is my commandment: love one another, as I have loved you. There is no greater love than this, that one should lay down one's life for one's friends. You are my friends, if you do what I command you. I call you servants no longer; a servant does not know what his master is about. I have called you*

friends, because I have disclosed to you
everything that I heard from my Father. You did
not choose me; I chose you. I appointed you to go
on and bear fruit, fruit that shall last; so that the
Father may give you all that you ask in my name.
John 15.11-15

Holy God, be in my mind
that I might let go of all that diminishes
the movement of Your Spirit within me.

Discerning God, be in my eyes,
that I might see You in the midst of all the
busyness that fills my life.

Loving God, be in my heart,
That I can be open to those I love,
to those with whom I share ministry and to the
whole human family.

Gracious God, be in that grace-filled
Silence that lies deep within me,
That I might live in Christ as Christ lives in me.
Anon

Once I knew you, but
Your love was more than I could bear

In my green and chrysalid days, and I fled
Into the familiar, carefully constructed protective
circle of my own devising
and hid there, in quiet desperation.
You sent many messengers to call me out, but
I was stubborn, afraid and persistent.
Yet now, in the midst of my anxiety, depression,
hurt,
my loss, despair and unfulfilled longing
I feel a strange disturbance
as the wind stirring dry leaves,
as though you yourself had found entrance to me
unawares,
And I feel a calling to rise,
to stretch out my hand,
to advance,
to go on pilgrimage again.
So now I seek to muster courage, strength and
hope
To meet the slowly rising surge of expectation
And, as I stand on the cusp of new life, new
promise,
I want to challenge the oppressive dark of gloomy
night
To be gone, to make way for this reborn glory of
God

Who desires with a deep passion
To stride into the emerging dawn of new
possibilities,
To walk towards its light,
Alive with the excitement of new discoveries to be
made,
new love to be found,
An immersion in the ecstasy of creation.
I desire to stand on the highest mountain
And contemplate the receding ridges which
beckon me,
And know I am alive, I am myself, and I am yours.
I want to journey and experience all
Until I find I have stumbled into the everlasting
arms of eternal love
When you will say to me
At last my peace is yours: be still.
I gave you the gift of restlessness
So you might find me, but
Now you can rest in what you have found.
And not only my protecting angels
But I myself will enclose you in the endlessly
immediate adventure
Of pure love, beauty and ecstasy.
Your struggle is over and won'.

Father, Creator, I am ready for the journey.

Let me only travel light that your friendship may
not be obscured
And I may know always where my trust is to be
placed.
Now may I be aware of your presence in face and
fountain
Without wanting to possess and so diminish.
May I without tension appreciate you in all of
your creation
with delight and wonder,
My lover, my end and my beginning, my most
faithful companion on the way.
Untitled Poem by Ian Corbett

It is crucial to remember that, when we are in situations of extremity or exposure and perhaps alone, or when our faith is tested almost to its limits, we have to hold on to what we know even when we cannot feel it, we have to remember that we are of the world even when we are isolated from it. For "no man is an island" and we are always woven into the fabric of humanity. In the Old Testament God speaks primarily to the people rather than to individuals themselves. In the Eastern Orthodox Churches the public prayer book is the only official source of private prayer. In the Creeds we now assert that "we", not "I", believe. God calls us into community and then addresses us. Monks withdrew to the Egyptian desert in the fifth century that they might be more involved in the world by listening to its deepest groaning and responding in intercession. In Africa today most effective evangelism targets groups rather than individuals. This must be recalled when we feel isolated and alone.

In his "The Church" Schillebeeckx reminds us that human beings are the evidence for the existence of God. There is no salvation outside the world – human liberation is the medium of divine revelation. This is sharply illustrated when we say to someone who has moved us, "you were a revelation to me". The Church should be the "brotherhood (and sisterhood) of God", as the Masai in Kenya call it, the communion of those who identify with God incarnate in Jesus, the Body of Christ. It has been said that "people are the words with which God tells his story" – people are the dwelling place of the Creator. Rabbi A J Henschel wrote that "God is compassion". Compassion is not pity but celebration, a way of life, a spirituality of forgiveness and creativity, the fire which the Lord has come to send on the earth. Merton used to say that prayer is impossible for those who do not try to cultivate compassion for others, who are, liberated from the prison of self-concern.

Christians believe that God poured himself into his creation in Jesus of Nazareth simply because he "so loved the world", and love must share itself. If Christ became Man it is because he wanted to be any man and every man. If we believe in the incarnation of the Son of God there should be no one on earth in whom we are not prepared to see, in mystery, the presence of Christ. In the sacrament of the Eucharist this pledge of the Creator is personally experienced and Heaven is open before us. This context of God experienced in his world, especially in our humanity, and in his particular laboratory, the Church, must be grasped and held, because it will be what sustains us when we are lonely and under duress. God often seems either hidden, obscured by the pettiness of the religious institutions that claim him, or a dim echo as in such phrases as "My God!" It is therefore vital to hang on to these perceptions gained in better times to sustain us in the desert, for "he is faithful who calls us".

We may prepare for such times by seeking out silence and solitariness in those better times, by entering into prayer and walking the hills. He who prays searches not only his own heart but he plunges deep into the heart of the world in order to listen more intently to the deepest and most neglected voices that proceed from its inner depths.

Prayer, then, is not primarily something that we do but rather openness to God's activity in us: in our humble waiting the Spirit comes to us, and we and God contemplate each other. We should not expect a false mysticism, special feelings or miraculous experiences. Emotions cannot be our guide here, but the faith and trust that God will pour into us his love. We may experience dryness or temptation but the Spirit feeds us. Doubts and difficulties can be overcome by remembering Mother Mary Clare's wise advice, "If you truly desire a life of prayer, the way to get it is by praying". Prayer is our love affair with God. Prayer becomes love as God looks at us and we at him. Father Benson wrote, "the soul in its littleness looks upon God in his greatness and loves him; and God in his greatness looks upon the soul in its littleness and loves it". Attentive silence is the key. God inhabits silence. Mozart said that silence is the most beautiful feature of music. Listening is as vital in prayer as in human relationships. If we fail to listen we are in monologue not dialogue, we do not hear, we do not learn, we do not communicate. How often could we say both to others and to the Creator, as Michel Quoist puts it in his *Prayers of Life*[55]: "Forgive me, Lord, for we were connected, and now we are cut off". Prayer requires time, regular daily periods, however brief. Our problem often is that we do not take the time to experience what we already possess, the gift of the Spirit. Also we often hold back because we are afraid of where such openness to God may take us. But, when the chips are down, we realize how much we need that connection, and to be grounded in the conviction that God's end for us is union with him in love.

As Mother Teresa said to Malcolm Muggeridge in his "Something Beautiful for God", "We need to find God and he cannot be found in noise and restlessness. God is the friend of silence...The more we receive in silent prayer...the more we can give...The essential thing is not what we say but what God says through us".[56]

So prayer is no casual occupation for any believer. But nor need it be a supreme effort, a thought which deters many. Archbishop William Temple once said, "we must learn to pray as we are and not as we are not". Therefore for some prayer will be mainly silent, for others a passionate outpouring of concerns as often occurred with St Teresa of Avila. Prayer does not guarantee success but a continuing connectedness to the Source of all being which holds us in the face of loneliness, guilt and despondency. When love is demanded of us, even of enemies, the prayer connection is what fuels us. Silence and solitude enable it. And when we can we need to share our discoveries with a "soul friend" with whom we can "review and refine our sense of direction" (Jim Cotter). Prayer can be a risky journey, and we are vulnerable, but it is the lifeline for those on the margins lest they go off the edge. It is how we become friends of God, the God who St Catherine of Siena tells us, "fell in love with us".

Such a God does not wish us to lacerate our souls with penitential whiplashes, crucifying ourselves by brooding over our sins or even by yearning for more experience and illumination, for satisfaction. He rather wishes to pour into us his silence and peace to soothe and heal our passions and imperfections. He wants dialogue and communion with us, to dwell in our poverty and weakness. Especially to those whose searching is in an undefined isolation outside the boundary of "spirituality", where traditional methods and books are not helpful, he moves to meet "outside the gate", welcoming in his compassion. This God who is love, as St John asserts, calls us to live and grow in that love by learning the wisdom of silent attentiveness. And one way into this growth, as part of our contemplation, is to enter into engagement with all that is pure, wise, profound and humane in every kind of culture. This can lead us to know and have confidence in the endless, unfailing mercy of God.

This is why prayer, spirituality, waiting upon God, just waiting – someone who knows me well gave me a sign for my desk which reads, "don't just do something, sit there" – above all, solitude is the place where we can find self acceptance, struggle for integrity, discover liberation – and face the chaos, anger, exhaustion or excitability within. In this space we encounter the "thin places" where the voice and presence from beyond confronts us. In this space we seek to identify the "Kairos", the signs of the times, God's call to us now. With "the mind in the heart", as the Eastern Orthodox put it, we pray to be granted new vision which will bring deeper understanding. We hope for a renewal of our creativity and compassion, and a rediscovery of the joy and passion of being called to be fully human and co-creators with God in his emerging world of justice and peace. We become freshly enabled and can say, "I am not what happened to me, but what I choose to become".

Being called – our vocation – solitude and silence open us up to our responsibility not just for ourselves but for others, for our world. We should indeed hesitate here for this will cost us, as it cost the Son of God. Someone wrote:-

> *The law kills the sinner:*
> *that is the way of damnation.*
> *Love kills the lover:*
> *that is the way of redemption.*

Much may be required from those of much discernment. We may need to strip down for action. Some may even experience a Franciscan call to total renunciation in order to fully serve the poor of the earth. For most of us the call will be gentler.

In my case God first showed me the world's need in its children, in a huge housing estate where nearly ten percent of the school where I taught was on probation. It was like being exposed to an abyss of want, but I was granted the vitality in their eyes and the warmth of their friendship as consolation. But the pain and hurt of humanity seemed endless as I was further led into ministry with Hell's Angels, in bars and prisons, and with the gay, lesbian, bisexual and transgendered community. I was being prepared all the time for the removal of all comfort and security as I was led to Africa, to Lesotho, one of the poorest countries in the world. But, because I now knew God was to be found in these little ones, the oppressed and forgotten ones, I was ready for the challenge of being one of God's many channels of grace in deprived situations. He was indeed gentle with me. I was to discover that I was to be renewed daily by his loving me back in the affection of those to whom I sought to minister. Africa is a good place to experience both the sea of human need and the ocean of God's love. As for the first, Africa is the continent of refugees and, meditating on the Flight into Egypt in his poem, "Among refugees", Albert Radcliffe concludes:-

> *When even God is made a refugee*
> *we can all feel abandoned on the road.*[57]

Or, as is said in American prisons, where a hugely disproportionate number of inmates are of African background – "If you ain't got the capital you get the punishment." As for the second consideration, we find that God always supplies the grace needed to accomplish the tasks he sets us: he never tests us beyond our capacities. As a hymn puts it:

> *Christ leads me through no darker rooms*

than He went through before.[58]

Part of our journey may involve our being led, as we enter the depths of the spiritual life, into a more agonized form of prayer which we might describe as "wrestling with God". The image of Jacob wrestling in Genesis 32 v 24ff is one of the most powerful images of prayer in the scriptures. Similarly Jeremiah's demanding answers from God in the so-called confessional passages of his prophecy (Jeremiah 20 v 7ff), and Job's accusing God in Job 3 v 1ff are arresting reminders of the need for total honesty and transparency in prayer. David Jenkins used to say that "God is in reality" – and only in reality, not in our illusions and evasions. He also said that "God is as he is in Jesus", reminding us of God's readiness to receive us like the father of the prodigal son (Luke 15 v 11ff).

The three goals that I identified for myself during a pre-retirement conference for clergy clearly were going to involve considerable dialogue with God if they were to be realized. The first was:-

"to know the ecstasy of being in love with, and being loved by, God, the world and myself; to experience all of God and Creation that I possibly can; to explore with an utter recklessness and deep passion, to walk in beauty and freedom".

The second was:-

"to become more a person in community than a person isolated; to search for and be open to a partner with whom to share the ecstasy and the passion".

And the third was:-

"to review, make connections and find some synthesis in my life, so that I may offer it meaningfully to God at the end".

I think I saw myself, as the last and unknown stage of my life began, a movement towards retirement and beyond, like the traveller in Carl David Friedrich's painting as he stands on the summit of a mountain contemplating all the further ranges still to come. I was nothing if not ambitious and would certainly need some deep spiritual reserves for the forthcoming pilgrimage. This would require of me a process of envisioning – identifying the core aspects of my identity and vocation; my passions, strengths and vulnerabilities; my goals and objectives. It would mean examining my work and its meaning and where my faith and my dreams might be leading me. I would have to look at my capacity for creativity and change partly by checking out how I handled issues in the past. And I would be confronted by some basic and inescapable questions:-

Who am I? (who has God created me to be?);

Who am I called to be? (what does God's heart yearn for me? How is the Holy Spirit restless in me right now?)

What are the good habits required to sustain my response to God's call and the Spirit's presence?

Who am I becoming? (how am I changing – what new identity is seeking to be born?)

It was a struggle to move towards answers to these life questions, demanding sacrifice of time, intellectual enquiry and emotional engagement. But some realizations dawned; particularly that God had both placed me and revealed himself where my deep passion and the world's great needs met. I could see that I tried always to say Yes to God and that God had always seen me through; that light had generally followed darkness and that had given me the confidence to endure and persist. By examining my past in order to enable my future I now understood

Soren Kierkegaard's maxim that "life is to be lived forward but understood backwards". I came, through this wrestling, to understand myself better as Henri Nouwen's "wounded healer" and was better able to embrace my failings and shortcomings and move on with a quiet confidence. Of course, not all issues were resolved, particularly that of close personal relationships, but I felt that I had entered into a deeper level of discourse with God, myself and the world.

But not all such striving will be as clear and positive in its outcome. Despair is always the great enemy raging at the gate, the inarticulate expression of the terror we cannot face, perhaps the terror of having to face up to being oneself. Or we may be tempted by the pursuit of ephemeral desires as a substitute for true joy, a ceaseless quest for new satisfactions. The fundamental theme of Ecclesiastes, writes Thomas Merton, is the paradox that, although there is nothing new under the sun, each new generation of mankind is condemned by nature to wear itself out in the pursuit of novelties that do not exist. Saint Gregory of Nyssa, commenting on the same book, observes how time weaves about us a web of illusion: we spin a whole net of falsities around us by the repeated consecration of ourselves to wrong values. Pascal remarks, "Distraction is the only thing that consoles us for our miseries and yet it is, itself, the greatest of our miseries". Distraction turns us aside from our ascent to truth.

If, like the Desert Fathers, we would find our own true selves in God then we tread a path that is largely uncharted but freely chosen because it is personal to us. We have to die to false values if we are to discern the inner, hidden reality of ourselves that is transcendent, mysterious and rooted in God. And, considering the dark times in which we live, it is a case not only of making time and space for our own spiritual quest but, in so doing, to save not only ourselves but the world. We are like those early Egyptian hermits who left the world as though escaping from a wreck because they knew they were helpless to do any good for themselves or others as long as they floundered about in the wreckage. Once they gained foothold on solid ground they had the capacity and obligation to pull the whole world to safety after them. But, of course, there is no guarantee of a successful outcome, and the demons know how fragile we are. One of the worst frustrations is to know ourselves blocked in our quest, separated from our source.

Sometimes we enter the profound darkness of depression. It is an old friend to me, difficult to define but characterized by prolonged periods of hopelessness. We are not depressed about anything but find ourselves in our own (and therefore lonely and isolated) valley of death. Acknowledging it is the first step, and the second is to seek some medical help, at least to relieve some of the immediate symptoms (often extreme exhaustion). Someone to be "there for us", as we say, is important, but not someone who will say very much. Job's "comforters" were most useful when they were silent. A presence is what is required. We should try to keep praying, maybe using the Psalms or the Jesus Prayer – nothing of any length. Try to remember the value of quiet time, even if it is now deathly quiet. It is in silence and stillness that God comes. When we do not remember the silence, the silence may remember us. If certain memories haunt the mind use them, do not let them use you; try to understand what they are saying to you now. Above all, depression is a question of endurance: it sometimes acquires a value, but only in retrospect. It renders us naked to ourselves but only in innocence do our masks fall away. We see hidden facets of ourselves. These can be fruitful in our future meditation. Depression can reveal to us what needs to be healed.

We are entering into discussion of the problem of suffering and the theological conundrum of theodicy, why a God of love permits suffering, "the roar which lies on the other side of silence". The great explorer of this dark area is the Russian novelist Fyodor Dostoyevsky: if you dare to read his vast *The Brothers Karamazov* you will never be the same again. There are many problems – the apparent inefficiency of intercessory prayer, the conclusion that God is either weak or cruel, the existence of free will. The problem of suffering becomes the problem of faith. Indeed, most suffering is not positive in outcome, and the idea of suffering inflicted as punishment is abhorrent to us.

I have to say that I have no more satisfactory answer to this central question of faith than any other writer I know. The only clue in justifying the ways of God to men lies in the relationship with him we fitfully glimpse in prayer. He's always there in our sadness and in our joy. He never lets us down and never lets us go. He suffers with us. Black South Africans, during the apartheid era, called themselves "a crucified people", perhaps recalling that the one most significantly crucified in Christian tradition was said to have risen again and therefore blazed a trail through the apparently closed circle of sin, disaster and death. The hope is that God in Christ will see us through our suffering by sharing it, bearing it with us, in perfect solidarity, so that, just as he has condescended to us in our sorrow, so we will in some way, either here or hereafter, being raised into the eternal joy of the Holy Trinity. Heaven is a logical necessity in the Christian dispensation. Whether it, and the linked theologies of Incarnation and Redemption, are an adequate response to the unfathomable depths of human degradation is a moot point. I can only cling to that elusive spiritual connectedness, that "still, small voice", which can yet be as ambiguous as any Greek oracle.

The dilemma becomes more profound when we encounter problems in making connections with the Creator. We now know that Mother Teresa spent much of her life without any sense of the presence of God. "The silence and the emptiness is so great", she wrote, "I listen and do not hear". She lived in a state of abiding spiritual pain. Words such as dryness, darkness, loneliness, torture, frequent her correspondence. It was a long, dark night of the soul and yet she abandoned neither her belief nor her work. She even came to love the darkness as a way of participating in Jesus' continuing pain over the sinfulness of humankind. She was particularly helped by a perceptive spiritual adviser who told her that there was no human remedy for her condition, that it is not necessary to feel the presence of Jesus to know he is there, and that her craving for God was a sure sign of his hidden presence in her life. Her pain could be a grace. And her life may be an encouragement to us in our lesser darkness. It may help us to realize that commitment, fidelity and vulnerability are more important than our feelings. She is a stunning example of faithful, self-emptying love.

What she shows us, however, in our present discussion is the centrality of holding on to solitude and silence and expecting them to be zones of revelation. If not always for Mother Teresa then for many in this stillness relationships can take on a new warmth and wonder, and we learn not to fear because God is discovered in the quietness. Suffering must be endured but if we go deep into it in the silence we may go beyond loneliness and emptiness into a sense of intimacy and shelter. Teilhard de Chardin wrote about descending into the obscure depths of the self and, to our surprise, finding God there (cf Psalm 139). It is the absence of silence that accounts for so much stress in our lives. The Desert Fathers advised going and sitting in one's cell – "and your cell will teach you all things". Being in the silence gives us space to listen, to dream, to integrate negativity and find harmony, to be kind to our failures and free ourselves of regret, and to be generous – even learning to love our enemies. In this rich and creative solitude the torment subsides. The longest and most exciting journey is the journey inwards. Cardinal Newman said that to grow is to change, and that to grow perfect is to change often. Each day is an adventure, every place potentially sacred, as the old Celtic prayers suggest. Time given to silence and solitude enables this growth and development. As some African porters for an over-eager colonial official declared when they refused to go further: "we have moved too quickly to reach here - now we need to wait to give our spirits a chance to catch up with us".

6. Endings and Beginnings

And the last enemy that shall be overcome is death

We are all afraid of death, or at the very least of dying. Again those silent and solitary times, whether chosen of forced upon us, come to the rescue. I draw very much on the wise thought of John O'Donohue[59] here. *"The fall of a person's life can be a time of great gathering: it is a time for harvesting the fruits of your experiences".* As the body loses strength the soul seems to gain it. *"The beauty and institution of old age offers a time of silence and solitude for a visit to the house of your inner memory".* We may revisit the past in an attempt to make sense of it, to integrate the elements of a perhaps fragmentary life. We may examine what we have neglected, what inner wounds cry out for healing, what anger and resentments we are nursing, and how we have lacked compassion for ourselves. "Je ne regrette rien" sang Edith Piaf – that is our goal. We should not be anxious for what is to come. *"How you view your future actually shapes it – expectation helps to create the future".* The serenity of old age should not be a myth but should creep upon us unawares. We have a wisdom to share, and a stability that should enable an easier openness to life – to God, self, the other and the world. And as we are filled with gratitude for what has been, what is, and what is promised, we can learn to let go and "let God".

Death itself can be prepared for by regarding life as a succession of little deaths, as we seek to let go of material excess and possessiveness in relationships so that, at the end, death is something we do rather than something that happens to us. It is when we say to God, *"here I am, take all that I am, I now hand over my entire self to you".* Death should not come to us as a stranger or a robber but as a friend. Life is short, yet in its span we have come to know something of the mystery of both ourselves and God and so can, perhaps, now offer it back to its Creator. It is true that ultimately we die alone, and that is a solemn moment, but dying well takes a good time, both in preparation and in the unhurried departure of the soul, which may hover around beyond bodily expiry. There is a very thin veil between this world and the next as most indigenous people know. In many traditions the dying person will know themselves visited by departed friends to welcome him home. The dead are our nearest neighbours, just over the horizon. We are given all we need to die without fear. Death is the liberation of the self so preparing for it is not a case of anticipating extinction but of living life to the full. Death is not an end but a rebirth, in each instance physical and spiritual, from darkness to light. We see death from only one side. The body goes home to the earth, the spirit to its Creator. The dead are close, all around us, and the eternal world interpenetrates our own temporal existence. When my seminary principal would return from a mid week celebration of the Eucharist at a nearby church we would always ask him at breakfast how it had gone and how many communicants were there. He would always return the same answer – that the church was full but the congregation was largely invisible.

Death is the one certainty of life. It should always be our care to contemplate it, not only to prepare ourselves but to assist us in preparing others. Death for the unbeliever can only be a terribly final snuffing out of life. Nothing is more difficult for the priest than counselling atheists and agnostics at the end of their lives. Some people can heroically meet death face to face but cannot depart this life with the joy and peace that should be theirs. We have faith that the God who has conquered death will receive and surprise them.

The future is more beautiful than all pasts
Author unknown

Conclusion

Through all the blessings and vicissitudes of life two convictions have never deserted me. Firstly, that, whatever doubts and darkness I may have endured, there is a Creator to whom I feel compelled to respond. Secondly, that the glory of the universe, and of human life within it, lies in its diversity.

Or, firstly in the words of Dag Hammerskgold:

> *I do not know who – or what – put the question. I don't know when it was put. I don't even remember answering. But at some moment I did answer Yes to Someone – or Something – and from that hour I was certain that existence is meaningful and that, therefore, my life, in self-surrender, had a goal. From that moment I have known what it means "not to look back" and "to take no thought for the morrow.*[60]

> *So do not be afraid of the darkness: just as the summit of the mountain recedes from sight as we climb nearer "so the closer we come to God the darker our faith may become, undiluted now by the half-light of created images and concepts. In the culture of fear that has come to characterise western society since 9/11, together with a false*

ethic of safety that follows in its wake – violence as a means of control – it may be more difficult to discern the hand of Providence in human affairs, so we need more than ever to keep the faith, our conviction, that our lives and our world constitute a coherent story, a drama, in which God and humankind together drive the story toward its proper conclusion.

Scott Bader-Saye[61]

R. E. C. Brown, in *Love of the World*, says:-

We cannot make ourselves safe but we can be safe in God in whom we live and move and have our being. He will always receive us so long as we are ready to receive him.......In life there is nothing more dangerous than acting to secure your safety; you must run both the risk of society and the risk of solitude: faith gives us boldness to banish caution.

What paralyzes life is failure to believe and failure to dare. The day will come when, after harnessing space, the winds, the tides and gravitation we shall harness for God the energies of love. And, on that day, for the second time in the history of the world we shall have discovered fire.[62]

Teilhard de Chardin also wrote:-

There is only one road that can lead to God and this is fidelity, to remain constantly true to yourself, to what you feel is highest in you. The road will open before you as you go.[63]

A Franciscan Blessing

May God bless you with discomfort at easy answers, half truths, and superficial relationships, so that you may live deep within your heart. Amen.

May God bless you with anger at injustice, oppression, and exploitation of people, so that you may work for justice, freedom and peace. Amen.

May God bless you with tears to shed for those who suffer from pain, rejection, starvation and war, so that you may reach out your hand to comfort them and turn their pain to joy. Amen.

May God bless you with enough foolishness to believe that you can make a difference in this world, so that you can do what others claim cannot be done. Amen.

And the Blessing of God, who Creates, Redeems, and Sanctifies, be upon you and all you love and pray for this day, and forever more. Amen.

A Celtic Blessing

May the peace of the Lord Christ go with you,
wherever he may send you,
May he guide you through the wilderness,
protect you through the storm.
May he bring you home rejoicing
at the wonders he has shown you,
May he bring you home rejoicing
once again into our doors.

When I look back upon my life nigh spent,
Nigh spent, although the stream as yet flows on,
I more of follies than of sins repent,
Less for offence than love's shortcomings moan.
With self, O Father, leave me not alone –
Leave not with the beguiler the beguiled;
Besmirched and ragged, Lord, take back thine
own:
A fool I bring thee to be made a child.
George MacDonald[64]

APPENDIX I

from the Revd Canon Ian D Corbett MA, M Sc.
Canon Missioner
Anglican Diocese of Botswana

Tel. Botswana 352115
c /o Anglican Diocesan Office
P O Box 769
Gaborone
BOTSWANA
September 1993

Dear

This is by far the most difficult letter I have ever tried to write, containing, as it must, elements of painful news, confession and 'apologia pro vita mea'.

The first awkwardness I feel is that some of you do not yet know the trauma I have been undergoing this year. I cannot face telling the whole story yet again, so let me merely explain that my long silence is a consequence of my having had my contract in Zimbabwe terminated without notice by my bishop, who plotted secretly with the immigration authorities to have me expelled from the country. No reason has been given, then or since. I fled first to South Africa, and then Botswana, before returning to England, where this is being written.

The update is that the Bishop of Harare has ignored the ultimatum from the Archbishop of Central Africa (in Botswana) to summon the Appeal Tribunal to which I am entitled, and so now has to be indicted by the Archbishop for his defiance. This could result in his suspension so the situation is very grave. The Archbishop has been strongly affirming and supportive of me, and we have decided, whatever the legal outcome, that it would be impossible for me in practice to work again with such a man, so I have been happy to accept his offer of a similar post here in Botswana, based at the cathedral in Gaborone. I am just about now in a state ready to look forward to this with great enthusiasm. 'Let today embrace the past with remembrance and the future with longing' (Kahlil Gibran). And I shall be well placed geographically to keep in touch with friends in Lesotho and Zimbabwe.

After all this upheaval, which included my being quite ill again earlier this year, my uppermost feeling now is one of great thankfulness, firstly to all of you who were aware of my predicament. Your letters with their persistent care and concern were a lifeline: many of them I know I shall always keep and treasure and some of them helped the tears to flow therapeutically just when my own state of shock and my automatically strong reflexes of suppression were such a block to healing. Without this experience, I should never have realised just how much I am loved, and held in this love: I cannot understand how you can all be so extravagantly generous in your affections when I cannot love myself, but I have to accept it and acknowledge my need of it, with the profoundest gratitude and humility. 'Your friend is your needs answered' (Kahlil Gibran). Friends in Zimbabwe as well as in England were equally solicitous, and if you could have seen some of the scores of letters from all over Mashonaland, especially from the youth, so affirming and loving that I could never reveal then, you would realise how mistaken my bishop must be in his judgement. Perhaps love knows its own depths only in the time of separation. Not least I am deeply grateful to Norma and Neil in South Africa, and to Judith and Tim in Botswana – true friends of long standing, who nursed me through this crisis by their steadfastness and patience at a very critical tine.

Secondly, I am thankful to God, who does not let me down and does not let me go. It seemed at the time the action of a nest cruel God (as Iago sings in Verdi's 'Otello') to tear me away from Zimbabwe so soon, and when I had not even recovered from leaving Lesotho. But He knew that it was at just such a tine of confidence in my African ministry that I was mature enough to be hounded by Him, stripped bare of my defences, prepared for the furnace and reforged more in conformity with His will and image: that, at least, must be my hope as He has forced me to a painful confrontation with myself and His boundless demand. He has enabled me, through all this, never to doubt His ultimate graciousness or feel insecure in my 'I – Thou' relations hip with Him, even when I have known the heat of His wrath, which is but a facet of His burning, passionate, irresistible love. I do at present experience great difficulties with the Church, which has revealed itself in my own life to require a shaking of its foundations, to be declared a site of struggle, and my prayer life is fractured and intermittent. But Him I could never doubt. And I now see that, in a very small way, He has enabled me to draw closer to Africa in that I have experienced just a little of the lot of most Africans – homelessness, joblessness, resourcelessness – and, if that is His intention, I gladly embrace my condition. Not so much is God in my heart as I am in the heart of God.

Indeed, thirdly I am grateful to Africa and African who have sustained me through this dark night: without the inspiration of the land and the unquestioning love of so many people expressed only as Africans can, I think I would have broken down completely and perhaps ended my ministry here – Africa, which alternately succours you and sucks you dry, Leaving such people is a great ache and burden for I have been neither a stranger nor a guest among them, but a son and a friend (in Zimbabwe).

I have never sought to avoid suffering for those to whom I am committed and I must now turn to this as my next theme. For even as love crowns you, so he also crucifies you – the pain of so much tenderness. I am in a very fragile state physically, mentally, emotionally and spiritually – drained, perhaps wounded by my own understanding of love. I suspect I have never really recovered from the chain of illnesses I contracted during my latter years in Lesotho, as the strains of an impossible work – load and the sheer demand of Africa took their toll. For the exposure at once to so much beauty (the mountains and the people) and to so much sheer total need was overwhelming. You will remember that I then had to face the collapse of my work after I left, owing to a quite unsuitable replacement, and now, of course, the collapse of the work in Zimbabwe, especially the youth work to which I was so devoted. In fact, I can now see that from 1990 onwards I have been undergoing something of a prolonged, insidious nervous breakdown, and I began a huge new task in Harare carrying this heavy burden. Neither I nor the doctors realised this while I was on leave last year, though I suspect that some of you did. I can scarcely bring myself to say this, but perhaps if I had been able to persevere with such challenging responsibilities in Zimbabwe I could have collapsed this year anyway. Has God, in fact, been protecting me by withdrawing me now? Nevertheless, for the first time in my life, I do feel anxious about my health; despite months of inaction this year, while admittedly being under great stress, I still feel exhausted and ill. If it is not M.E., then I must need more counselling in the widest sense, than I suspect. The trouble is that, because the events of the last two years have left me in a condition of shock and numbness, it is difficult to be aware of what I really feel or think or want.

I am aware of a brokenness, and with it a sense of my own pathetic crucifixion on the altar of love, having perhaps reached out to too many and therefore failed some. But I also know I do not really agree with this prudent caution, and my being in Christ tells me I am not wrong to pour mys elf out as He continually does. Perhaps it is just the inevitable failure and pain I find difficult to bear. Yet I am coming to find the courage to accept that this sort of weakness is precisely what God can use and turn to strength. I have tried to do too much for Him and not enough in and with Him, too much for others rather than with them. But the pain of giving is a sort of baptism: we give to live, for to withhold is to perish. Indeed, despite all the problems, I have to admit that the poor quality of my past oral care acquired new depths in Lesotho, and that, despite my habitual underpreparedness, my teaching and preaching attained greater potency in Zimbabwe: God was able to use me either despite or because of my exhaustion, my fallen defences rendering me perhaps more transparent to Him. I can now see Him speaking through rather than healing such brokenness: wholeness does not necessarily imply cure. And the deeper that sorrow carves into your being, the more joy you can contain (Kahlil Gibran).

I have too, to face my pride and my anger, the humiliation and resentment at having a lifestyle that requires justification exposed, at having work terminated, at the brutal severing of so many relationships that matter – all in terms of the bishop's action, so publicly done and with little hope of effective restitution. I still find it impossible to try to express the hurt at being forcibly separated from so many in Zimbabwe bound to me by mutual need and, giving of ourselves, the trampling in the African dust of so many 'little ones' through whose eyes Christ shone, yes, the blasphemy of the Church' itself spitting in the face of its Lord. I know that Neil and Norma in Natal, having just fostered a Zulu boy will understand when I say that, after all this, being cloistered in the white highlands of Pieter-maritzburg seemed at times like an imprisonment, being out off from African love and laughter just when I needed it most. The Shona say 'friendship is kinship'. I think I can now begin to face and accept all this in a new way and try to do something with it. Confessing it to you is at least a start!

But I must come to this central issue of relationships, for me the core of both life and gospel, and what, of course, binds me to you – that God is Love (St John), that ultimate reality is gracious (Tillich), that the relationships between agents are more important than the agents themselves (Whitehead), that 'a person is a person through other persons' (a saying common in the cultures of southern Africa, the principle of 'ubuntu', humanness or togetherness). The awful irony in the whole of the Corbett Affair is that I suspect Bishop Hatendi saw something of this truth in me but misinterpreted it. I referred above to the issue of 'life style': this is the word the bishop has gossiped to others about me, and perhaps contains the essence of his fear of me. I assume that he thinks that I have too many of what the old confessional manuals used to call 'particular relationships'. For me, this is what life is about. You cannot love in general (the Greek word 'agape', used occasionally by St Paul) if you do not love in particular (the Greek word 'eros'): indeed, I strongly suspect that even for God Himself there is little distinction between the two. When two people discover each other in mutual wonder, acceptance and affect ion, they create a dynamo of love which knows no bounds, which opens out into the universality and fullness of life itself and becomes part of the loving of God Himself. This connection between the love of God and the love of lovers is suggested by two quotations which have burned themselves into my mind.

Othello says to his Desdemona, 'When I love you not, chaos comes again' when his jealousy flames to threaten their bond, it seems to poison the whole environment, primeval chaos replacing the order of the Spirit's creativity. Thinking of his Beatrice, the poet Dante writes: 'Already my heart and will were wheeled by love, The love that moves the sun and the other stars'. Again, the passionate love of human relating is part of the continuum, the spectrum, of divine love in its totality. D H Lawrence even suggests that sexual union at its most profound is a type of Holy Communion. To me the friend has always been the most meaningful gate to heaven, the most sure route to the heart of Jesus, rivalled but not surpassed by the more conventional ways of prayer and worship. If I have any gift at all, it is for befriending, and for being able to elicit a quality of trust ibm others. Literally every day I am bowled over by the beauty and worth of people, of perfectly ordinary people, who, to me unbelievably escape the attention of others. And I have always believed in exploring any opport unities for human converse that present themselves in a world growing ever more dehumanised and brutalised: they are almost signs of defiance, protest, hope and joy in a bleak and barren universe. Sometimes I expose myself to too much loving, often ignoring convention, and therefore frequently I must fail people, but the biggest effort in my life is to try to ensure that where death rather than life results, the hurt is mine to bear rather than the others. In the tunnel of the last two years, where life has seemed to close in, my own neurosis has driven me to err on the side of too many personal adventures because of my desperate need of affirmation, affection and tender loving care when I have been unable to love myself. But even where I have taken so much I have also tried to give. Yet my loving has developed a pathology which I hope I am now correcting. However, I would still defiantly say, better the sins of love than the sins of hate. And that loving has been my lifeline, my survival, even my intimation of divine glory in the place of human darkness. Also, without being so fed, I could not draw upon the depths of love that fuel a very pro – active ministry. Clearly, conservative bishops will always find me unsound, a threat, a subversive I am not a system man, and shall never achieve the sort of position in the Church which would enable me, in grace, to try to mould it into something a little more accepting and forgiving. I am always, likely to be its victim, and, if all this is indeed the matter of the Bishop of Harare's panic, then I suppose I have been blessed in not suffering Episcopal censure much earlier in my career God bless the Bishops of Manchester and Lesotho! It was T S Elliot who observed that man 'cannot bear too much reality', and the institutional church has always persecuted love. It was one of the great privileges of my life on a walk with David Jenkins, Bishop of Durham, to weep with him for the Church's inability to ever have understood the love of Christ. 'Christianity has not been tried and found wanting: it has never been tried.' 'Only a crucified God can help', Bonhoeffer wrote from prison and not even the Church can accept that.

My basic contention is that only the person who knows the grace of deep, uninhibited, passionate relationships can love the world in service and ministry the one fires the other, or else the latter becomes a case of patronising charity. I would claim that many great Christian lives support this. Certainly it is in my attempting to live out, terribly inadequately, these twin commitments to the individual and the world, particularly those marginalised within it, that I have discovered the passion of God, in both senses of the word. How can a God who empties himself into his creation (Philippians 2 vv 5 – 11), who enters it incognito and is 'edged out of his own world on the Cross'

(Bonhoeffer again), love us with anything less than a mighty passion? And how can a God who forsakes his power and wagers everything on the invincibility of His love, and who then stakes the future of His creation on eliciting our response (waiting, suffering – His Passion – from His being tried in Jesus by us His creatures until now), not love us with an unbelievable intensity, like that of the lover? This is a God who became one of us, identifies with us (the God with a human face), and who still suffers and loves in us (not least in the dispossessed of Africa). To me, the most potent symbol of God in the New Testament is Jesus washing the disciples' feet (John 13). Jesus even talked of our feeding on Him (John 6), rather as British lovers sometimes say to their loved ones, 'you look good enough to eat'! Well, I want to follow a God like that, and take you with me. Of course, there are moral parameters to loving that cannot concern us here.

Society always fears moral anarchy, but it is most afraid of truth permanently off the leash, the love that threatens its structures of control. Society distrusts, too, love that dares to speak its name across barriers of age and class. Those to whom I am closest are usually younger than me. That is because I cherish their capacity for enthusiasm, passion and exploration, and find myself ever rejuvenated by innocence and confidence not yet corrupted by cynicism, despair and more experience than they can bear. Indeed, I sometimes think that theirs is the only real world and that there is no adult world at all. 'Youth is reckless, generous and valuable, but the world of wise, mature and organised adults, for which youth is supposed to be a preparation, does not exist' (Peter Lennon on the student revolution, Paris, May 1968). Well, 'the sixties' was the most formative era for me! I suppose I do seek more to be like the young than to make them like me.

Yet as the original sin of humankind is not to love enough rather than to love too much, I have been content, at times, to risk loving unwisely rather than not to love at all. I don't regret that. I am more conscious of loving with 'too small a heart', a memorable phase I recall from an otherwise insipid, forgettable paperback novel bought from a railway station bookstall. I also remember great words of John Donne:

'Whom God loves He loves to the end: and not to their end, and to their death, but to His end, and His end is that He might love them more.'

My dilemma now is that I feel a 'burnt out case', as Graham Greene put it. Yet I know, and try to internalise the thought that God can use my brokenness as He can use nothing else, and also that I find myself bound to Africa as surely as Captain Nemo to Melville's Moby Dick. 'Africa always wins' is a rather resigned white settler saying! I cannot have a career, but I can continue to wait upon Africans in this terrible aftermath of what we have done to them, when the whole continent survives on the edge of catastrophe. But as Rob Haarhoff, a dear friend in Zimbabwe, says, 'all problems are opportunities'. So even as I write, there immediately floods into my mind the open faces of the children playing with their ingeniously crafted wire cars, the elegance and warm companionship of the youth, the friendly motherliness and insistent greetings of the village women as they go to the fields, the stories and shared experience of the old men round the fire at night, the vigour and rowdiness of the shebeens, the brilliant panoply of jewelled stars set in the blackest of African skies, the cacophony of bird song at dawn, iridescent and dust – swathed sunrises and sunsets, the cataclysmic storms that try to deafen and blind, the distant singing of shepherd boys, the eternal mountains, the endless bush, the cry of the fish eagle...Africa beckons. As a white, my models and heroes remain the more distant and, the most recent, omitting the period of the 'scramble for Africa', namely the Protestant missionaries in Lesotho and Albert Schweitzer in the Congo, who alike sought to understand, respect, learn, love and serve, rather than patronise, prejudge, dominate, exploit and manipulate. There is so much to learn from Africa, and I am only a beginner.

I wanted to be honest with you. I find this very hard as I scarcely know myself. And what I have here set down cannot be all the truth, and may even misrepresent it. The problem of Moses and Aaron again, how to express truth in words.

Forgive me.

With love and prayer.

APPENDIX 2

LEADERSHIP IN MISSION

PART 1: SIX IMPERATIVES

I take it to mean that 'domestic mission' implies a movement of the local church towards a group or area that is of a markedly different culture than that of the congregation reaching out. This applies equally to ministry with ethnic minorities as to certain aspects of youth work or industrial mission. I also have a conviction that certain basic principles of operating remain the same whether the missioner-in-charge is of a culture of the sending or that of the receiving group. Many mistakes have been made in recent years by missioners ostensibly of the tradition of the receiving group being so inculturated by the sending group that they have in practice lost touch with the customs and thought of the group of which they were once a part.

The first imperative is that the missioner listens. Too much of the history of missions is a tale of 'salvation models' being imported into indigenous cultures, a one-way traffic where the missioner assumes moral superiority and greater knowledge than those to whom he is sent. It accounts, for example, for why early European missionaries to the Americas thought that native peoples had no religion when they saw no buildings for it and discovered the very word did not exist in their vocabularies. Rather must contact be in the nature of dialogue, in which each party listens and shares, and mutually decides what sort of communication is desirable.

This heralds the second imperative, which is that the missioner himself must be prepared to be evangelised. Even liberal Christians tend to assume that, in the end, if this dialogue takes place, the other side will see the light and want conversion. But in truly open conversation either side may be convinced by the other. I found that my whole prayer life was reinvigorated by learning how to pray with the native peoples who welcomed me. We also tend to assume that a pristine gospel exists somewhere out there in the ether that merely needs to be pulled down into our situation to be understood and accepted. But the gospel has always been inculturated, that is, expressed in the form of its receiving culture, whether Hebrew of Greek. It is our task to re-express it in different cultural forms as it goes global so that it may be "understanded of the people". In the process we any find our own expressions of belief challenged and in need of modification.

The third imperative is, don't evangelise! Mission precedes evangelism. The World Council of Churches has defined mission as bringing all the resources of God to bear upon all of human need'. Particularly in situations of extremity we offer the love of God in practical form without stint and without conditions. 'Nothing can separate us from the love of God' - or shouldn't! There will be times, however, when it is appropriate to give an account of our involvement, especially when asked, and it is then that evangelism happens - but, again, by conversation and dialogue, not by argument and hectoring which is an affront to the hospitality with which we are normally received. Missionaries tend to be better at the gospel that at the cultures they enter, and they need to be good at both. Adequate preparation is vital.

Fourthly, the local culture must be respected and entered into. This is a slow process of learning when we may appear to be doing nothing. And this involves at least some attempt to learn a foreign language where appropriate. Native American languages are usually very difficult for outsiders, but even a poor attempt to speak is appreciated, and a study of the language reveals much about ways of thinking and believing. If you cannot express your faith in similar ways it will not be heard and understood in the local culture. You will perhaps spend more time in learning than in doing what you thought an effective missionary should.

The fifth imperative is that leadership style must reflect that of the local group. Sitting in a large circle guarantees more democratic participation than sitting in serried ranks and this is the norm among Native American and many African societies. Examine how women and children may participate: they may exercise more equality than you would expect. Leadership is best exercised collaboratively and in community. We often fall back into 'the teacher (or Father) knows' mentality because we lose patience with the time required for more consultative procedures. First peoples operate on an expansive time-scale and so, often, do young people of all traditions.

The sixth imperative is, as has been suggested, substantial preparatory training. The missioner needs to be a person of great self reliance: he or she will often be in situations that cannot be foreseen and in which no support is ready to hand; acquiring survival skills may be as important a part of training as acquiring theological skills. Secondly, the missioner needs a personal spirituality of real depth to sustain him or her, a capacity to live with and out of silence, a regular pattern of prayer, a still centre and beliefs that have been tested in the trials and tribulations of life. The missioner then requires a breadth of learning, both in study and in situ, that is not skimped or done down, as is the present trend. Not a minute of extensive preparation is wasted. Without it people's lives may be damaged and wasted - as has often been the missionary's legacy.

God himself is the Great Missioner. God is in perpetual engagement with the created world, seeking always to bring order out of chaos, good out of evil. God seeks our cooperation in this task, and works with and through us, or, if we fail to respond, entirely without us. But the mission is God's, not ours, and is to be done in God's way, not ours. We are given as models the Suffering Servant of Isaiah, the taking on of our humanity by God in the Incarnation, and the waiting upon the Father of Jesus in his Passion. We are not given the model discerned in the angry, impatient priest by so many first peoples over the ages of a wrathful and vengeful God in comparison to whom their traditional deities were preferable. So let us now move with a new modesty and grace, humbly recognising that in those to whom we minister God is already present and in their faces smiles out at us.

PART 2: THREE QUESTIONS

Of what I have just written I am confident. I am also sure of what I now offer for reflection, while being aware that these issues are enough to deter the most conscientious outreach worker. I am not confident of the answers.

The point about missionaries being open to change as much as their charges raises a huge potential problem. It could be that the missioner will find himself in conflict with the sending body over adopting measures that, while making perfect sense in context, may appear strange and unsettling to those in ultimate authority. So sending bodies ideally need to have a real understanding of the issues we are considering. Furthermore, it could be, in certain cases, that, if a truly indigenous local Christianity emerges, it may not look totally like its origins. For example, where an indigenous form of Navajo Christianity to develop, I feel that Jesus would not appear quite as unique as in traditional western expressions. He would be one of the 'Yei, the Holy People, probably chief among the Yei, but not the absolutely unique Son of God that we know. Indeed, the Navajo already experience a multiple incarnation in the masked dancers on the last night of the Yeibichei ceremony. We are faced with the dilemma, is this acceptable? Are we willing to travel this road? Are we ready to be the midwives of a new and different sort of Reformation?

Then, again, native peoples are shaped by their relationship to the land, and some disaffected youth groups by the security they find in their ghettos. Yet this sort of identity is not understood by Western, urban Christians who have lost this sense of attachment, this ability to live as part of the natural world rather than as its exploiter. So we do not understand one of the vital components of the lives of many of those to whom we would seek to minister - unless, perhaps, we can find the courage to sit alongside them, learn from them, and find our own lives enriched. The Hopi, for instance, have opened more of their traditional ceremonies to outsiders because they are convinced that they have knowledge of how to live in the world that all of us need to participate in if we are not to destroy it.

But the most frightening thing of all is that the true missioner inevitably becomes what has been described as a social martyr': cut off to a large extent from his own roots yet never able to become frilly a member of the group to which he goes the missioner is stretched between the two, one might say in a cruciform position, belonging to neither the one nor the other. He will commonly he misunderstood, sometimes shunned, sometimes reviled. Yet for the sake of the work he must endure. Minorities are only too used to well-meaning rich and/or white people bursting into their lives, usually uninvited, promising the Earth, and then not standing the pace and disappearing. Endurance is the key mark of the missioner but it may come at great cost. The isolation can be a heavy cross to bear.

Any candidate must consider these issues. Any sending body must know into what situation they are dispatching people. No obvious success can be expected. Even youth situations can be fraught with danger. In my ministry with bikers in the seventies I had to submit to all sorts of hair-raising escapades - on bikes - to become accepted by the group, arid only then could work begin. Young pudeople stand a better chance of surviving these challenging vocations and this is in itself a great challenge to the whole Church in its nurturing of its youth.

In fact, we need, as never before, missioners of the character and vision of those who brought the faith first to Europe and then across the seas, but also missioners who would perform the task with more understanding and compassion than they often did. This is the real call of God to the Church today.

The Very Revd Ian D Corbett MA, MSc

REFERENCES

[1] Philip Wetherell, *When you are Dying: A personal exploration of life, suffering and belief*, 2011 Gilead Books Publishing

[2] Letters of Sigmund Freud, *To Edward L. Bernays*, August 10 1929

[3] Thomas Merton, *Thoughts in Solitude*, 1958 Farrar, Straus & Cudahy New York permission applied for Curtis Brown Ltd New York

[4] Moss Campion in Mountain Gazette No. 85 published by Sumitt Publishing, Boulder Colorado

[5] One of the reasons I was convinced that the theft was an inside job was the support of a local medicine man. One of my students, in whom I had confided, pressed me to consult one in whom he had confidence. He was not what I expected – an ancient seer – but a young man in blue overalls. We chatted, and, at a silence, I judged this to be the time to explain my problem – but no, he would tell me why I had come. I had been robbed – and he knew the exact amount of money. He went into a sort of trance and accurately described my study, from where the money had disappeared. He then described a person entering the room who seemed to be very like the one I suspected – and then his vision faded. I don't know whether an extra payment would have yielded more but that was enough – no proof but serious confirmation.

I was to consult medicine men much more later when I was in North America. My experience has always been positive and good, whether in seeking cures for high blood pressure or psychological problems – the latter particularly effective all Navajo ceremonies are concerned with healing. I have seen others totally cured of physical complaints. I cannot explain the medicine but I can vouch for its effectiveness. I went to traditional healers more than to doctors and was unfailingly helped. It was a privilege to be recognised by them and work with them.

6 I was a rather wild young curate. In my first parish a night club opened that demanded ties be worn. I and a cub reporter from the 'Famworth Journal' thought this ridiculous in this day and age and so went to seek admission with me wearing my dog-collar. We were refused as we had no ties, so I then threw my scarf aside revealing my collar. The doorman was distinctly unimpressed and said, 'It wouldn't matter, sir, if you was Georgie Best, you wouldn't get in here without a tie'. Even back then it was clear that football players enjoyed much higher prestige than clergy! When this incident appeared in the press indignant readers wanted to know why a clergyman should want to enter a night club anyway.

In Bolton, where I was student chaplain, I also became chairman of the Octagon Theatre Youth Group, and we wanted to put on a subversive piece of experimental theatre in the pedestrian precinct in answer to the army's having staged a recruitment exhibition there a week or two before. We needed the permission of the Watch Committee, which in those days could censor public performances if considered distasteful, as the rock group we were using would need to plug into the Town Hall's electricity supply. Permission was refused so, in anger at this injustice when the 'professional killers' had been allowed their recruitment opportunity, we staged a mock funeral procession for free speech. One Saturday, when the precinct was busiest, every hour a funeral procession took place. The coffin was labelled 'Free Speech', the bearers were gagged, and I walked in front in my funeral gear as at a real burial. This raised a lot of anger as well as support and it is perhaps all many people in Bolton remember me for. All praise to the Technical College for allowing us to perform on their premises. I gained further notoriety in an ill-judged riposte in the Bolton press to my nemesis, a fierce evangelical minister called Canon Butlin. He had asked people to come to the precinct and bum their pornography in return for being handed a Bible. It attracted little support and I suggested that he would have had more success if he had asked people to burn their Bibles and be given pornography. That did not go down well. I was also a founder member of 'Bolton Free Press' and was often dodging the police and angry opponents as, with my colleagues, we flitted round town selling it on the streets. I remember that a critical review of Bolton pubs nearly got us lynched! But the political content was often sharp and probing.

[7] Raimundo Panikkar *The Unknown Christ of Hinduism* 1964 Dartmon, Longman & Todd

[8] When I was appointed Warden of Lelapa la Jesu, the seminary in Lesotho, it was under the auspices of the United Society for the Propagation of the Gospel, an Anglican missionary society. So I had to be interviewed by them. I had decided by this lime that I was not prepared to deny my sexuality any longer, and so was frank when this issue arose. Two of us were interviewed that afternoon. The other guy was summoned in about five minutes and told he had been appointed to the position he had applied for. Half an hour later I was still waiting. The committee was clearly having a difficult discussion. I was eventually recalled and told – all credit to them that I had also been appointed but, in my case, I was asked if I would mind seeing a psychiatrist. She turned out to be a Miss Marple look-alike who had been a missionary in India and, I presumed, had some psychiatric qualification. But she could not get round to asking me a direct question on the key issue and I was not inclined to help her. After going round in circles for some time she started to talk of the problems of single people working abroad but again ran out of steam. She next suggested I might take up a hobby to divert myself from certain [still unspoken] desires and anxieties. By this time 1 was at the handkerchief-chewing stage trying to hide my amusement, but I asked her what she had in mind. Bird watching, she ventured, as this could be done at any time, including early in the morning and late at night. I felt like telling her I did not usually feel too aroused early in the morning but I desisted. And there the interview ended, in a certain degree of embarrassment.

Later, when the society asked me if there was any special resource I needed for my work in Africa I requested a pair of binoculars – but this was refused.

[9] Vincent J. Donovan *Christianity Rediscovered*, 2001 SCM Press

[10] Ruth Hutchinson is one of my heroes. She took early retirement from the National Health Service in England and offered her services to medical mission work in Zimbabwe. She went as an anaesthetist to Harare and was soon Senior Anaesthetist to all the hospitals in the capital. She was held in tremendous respect, not least for her ability to identify at sight really urgent cases in long hospital queues: 'see that man at once – he'll be dead by the time his turn arrives!' She was now working harder than she ever had before, but her passionate dedication to the Shona people did not stop here. With a Shona friend in her local church in Mabelreign she observed the problem of many highly educated teenagers emerging from a then admirable school system and being unable to find jobs. At that time a civil war was still raging in Mozambique but the government was making heroic efforts to maintain health and education provision, including the replacement of Portuguese by English as the second language. So Ruth and her friend decided to establish a project which would place Zimbabwean teenagers in Mozambiquean secondary schools for a year to teach English, both therefore meeting a shortage of teachers and giving the youth valuable work experience. Hence, after a long week in the hospitals, Ruth would drive across the huge country late on a Friday afternoon, sleep in

her vehicle near the border, cross into Mozambique, visit schools to persuade head teachers to employ and accommodate her youth, and then return to Harare on Sunday. This crippling schedule would then be repeated as she delivered the young people, then went with school supplies and constantly made return visits to check on her charges, often on horrendous roads. It was an immensely successful operation against tremendous odds. Sometimes when Ruth arrived with her young teacher the head teacher would have changed his mind so she then had to travel to find another whom she could pressurise into taking on her now spare candidate. At least once she was forced to take cover in a school as bullets flew around in a war engagement she had stumbled into. On another occasion she was arrested at the border on suspicion of smuggling explosives; she was in fact taking chemistry supplies for a school. Later on, as conditions in Zimbabwe worsened, she was actively involved in schemes to distribute food to communities which did not support the ruling party: this was illegal. When I last stayed with her she took me to the airport early in the morning explaining to me what she would have to do if we were accosted at traffic lights by thugs or stopped by the police or military. She was fearless. Her house was burgled arid she lost many of her possessions. And amidst all this she organised an international conference of anaesthetists in 1-larare! To my relief she has at last retired to England. I am so proud to know her, an unsung saint of our times.

[11] Samuel Beckett, *Selected Works of Samuel Beckett* 2011 Grove Press, permission applied for

[12] My difficulties with Bishop Mark were not quite over. I completed my time in America with a welcome sabbatical term at a world leader among Anglican training colleges, Virginia Theological Seminary, Alexandria, next to Washington, D.C. This was a very happy and refreshing time, learning much from Dean Ian Markham and his staff and enjoying student life again. Whilst there, I sent the Presiding Bishop of the Episcopal Church of the U.S.A. Katherine Jefferts-Schori, a report of my experiences in Navajoland. I was invited to discuss it with her staff, and I was not sparing with my criticism. I eventually returned to England, to semi-retirement as a part-time, unpaid priest in Clevedon, North Somerset, near my brother and his family – another happy period, during which I was able to revive my capacity for organising arts festivals. I soon heard that Bishop Katherine had removed my disturbed successor and the bishop! I was quite taken aback, though obviously she had acted not on my advice alone. However, Bishop Mark was to have his revenge. When I applied for the Clevedon post I had to request a testimonial from my previous employer, namely Bishop Mark. Imagine my surprise when, after a good interview in the benefice, Bishop Peter of Bath and Wells wrote to say that he felt he could not confirm the appointment because of the reference given over the telephone by Bishop Mark. This was a serious matter as a negative report could have prevented me accessing a position anywhere. I discovered from the Bishop's chaplain

that I had been accused of, among other things, having an uncontrollable temper and showing premature signs of senility, features more readily identified with my successor! I asked several influential people, including Dean Markham, to write on my behalf, and in the end a reference was accepted from the previous acting Bishop of Navajoland. Rustin Kimsey, who knew me well. When challenged by this body of contrary opinion Bishop Mark 'thought' he had supported my application and denied having made any of his previous accusations. Extraordinary behaviour from a bishop! He still allegedly ministers to all First Nations people in all of Canada: well, it sounds impressive. He has yet to visit the area I used to serve in Saskatchewan.

[13] Great Barr Comprehensive School, where (taught, was one of the worst secondary schools in Birmingham. A significant number of its pupils were on probation. The City of Birmingham Teacher Training College advised its students not to apply there. All the senior staff were of Grammar School background, except the Deputy Headmistress who had been a Primary School Head and had to be offered a comparable post when her school was demolished to make way for the Comprehensive, and the place was run like a failed Grammar School. Her job was devising the school time-table, which she did so well that one year I had to take a second year history class and a third year games period at the same time! The entire capitation budget for the remedial department of the whole school was a hundred pounds and the Head of Department

supplemented it with his own money. The Headmaster, Oswald Beynon, was a strange man who claimed to have trumped the achievements of any member of staff who talked with him so he told the Head of Physical Education that he had run for Wales competitively, and the Head of Music that he had conducted the Halle Orchestra – though he was tone deaf – neither of which was true. He was scared of our admittedly sometimes wild pupils and, if asked for permission for school trips, would delay so time passed and the event was impossible to organise. Hence, I and a fellow English teacher would arrange such matters entirely without permission, especially theatre outings to widen our pupils' experience. So the kids would go home as usual in the afternoon, then creep back into school about half past five, after which a coach would appear at the end of the drive, the kids would run down the drive and into the coach, and we would be off, quite undetected. Parents would meet their offspring outside the school when we returned. What would have happened had there been an accident on the motorway I dread to think! At the end of my last term the senior pupils played a great prank to which I was privy. Notes were smuggled into class registers telling staff to send their classes to Middle School hall. So the entire school, of two thousand students, descended on this limited space causing utter chaos and entirely disrupting the last day. Two of the ringleaders were rather pointlessly expelled! The state of the school tended to throw together junior staff mid older pupils in the face of the common enemy, and some students have remained close friends and

I later officiated at several of their weddings. When I left to pursue ordination training so did a third of the staff! The staff farewell party took place in a series of doubtful bars and culminated in letting down the tyres on a parked police car, a visit to a strip club and an Indian meal at two in the morning! We knew how to celebrate, I mused, as my drunken driver for the night tacked or zigzagged like a yacht down the Bristol Road, taking me home around four a.m.

[14] Alan Ecclestone, *Yes To God*, 1990, Darton,Longman & Todd Ltd, reprinted by permission

[15] Louise Erdrich, *The Plague of Doves* ©2008, reprinted by permission of Harper Collins Publishers

[16] Arthur O'Shaughnessy, *An Ode* 1873 Appleton's Journal New York, NY: D. Appleton & Company

[17] Thomas Merton, *No Man is an Island* 1974 Burns & Oates Ltd, permission applied for

[18] Meister Eckhart *Selected Writings* 1994 Penguin Classics

[19] *Praising God of Many Names* by Mechthild of Magdeburg, 13th-century Christian mystic

[20] Mary Sojourner, *Bonelight: Ruin and Grace in the New Southwest* ©2002 All rights reserved, reprinted with permission, University of Nevada Press

[21] Barry Lopez, *Rediscovery of North America* 1992 Vintage Books USA, permission applied for

[22] http://www.twinrocks.com, used by permission

[23] This extract appeared in a magazine article but neither this author or Mary Sojourner remember when or where it was published

[24] Lord Baden-Powell of Gilwell, *Alone in the Andes* from *Rovering To Success A Book Of Life-Sport For Young Men* 1930 Herbert Jenkins Limited London

[25] Rainer Maria Rilke, *Duino Elegies* (A Bilingual Edition) 2006 translated by David Young W. W. Norton & Company

[26] The author has credited this to Terry Tempest Williams but only has a vague recollection of a lecture in Moab Utah.

[27] W. H. Auden, *The Age of Anxiety: A Baroque Eclogue*, 1947, first UK edition 1948 Faber & Faber

[28] Thomas Merton, *Thoughts in Solitude*, 1958 Farrar, Straus & Cudahy New York permission applied for Curtis Brown Ltd New York

[29] Thomas Merton, *The Wisdom of the Desert* ©1960 The Abbey of Gethsemani Inc. Reprinted by permission of New Directions Publishing Corp.

[30] C.S. Lewis *The Weight of Glory* ©C.S. Lewis Pte Ltd 1949, reprinted by permission

[31] Pierre Teilhard de Chardin, S.J., *Le Milieu Divin, essai de vie intérieure*, Ed. du Seuil, Paris, 1957

[32] 1 Thessalonians 5:24

[33] Charles Williams, *Descent into Hell*, 1937, Faber & Faber

[34] See: Eileen C. Sweeney, *Anselm of Canterbury and the Desire for the Word*, 2012 CUA Press

[35] Kahlil Gibran, *The Prophet*, 1923 © The Gibran National Committee (GNC), Bsharri, Lebanon, Public Domain

[36] Christopher Hassall 1954 *Troilus and Cressida libretto / Chaucer-adaptation* - Opera by Sir William Walton

[37] Thomas Merton, *The Seven Storey Mountain*, 1948, Harcourt Brace Jovanovich, permission applied for

[38] Brenda Meakins, Lesotho 07/03/1988, reprinted by permission

[39] Albert Radcliffe, reprinted by permission

[40] The Most Reverend Desmond Tutu, Archbishop Emeritus of Cape Town in a private letter to the author

[41] C. Day Lewis, *The Complete Poems of C. Day Lewis* 1992 Stanford University Press, p. 546, Poem "Walking Away"

[42] T.S. Eliot, *Four Quartets, East Coker* 1940

[43] George Herbert, 1652 *Jacula Prudentum 245* a collection of proverbs collected by Herbert and published as part of *Herberts Remains*

[44] Dietrich Bonhoeffer, *Letters and Papers from Prison* 1967 London SCM Press

[45] Samuel Beckett, *Malone Dies*, 1956 New York Grove Permission applied for

[46] Mary Oliver, *In Blackwater Woods*, 1993, New and Selected Poems Volume 1, Beacon Press, permission applied for

[47] Thomas Merton, *The Collected Poems of Thomas Merton*, 1980 p380 New Directions

[48] Thomas Merton 1980 op cit p381

[49] Thomas Merton 1980 op cit p387

[50] Barry Lopez, 1992 op cit

[51] Tuam Herald, Summer 2004, reprinted with permission

[52] Jean Vanier, quoted in an article by Sue Careless, December 1st 2000, *Challenged to become Good News*, Anglican Journal

[53] Mary McAleese, 1998 *Céide* Autumn

[54] Tim Cook (Editor) *Practical Compassion: Merfyn Turner 1915-1991*, 1999 Privately Published

[55] Michel Quoist, *Prayers of Life*, 1965 Gill & Macmillan

[56] Malcolm Muggeridge *Something Beautiful for God: Mother Teresa of Calcutta*, 1971, HarperCollins, permission applied for

[57] Albert Radcliffe, *Among Refugees*, used by permission

[58] Richard Baxter 1681, *Lord, it belongs not to my care*

[59] John O'Donohue, *Anam cara: A Book of Celtic Wisdom*, 1998 Harper Paperbacks, Permission applied for

[60] Dag Hammarskjöld *Markings,* 1964

[61] Scott Bader-Saye, *Following Jesus in a Culture of Fear (The Christian Practice of Everyday Life)* 2007 Brazos Press reprinted under Baker Publishing Group 'fair use' guidelines.

[62] Charles Brown, *Love of the World*, edited by the author, reprinted by permission

[63] Teilhard de Chardin *Letter of 11th June 1926* in Letters to Two Friends 30-31

[64] George MacDonald, *The Poetical Works of George MacDonald* (Volumes I and II) 1893